The White Minority
in the Caribbean

THE
White Minority
IN
THE Caribbean

Edited by Howard Johnson and Karl Watson

Ian Randle Publishers
Kingston

James Currey Publishers
Oxford

Markus Wiener Publishers
Princeton

First published in Jamaica, 1998 by
Ian Randle Publishers
206 Old Hope Road, Box 686
Kingston 6

ISBN 976-8123-10-9 (paper)
      976-8123-67-2 (cloth)

A catalogue record of this book is available from the National Library of Jamaica

First published in the United Kingdom, 1998 by
James Currey Ltd
73 Botley Road
Oxford OX2 0BS

British Cataloguing in Publication Data
The white minority in the Caribbean
    1. Whites - Caribbean Area 2. Caribbean Area - Race relations
    I. Johnson, Howard II. Watson, Karl
    305.8'034'079

    ISBN 0-85255-746-9 (paper)

First published in the United States of America, 1998 by
Markus Wiener Publishers
231 Nassau Street
Princeton, NJ 08542

Library of Congress Cataloging-in-Publication Data
The white minority in the Caribbean / edited by Howard Johnson and Karl Watson.
    p. cm.
    Includes bibliographical references.
    Contents: White women and a West India fortune : gender and wealth during slavery / Hilary McD. Beckles -- Salmagundis vs Pumpkins : white politics and creole consciousness in Barbadian slave society, 1800-1834 / Karl Watson -- The white elite of Trinidad, 1838-1950 / Bridget Brereton -- Bay Street, black power, and the Conchy Joes : race and class in the colony and commonwealth of the Bahamas, 1850-2000 / Michael Craton -- The culture of the colonial elites in nineteenth century Guyana / Brial L. Moore -- The white minority in Jamaica at the end of the nineteenth century / Patrick Bryan -- In the name of the people : populist ideology and expatriate power in Belize / Karen Judd -- Ethnicity and social change in Curaçao / R.A. Römer -- French republicanism under challenge : white minority (Béké) power in Martinique and Guadeloupe / Fred Constant.
    ISBN 1-55876-161-6 (alk. paper)
       1-55876-184-5 (cloth)
    1. Whites--West Indies--History. 2. Whites--Belize--History. 3. Whites--Guyana--History. 4. West Indies--History. 5. Whites-West Indies--Ethnic identity. 6. Social classes--West Indies--History. 7. West Indies--Race relations. I. Johnson, Howard, 1945- . II. Watson, Karl S., 1944- .
    F1629.W47W5 1997
    972.9'004034--DC21
                                                                    97-26833
                                                                        CIP

Cover design by Robert Harris
Printed and bound in the USA

Contents

Acknowledgements

This book has undergone a long period of gestation. The idea was first mooted by Karl Watson in 1990. The contributors who have written on the major Anglophone Caribbean territories, largely self-selecting on the basis of their research interests and published work, were contacted in 1992-93 and agreed to participate in this venture. I should like to thank those contributors who met the earliest deadline, for their patience. The effort to extend the coverage beyond the core group of English-speaking territories depended on the generosity of colleagues. I am grateful to Alain Buffon, Nigel Bolland, Gert Oostindie and Flora Poindexter for their recommendations on potential contributors. Finally, Gail Brittingham and Ruth Toole provided vital word-processing skills at different stages of this enterprise.

Howard Johnson
August 1997

Introduction

HOWARD JOHNSON

Since the 1960s the historiography of the Anglophone Caribbean has focused primarily on the exploration of the historical experiences of the black, and in some territories Indian, majority. This pattern of research and publication is explained by the convergence of historiographical trends and political developments which have affected most territories in the region. With the emergence of the 'new' social history, the emphasis shifted from historical writing which generally privileged the white elites to one committed to recovering the past of the non-elites whose existence had been largely ignored. Equally important as influences on historical scholarship were the political developments such as decolonisation, which generated nationalist feeling, and an increased black consciousness, a heightened awareness of the Caribbean as a part of the Third World, and the experiment with democratic socialism in Jamaica which directed attention on the plight of the black 'sufferer' throughout that island's history. One effect of the process of decolonisation, and the national pride which it engendered, was the promotion of the search for a usable and epic past by identifying forms of resistance to the institution of slavery and to colonial rule.[1] With the sharply increased interest in giving agency to the 'subaltern', the white minority, especially in its role as a social, economic, and political elite, has become peripheralised in historical discourse.[2]

The emphasis on the dominated class which is relatively new in historical scholarship has traditionally formed the subject matter of anthropological research that has generally centred on the disadvantaged and the dispossessed. There has, however, been an increased recognition on the part of anthropologists of the importance of integrating elite groups into the main concerns of their discipline.[3] In 1969, for example, Laura Nader argued that anthropologists could benefit from studying 'up' as well as 'down': 'What if, in reinventing anthropology, anthropologists were to study the colonizers rather than the colonized, the culture of power rather than the culture of the powerless, the culture of affluence rather than the culture of poverty.'[4] In the context of anthropological scholarship on Jamaica, Carol S. Holtzberg and Lisa Douglass have produced studies on sections of the white elite.[5]

This collection of essays by historians, anthropologists and a political scientist represents an attempt to place a discussion of the white minority in the Caribbean in the mainstream of the social scientific literature on the region. This is especially important because white minorities (particularly in their 'elite' dimensions) continue to exercise a political and economic influence disproportionate to their numbers. The sustained emphasis on the contributions of the subordinated classes, an important feature in the formation of national identities, can provide only a corrective and not an alternative to the earlier concentration on the elites.[6] In the contemporary Caribbean, as several of the essays indicate, white minorities shape the social and economic framework within which the lower classes operate and influence policy-making despite the advent of black democracies. Although the focus will be directed on the white minorities, especially as they functioned as political, social and economic elites, the discussions will not exclude a consideration of the other social groups with which they interacted. Neither the dominant nor the dominated exist independently of each other for the process of subordination/domination is one in which both groups are involved. Thus E. J. Hobsbawm has commented: 'class defines not a group of people in isolation, but a system of relationships, both vertical and horizontal. . . . Research on class must therefore involve the rest of society of which it is a part. Slave-owners cannot be understood without slaves and without the nonslave sectors of society'.[7]

The essays in this volume range from a discussion of the white minority in the slavery era to a consideration of the contemporary role and status of white elites in the postcolonial context. The territories surveyed in this collection (including the insular Caribbean as well as the mainland polities of Belize and Guyana) have had important common historical experiences. Most of them share parallel social and economic structures which are often the legacy of slavery, the plantation economy and the colonial experience. It is for those reasons that Sidney W. Mintz has argued that the Caribbean has a distinct identity both as a geographical and socio-cultural unit. It is important, however, to recognise that despite certain commonalities, Caribbean societies 'do not form an undifferentiated grouping'.[8] Curaçao, for example, proved to be unsuited to plantation agriculture, and thus its economy was initially based primarily on commerce rather than agricultural staples. The economies of Belize and the Bahamas were also based mainly on extractive industries.

This collection has attempted to avoid a problem endemic in Caribbean scholarship — the tendency to examine issues entirely in the context of the boundaries imposed by

European empires in the Caribbean. It is intentionally pan-Caribbean in scope, for it includes a discussion of both French and Dutch territories and an examination of developments in Belize which has been traditionally overlooked in the scholarly literature.[9] Although contributors were asked initially to consider the strategies adopted by white minorities to maintain social, political and economic power in the post-emancipation years, there has been no attempt to dictate the emphasis or the perspectives which they have taken. The contributions are ultimately a reflection of the research interests of their authors.

The first two essays discuss the white minority in the context of Barbadian slave society. Hilary Beckles provides a gendered analysis of the involvement of white women of the 'middling' class in entrepreneurial activities. Using Richard Pares' male-centred analysis of entrepreneurship in *A West India Fortune* as a point of departure, he traces the careers of the women in the Fenwick family in a process of fortune-seeking which paralleled those of their male counterparts. Challenging the historiographical exclusion of women in these activities, Beckles argues that women, like men, dreamt of making fortunes in the West Indies but more importantly pursued fortunes 'as independent and autonomous agents'. For the Fenwick family Barbados was only a temporary sojourn, for as Beckles observes: '. . . Barbados, in spite of offering the family an opportunity to restore and advance their financial interests, could never be considered a place of final settlement'.

The white Barbadian society to which Karl Watson directs his attention is, like that which Beckles discusses, internally differentiated along class lines. However, by contrast, Watson discusses the world of the Barbadian settler rather than the white sojourner. He describes the political divisions among the white minority along class lines in a community which closed ranks when the non-white population (particularly the slave majority) challenged their dominance. This was a white community which had by the early nineteenth century undergone the process of creolisation and developed a proto-national identity, separate from their British heritage, as 'native Barbadians, secure in their identity, proud and conscious of their achievements and traditions'.

In a panoramic discussion of the white minority in Trinidad, Bridget Brereton argues that this group constituted a true elite, 'dominant in the economic, social and political life of the island'. Unlike Barbados, she contends, there was no distinct category of 'poor whites' in Trinidad. The white community in Trinidad, she demonstrates, was divided more along lines of divergent cultural traditions and ethnicity, reflecting the successive migration of diverse groups of European immigrants. Brereton's wide-ranging discussion traces the evolution of inter-ethnic relations within the white community and discusses the social development of the white elite in the areas of cultural and associational life, domestic relations and their self-identification. She argues that the resilience of the white elite is explained by their ability to adjust to changing economic circumstances. Thus they diversified their economic holdings out of sugar and cocoa production into areas such as industry, real estate development and finance in the years after the Second World War. The cohesion of this white elite, Brereton suggests, was prompted by the challenges from the brown middle classes and the labouring people in the decades after 1920. This solidarity was also maintained throughout the period examined by a 'densely connected network' of family and friends. Brereton argues that the white Creoles of Trinidad had a double consciousness: an identification with Trinidad where they had been settled, in some cases since the eighteenth century, and an identification with the European countries – Britain and France – from which their families originated. In a concluding comment she notes that the white elite continues in present-day Trinidad 'an important, often privileged, and at times controversial role in the nation's affairs'.

In his essay on the Bahamas, Michael Craton traces the power of white Creoles in the colony and later nation state from the time of their initial colonisation of the islands. This minority remained 'sufficiently large and politically well-organised' to ensure their dominance in social, political and economic life into the 1960s. In a discussion which traces the fortunes of the white minority through successive economic cycles, Craton delineates the social differentiation within the white community which was widely dispersed among the several islands of the archipelago. He argues that the racial divide was most clearly defined in this of all the British colonial territories in the Caribbean. The incursions of external capital in the twentieth century resulted in the cohesion of Bahamian whites, the 'Conchy Joes'. This dominance of the local whites was broken in the late 1960s with the political control of the black majority. In his assessment of contemporary developments in the Bahamas, Craton suggests that the polarisation of the races which was so much a feature of the decades of the 1950s, 1960s and 1970s has declined and has been increasingly superseded by class differences. This development, he argues, does not threaten the native whites' 'cherished sub-ethnic identity'. Craton ends by discussing their possible role in Bahamian society in the twenty-first century noting that the current government has involved both white and black Bahamians in a programme of national reconstruction.

The following two papers focus on the white minority in the plantation societies of Guyana and Jamaica in the nineteenth century. Brian L. Moore examines the culture of the colonial elites in Guyana which, he argues, was 'an essential softer side of imperialism aimed at achieving consensus while preserving existing social inequities'. In the post-emancipation years, culture thus complemented the use of force in maintaining social stability. Although recognising the social divisions within the white community, Moore argues that there was cohesion among members of this group which was primarily urban-based. According to Moore,'this elite class had almost absolute dominance over the colonial polity and economy.' His central argument is that members of the white minority were anxious to establish imported cultural norms in order to create a sense of unity among the disparate elements in the racially and ethnically divided colonial society of Guyana. Thus the emphasis on loyalty to the British sovereign provided a unifying symbol to which both blacks and whites eventually subscribed. In the colonial context of Guyana, British culture instilled middle-class values and prejudices from the metropolis and served as an instrument of social control.

In his discussion of the white minority in Jamaica, Patrick Bryan presents a picture of a socially differentiated white community which was, however, aware of existing 'in an island of dark men'. He provides an analysis of the attitudes of the white minority on race and their relations to the rest of the colonial population, placing them in the intellectual framework of late nineteenth-century Social Darwinism and Positivism. There was, he suggests, no single position on how the black majority should be treated although there was general concurrence on their cultural and racial inferiority. The white group possessed, in the Jamaican context, social authority regardless of their class position or occupation. Finally, he argues that members of the white community saw themselves as Englishmen regardless of the length of their association with the island, identifying more directly with their property than with their fellow Jamaicans.

Karen Judd reviews the history of colonial exploitation in Belize, which by the 1850s saw the colony firmly controlled by the British banking houses and their allies in the Colonial Office. She argues that the Colonial Office's efforts to protect the largely black population from unscrupulous British developers resulted in a virtual absence of infrastructure and an economy almost entirely dependent on timber extraction until the mid-twentieth century. The effect of this administrative paternalism was not only to deny the majority of the Belizeans a livelihood, but also to perpetuate the ability of the foreigners to extract labour and profits while failing to develop the country, a situation which continues.

Although there was always a small settler class in the colony, Judd contends that the composition of that group changed over time. Members of the resident white families pioneered the diversification of the economy in the post-war years to include sugar and citrus production, but have prospered only by establishing links to international capital. The economic dominance of this small group of whites, Judd asserts, has been obscured by the contemporary Belizean debate about the nature and origins of a creole (now predominantly black) elite that has historically dominated political life.

R. A. Römer's discussion of Curaçaon society describes the gradual erosion of ethnic boundaries and racial divisions. The tripartite social structure, characteristic of Caribbean slave societies, remained intact after the abolition of slavery in 1863. By the twentieth century, however, the divisions between the whites and the non-white coloureds had blurred as the coloureds were gradually assimilated into the European group, adopting Protestantism which was regarded as the white religion. The establishment of the Royal Dutch Shell Company's refinery in 1915 had far-reaching effects on the social structure and ethnic and racial relationships. It resulted in the influx of metropolitan whites which led to a re-evaluation of the concept of whiteness as locally understood. The entry of black Caribbean immigrants also had a disturbing influence because the majority of them were Protestants, a religious affiliation associated with whites. According to Römer, the presence of the newcomers led to a heightened awareness of a 'creole culture' shared by the local whites and the coloured middle classes. One consequence of the social changes was that the Sephardic Jews (who had maintained their separateness as an ethnic group) became integrated into the wider Curaçaon society by participation in a more secular cultural tradition. Römer suggests that Curaçao, which was in the early twentieth century stratified along racial and ethnic lines, has gradually developed into a society divided primarily along class lines.

In a discussion which distinguishes between the historical experiences of Martinique and Guadeloupe, Fred Constant establishes the ability of the white minority, the *békés*, to adapt to changing political circumstances and maintain their power base in predominantly black societies. When French Republican reforms introduced male adult suffrage in 1870, the propertied whites retained their ability to shape political decisions by taking advantage of the divisions among mulatto politicians and the lack of political experience among the former slaves. The *grands békés* also benefited from the integration of Martinique and Guadeloupe into the French administrative and political system in 1946. The increased inflow of French government funds has allowed the white creoles to modernise sugar production, diversify their agricultural holdings and extend their economic interests in tourism, real estate and the import/export trade. As Constant demonstrates, the *békés* have benefited from the territories' status as part of the French state while, on occasion, using arguments about 'local autonomy and territorial identity' to obtain additional concessions. In recent years, Constant argues, there has been a rapprochement between young *békés* and the 'wealthy, educated milieu of colour', one which is, however, limited to the business world rather than to the social sphere.

Although the contributors to this volume have approached the subject of the white minority from diverse perspectives in different territories, common features and emphases have emerged from these discussions. The authors have argued that the white minority was not monolithic but was significantly differentiated along class, gender and ethnic lines, as well as by creole or European origins and identity. These differences were, however, usually submerged in response to challenges to the social and economic dominance of this group. As several essays indicate, the composition of the white elite changed as newcomers to these societies were recruited to membership in this group. It is also clear from several of the discussions, including those of Brereton, Craton, Judd and Römer, that the definition of 'whiteness' has changed over time.[10] As Stuart Hall has written of the Anglophone Caribbean: 'Race is not a "pure" category in the Caribbean. . . . In the Caribbean, even where a strong white local élite is present, race is defined socially.'[11] In their analyses, the contributors have traced the shifting patterns of race relations between the white minority and other groups in several Caribbean societies but there is also agreement, among those who have discussed the contemporary position of the white minority, that whites remain a dominant minority. The resilience of this group owes much to their continued access to domestic and foreign capital and links to political power, allowing its members to adjust to changing conditions in the predominantly black societies in which most continue to reside.

Notes

1. See Hilary McD. Beckles, 'The 200 Years War: Slave Resistance in the British West Indies: An Overview of the Historiography', *Jamaican Historical Review,* 13 (1982), p. 1.

2. The term 'minority' in this context refers to a small group of persons differentiated from the majority group by race. Although widely used in the sociological literature, the term is surrounded by conceptual confusion. For a lucid discussion of this point, see Hans van Amersfoort, ' "Minority" as a Sociological Concept', *Ethnic and Racial Studies* 1 (1978), pp. 218-34.

3. Political scientists and sociologists took the lead in recovering the ruling class and political elite theories of Gaetano Mosca and Vilfredo Pareto from the 1930s. They published work on elites in a variety of contexts, notably Latin America. An early example of this trend is Seymour Martin Lipset and Aldo Solari (eds), *Elites in Latin America* (New York, 1967). Examples of work on elites in the anthropological literature include the seminal volume edited by George Marcus, *Elites: Ethnographic Issues* (Albuquerque, 1983); Diana Balmori, Stuart F. Voss, Miles Wortman, *Notable Family Networks*

in *Latin America* (Chicago, 1984); Larissa Adler
Lomnitz and Marisol Perez-Lizaur, *A Mexican
Elite Family, 1820-1980: Kinship, Class, and
Culture* (Princeton, 1987); Gary Wray
McDonogh, *Good Families in Barcelona: A
Social History of Power in the Industrial Era*
(Princeton, 1986).

4. Laura Nader, 'Up the Anthropologist —
Perspectives Gained from Studying Up in Dell
Hymes' (ed.), *Reinventing Anthropology* (New
York, 1974), p. 289.

5. Carol S. Holzberg, *Minorities and Power in a
Black Society: The Jewish Community of
Jamaica* (Lanham, MD, 1987); Lisa Douglass,
*The Power of Sentiment: Love, Hierarchy and
the Jamaican Family Elite* (Boulder, 1992). In
the case of Jamaica, political scientists have pioneered a discussion of predominantly white
elites. See the essays by Peter Phillips and
Stanley Reid in Carl Stone and Aggrey Brown
(eds), *Essays on Power and Change in Jamaica*
(Kingston, 1977). For important pioneering his-
torical research on the white elite in the
Barbadian context see Cecilia A. Karch, 'The
Role of the Barbados Mutual Life Assurance
Society During the International Sugar Crisis of
the Late Nineteenth Century' in K. O. Laurence
(ed.), *A Selection of Papers Presented at the
Twelfth Conference of the Association of
Caribbean Historians, 1980* (St Augustine,
1986), pp. 95-133; 'The Growth of the Corporate
Economy in Barbados: Class/Race Factors,
1890-1977' in Susan Craig (ed.), *Contemporary
Caribbean: A Sociological Reader* (Port-of-
Spain, 1981),1, pp. 213-42.

6. For an early appeal, in the British context, for
social historians to integrate elites into their discussions see Harold Perkin, 'The Recruitment of
Elites in British Society since 1800', *Journal of
Social History* 12 (1978), pp. 222-35.

7. E. J. Hobsbawm, 'From Social History to the
History of Society' in M.W. Flinn and T.C.
Smout (eds), *Essays in Social History* (Oxford,
1974), p. 15.

8. Sidney W. Mintz, 'The Caribbean as a
Socio-Cultural Area' in Michael M. Horowitz
(ed.), *Peoples and Cultures of the Caribbean: An
Anthropological Reader* (Garden City, New

York, 1971), p. 18.

9. For a recent criticism of the insularity of
Caribbean scholarship see Michel-Rolph
Trouillot, 'The Caribbean Region: An Open
Frontier in Anthropological Theory', *Annual
Reviews of Anthropology* 21 (1992), pp. 34-35.
For an earlier perceptive critique of the insularity of Caribbean historical scholarship see Eric
Williams, 'A Bibliography of Caribbean History,
A Preliminary Essay, Part I: 1492-1898',
Caribbean Historical Review, iii-iv (1954), p.
208. Eric Williams commented: 'International
politics, in putting asunder what geography has
joined together, has had the effect in the field of
historical research, of destroying the essential
unity of Caribbean history and of segregating the
scholars who have made this area their field of
specialisation . . . . Linguistic difficulties aggra-
vate a problem deeply noted [*sic*] in nationalism
and insularity.'

10. The variations in the white somatic norm
image in the Caribbean have long been noted by
Harry Hoetink. See, for example, *Caribbean
Race Relations: A Study of Two Variants*
(London, 1967); 'The Dominican Republic in the
Nineteenth Century: Some Notes on
Stratification, Immigration, and Race' in
Magnus Mörner (ed.), *Race and Class in Latin
America* (New York, 1970), p. 115. In a study of
creole Louisiana, Virginia R. Dominguez has
pointed to significant changes in racial bound-
aries in Louisiana and Puerto Rico. See *White By
Definition: Social Classification in Creole
Louisiana* (New Brunswick, 1986), pp. 266-67,
273-75.

11. Stuart Hall, 'Pluralism, Race and Class in
Caribbean Society' in UNESCO, *Race and Class
in Post-Colonial Society: A Study of Ethnic
Group Relations in the English-Speaking
Caribbean, Bolivia, Chile and Mexico* (Paris,
1977), p. 170.

*My thanks to Karen Judd who made helpful com-
ments on the penultimate draft of this introduction and suggestions for further reading in the
anthropological literature.*

1

White Women and a West India Fortune: Gender and Wealth during Slavery

HILARY McD. BECKLES

Surprisingly, opportunities have not always been taken to contest, from the perspective of gender, well-known dominant concepts in the recent historiography of Caribbean slavery.[1] Debates that should arise, for example, from feminist criticisms of privileged texts, such as Richard Pares's 1950 seminal *A West India Fortune*, have not taken place. One result is that mythic representations of women's experiences and identities within the literature have survived as stable conceptual constructs outside the reach of critical discourse. *A West India Fortune* illustrates this state of affairs, and is selected here as a point of departure only in so far as it illuminates an area of interpretation not visited by scholars of either women's or gender history.[2] The term 'gender' is used here in reference to the social organisation of the relations between the sexes, and to denote the social meanings attributed to sexual differences.[3]

Pares elegantly recounts the journey of the Pinneys, a financially-broken yeoman family from Dorset in England, as they accumulate an enormous amount of wealth in the Leeward Islands from the end of the seventeenth century to the mid-eighteenth century. It is an account of the imperial white, Non-Conformist, Protestant male as he transformed, and is reshaped by, the West Indian colonial frontier that had made black slavery the basis of all its economic and social arrangements. The Pinney men, starting with Azariah, and continuing with his son and grandson, are presented as successful representatives of England's superior entrepreneurship, as well as the creators and patriarchs of a dynamic and profitable economic system that contributed in no small measure to the revolutionary refashioning of the modern world. The Pinney women, however, are located, when identified, on the margins of the entire accumulation affair. The general thrust of the analysis furthermore suggests that the lure of a West India fortune, which had gripped the heart and soul of the propertied classes in English society, had engendered positive responses only from enterprising menfolk.

Little is known about the motives and experiences of single white women from the 'middling classes' as participants in the West India enterprise. During the seventeenth century, when the 'sugar plantation' revolution swept the islands of the Lesser Antilles, labouring white women figured prominently in the records of indentured servitude. The collapse of the white indenture system, under the impact of black slavery, meant the removal of the principal mechanism used by labouring white women to settle in the West Indies. Those who came were mostly driven by destitution, and arrived as bonded labourers without social honour and with minimal legal protection. Most of them worked on the sugar estates, and apart from the few who secured social mobility through marriage or other relations with propertied white males, they emerged from bondage only to contribute to the 'poor white' lumpen proletariat that eked out a living in the 'outback' of the plantations and inhabited the urban slums.[4] Much less, furthermore, is known of those white women who, as part of the rural gentry and urban middling classes, chose the West Indies as a place to repair broken domestic economies or pursue new fortunes.

In this essay, the journey to Barbados in the early nineteenth century of a 'respectable', English, female-headed family is placed at the centre of the discourse represented by Pares's text. The purpose of the examination is not so much to destabilise his argument and assumptions, but to advance a proposition that speaks critically about the way social experiences of women have been historicised and how as a result the history of West Indian slave society has been written. To some extent, it is motivated by a considerable conceptual curiosity, and driven in part by an unshakeable suspicion about the ideological perspectives that have informed and fashioned the canons of West Indian historiography. By placing a gender history reading within the analytical 'calaloo' of race, colour, class and identity, not only is the white woman called forth – to account rather than by accounts – but also the complexities of human experiences involved in pursuing West India fortunes can be discerned.[5]

Unlike Azariah Pinney, preacher, small landowner and lacemaker, who found himself marooned in Nevis in 1685 serving a ten-year transportation sentence for his involvement in Monmouth's Rebellion, Eliza Fenwick arrived in Barbados in 1811 seeking to repair her family's domestic economy that had been shattered by the separation of her parents, John and Elizabeth Fenwick. Her father had been a business failure, leaving the family ruined and at the financial mercy of concerned friends. While he continued to fall deeper into debt to various London money-lenders, and occasionally going off to Ireland on unsuccessful business ventures, his wife, adult daughter and his teenage son eventually became involved in the colonial enterprise as colonists'.[6]

The collapse of Mrs Fenwick's marriage forced her to consider ways to generate an income in order to 'extricate' herself from the 'torture' of seeing her husband 'perpetually struggling against a tide that so fettered and manicled, he could not stem'.[7] She considered turning a profit from writing, but recognised that the distress caused by marital separation made this difficult. Finally, she resolved to open a school hoping to earn a living from teaching. Eliza, meanwhile, who had also considered teaching as a career, was well on her way to being a fulltime actress, performing at various theatres in the West End. Resolved to 'work and starve together' mother and daughter prepared collective survival strategies.[8] In 1811, after failing to secure parts for the Haymarket season, Eliza, now 23 years old, became distressed by her financial uncertainty. It was then that she encountered the colonial world in the person of Mr Dyke, a businessman from Barbados, who sought to contract her for his new theatre in Bridgetown.

The Barbados proposal, the Fenwicks thought, was far-fetched and not received with much enthusiasm. While it promised 'some remuneration in money', there was the burden of doubt about inhabiting an unknown colonial society.[9] Ireland was ruled out, but as Mr Dyke pressed his claims, Eliza and her mother soon considered themselves as having little choice. They discussed at length the nature of the Barbados undertaking, and sought counsel with London residents who knew West Indian conditions. It would be a family migration, pioneered by Eliza; her mother and Orlando, her younger brother, would follow. It would change the course of the family's life in ways unimaginable.

A Bridgetown theatre was a far cry from the Covent Garden and Haymarket Eliza had idealised, but it was an opportunity to gain further experience, promote her reputation as an actress and generate a reliable income. The financial package seemed agreeable. She would be assigned exclusively to Mr Dyke's theatre for eight months and tour Antigua with the company for the rest of the year. A salary of 6 guineas per week, paid weekly, was offered, in addition to lodgings at Mr Dyke's home for 2 guineas per week. On tour to Antigua the company would pay the expense of the voyage. An undertaking was made in writing by the 'Committee of Gentlemen Subscribers' to the theatre with respect to the payment of salaries. The Committee was chaired by Judge Beccles, son of the Attorney-General for the colony.[10]

Eliza arrived at Barbados, 'the Land of Promise', 'heaven', on 20 December 1811. The theatre, 'not half-finished', was scheduled to open on the night of Saturday, 28 December, with a play entitled *The West Indian and the Spoiled Child*. She described it as a 'handsome building on the outside, but is painted within in every colour that ever was invented or thought of. In the middle of the ceiling, over the 'Pit', 'is a great daub – King George riding in a chariot thro' the sea'. The 'prevailing colours', she noted, 'are crimson, scarlet, dark blue and dark green – very well chosen for a cold country!' Immediately, she had reason to question the details of Mr Dyke's financial calculations. The row of boxes, pit and gallery, when full, would produce £350 sterling. Mr Dyke, she thought, had said in London, £500. The green room and dressing rooms were unfinished, and would be small.[11]

These revised calculations, in addition to other unforeseen expenditures, caused Eliza to reassess her financial projections. In a letter to her mother dated 18 December 1811 she sets out her condition:

> I shall not make a fortune here the first year at any rate, if I do afterwards. I have half a hundred expenses I never dreamed of. I have been obliged to buy my bedstead. It cost 20 Dollars. There is not a bit of furniture in my room but that, a table and one chair, and I fancy if I have any more I must buy it myself. Drawers are £40 the set, so they are put out of the question. You may suppose how much I am distress'd being obliged to keep everything in my trunk .... Oh my money![12]

The 'seasoning period' was, however, short, and early in the next year Eliza seemed settled and surer of her financial affairs. 'Everything', she told her mother, 'turned out better than I had any hope of,' and 'I say this is the happiest period of my life.'[13] 'I am sure', she commented of Mr Dyke, 'if ever there was an honest man in the world he is one', and 'At the theatre I am the first personage and of course comfortable there.' 'I am certain (I think I am),' she concluded, 'that I shall reach the top. I have here every advantage (but one), and by devoting every hour I can call my own to the serious study of the stage.... I shall be advancing our interests better than by any present money I might gain by teaching.'[14]

Eliza was now ready to sponsor the immigration of her mother and brother. 'England has discarded us,' she proclaimed, and the choice was one of destination – America or Barbados. 'Yes, indeed, you must come here,' she implored her mother; 'I am sure there is a fortune waiting for you here, and easily earned. I have no time to teach. You would do wonders.' She instructed her mother to bring her brother, Orlando. 'We can keep him for three years,' she advised, 'But he must never become a Manager of Slaves.'[15] Mrs Fenwick outlined the details of her daughter's proposal to her friend, Mary Hays:

> Eliza with the beginning of the new year began the project of a school in Barbados
> FOR ME, upon the prudent consideration of making an experiment upon the pro-
> fessions of those who had loudly and long declared that if she and her mother open
> a school on the island, the greatest encouragement would be given, and that it
> must inevitably be a most profitable undertaking.[16]

She had earlier agreed to take 'a year to consider the plans' , which seemed attractive bearing in mind that supporting Orlando financially was beyond her reach, and that there was hope he could 'study and practise the Laws of Courts' in Barbados.

On 28 October 1814 Mrs Fenwick and her son arrived in Barbados.[17] Eliza was married to a Barbadian and had a daughter. She described the colony, as her daughter had done three years earlier, as the 'Land of Promise'.[18] In December, she informed Mary Hays:

> Our prospects, I am assured, are excellent, and one of the wealthiest men of the
> Island told me yesterday the only danger was of our having too large a school.
> Eliza and Mr Rutherford [her husband] are no less sanguine on the subject, but the
> dearness of living and the hideous expense of servants create fears in my mind
> . . . . Orlando is quite well, but I was misinformed in London respecting the ease
> of placing him in a Commercial House here. There are at this moment six young
> men of good families here waiting for a probable vacancy in a great Merchant's
> office, and another merchant, to whom I brought letters, tells me he is not only
> overstocked with young clerks, several of whom have given £100 premiums for
> their admissions.[19]

Notwithstanding the unfavourable prospects for settling a career path for Orlando, Mrs Fenwick shared the optimism other people expressed about her own circumstances as an educational entrepreneur. 'Prosperous I am likely to be', she professed, but the social process of wealth accumulation involved 'various and harassing changes' and a 'feeling of desolateness'.[20]

Within six months the number of pupils attending Mrs Fenwick's school for girls increased from 14 to 30, with the possibility of further increases. These were all day students, but several applications were made by parents for boarders. She was soon on the search for a suitable house to meet the demand for boarding. These developments occurred despite her admission that the school's 'prices are high, very high'. Day students, she stated, paid from 'ten to thirty or forty guineas per annum, according to what they learn'. These charges, she stated, 'are much higher than the other schools (which are to me surprisingly numerous)', but they kept her 'in the higher and wealthy classes', thus securing her 'from bad debts'. The school she described as being 'in fashion', and 'those rich families who do not send their daughters to England, give them to us'.[21]

The 'Barbados project' was going well for Eliza and her mother. The school was proving a business success, and projections for the future indicated that within two years the family would be 'clear of all debt, including the money sunk into . . . passage and preparation'.[22] Orlando, now 17 years old, had finally secured a placement for three years with a young merchant in Bridgetown who had extensive business interests in other West Indian colonies. In addition, Eliza was offered '24 guineas per week and clear benefits to join the Company performing in Jamaica'.[23] In July 1815 Mrs Fenwick reported 37 pupils, including one boarder at £100 per year, and 'several others spoken of as coming'. The family had moved into 'a very fine house' in order to accommodate the boarders, and the expectation of having 50 students by the end of the year was considered reasonable. The day school was now 'bringing in nearly £800 per annum'.[24] 'Thus, my dear Mary,' Mrs Fenwick wrote, 'our experiment has been attended with the happiest results'.[25]

The Fenwick enterprise cannot be accounted for within the dominant historiographic paradigms that focus exclusively upon the financial activities and entrepreneurship of white, agro-commercial males. Negating the significance of white women as colonising agents making autonomous ideological, social and economic inputs into the colonial system has resulted in a conceptual homogenising of the white community's experiences. The Fenwicks, like other white women, played important roles in shaping the urban and rural milieu of colonial society. As slave-owners, entrepreneurs and pro-slavery ideologues, they demonstrated by their ideas and social and economic actions considerable support for the colonial mission as an opportunity for betterment.

As business women, their search for autonomy within the structures of colonialism entailed the staging of various forms of contests. The militarism of empire and the patriarchal culture of plantation commercial organisations had assigned to white women a supportive, but not independent, role. These roles can be seen in the efforts of colonial patriarchs to insulate them, as much as possible, from the aesthetically crudest aspects of slavery. For example, in order to protect propertyless white women from the hallmark of enslavement, field labour, slave-owners were refusing by the early eighteenth century to employ them as fieldhands.

The society which the Fenwicks entered was already settled in its ideological representations of gender and sexual divisions of labour. Considerations of race and class had fractured any unitary concept of womanhood, and social relations were understood and shaped within this context. By the middle of the eighteenth century, most fieldhands in the English colonies were black women. In addition, from the beginning of the slave system laws were framed and implemented in order to dissociate white womanhood from the reproduction of children of slave status by linking it solely to the progeny of black women. The children produced by white women with enslaved black men, which was not as uncommon as generally believed, were born legally free. In this way the off-spring of white women could not experience the status of human property, nor suffer legal alienation from social freedom. White women, then, were constitutionally placed to participate in the slave-based societies as privileged and protected persons.

The linking of white womanhood to the reproduction of free status, the Fenwicks understood, meant that the entire ideological fabric of slave societies was conceived in terms of sex, gender and race. This was the easiest way for black slavery and white patriarchy to coexist without encountering major legal contradictions. They also knew that these relations made it necessary for white males to suppress and dominate white women, limit their sexual freedom, and at the same time, enforce the sexual exploitation of black women as a 'normal benefit' of masterhood. In so doing, white males valued black women's fertility primarily in terms of the reproduction of labour, and placed a premium on white women's fertility for its role in the reproduction of patriarchy.

The 'victim' thesis that seeks to explain the experiences of white women like the Fenwicks has severe conceptual limitations. These can be identified immediately by an empirical assessment of white women's autonomous participation in the shaping of eco-nomic and social relations. The Fenwicks were representative in many ways of the small business culture developed by white women in Bridgetown and other West Indian towns. It is necessary, therefore, to place them within its economic and social context.

The demographic and property data, for instance, show the extent to which slave ownership correlated with differences of class, race and sex. White males were the pre-dominant owners of slaves in the plantation sector. White women were, however, aggressive agents in the contest over landownership and slave-based production. Recent work by Mary Butler has shown that the Barbados slave registers for 1834 list 27 women as owners of sugar plantations comprising 6,241 acres and at least 3,870 slaves. They accounted for 11 per cent of the 241 persons who owned estates of more than 50 acres and supervised the affairs of 11 per cent of the total of 307 plantations of that size. At emancipation, when slave-owners were compensated for the loss of their slave prop-erty, their claims accounted for 37 per cent of the total submitted. Likewise, in Jamaica, Butler shows that white women owned or controlled approximately 5 per cent of the estates, and several ranked among the island's greatest landowners, some with proper-ties in excess of 1,000 acres.[26]

Different patterns of ownership and involvement can be discerned for the urban sector. White women were generally the owners of small urban properties and businesses, and these had higher stocks of slaves than the large, male-owned properties. In 1815 white women owned about 24 per cent of slaves in St Lucia; 12 per cent of the slaves on properties of more than 50 slaves; and 48 per cent of the properties with less than ten slaves. In Barbados, in 1817, less than five of the holdings of 50 slaves or more were owned by white women, but they owned 40 per cent of the properties with less than ten slaves. White women were 50 per cent of the owners of slaves in Bridgetown, on properties with less than ten slaves. In general, 58 per cent of slave owners in the capital were female, mostly white, although some were also 'coloured' and black. Overall, women owned 54 per cent of the slaves in the town.[27]

In 1821 the Fenwicks employed in their household eight slaves, five of whom they owned (two men, two boys and one woman) and three hired (three women). Mrs Fenwick found from experience, unlike other town dwellers, that male slaves were easier to manage, and were more productive within the domestic economy.[28] White women, however, tended to own more female slaves than male slaves. In Bridgetown, in 1817, the sex ratio (number of males per 100 females) of slaves belonging to males was more than double that for female slave owners at 111 and 49, respectively. The sex ratio of slaves belonging to white females, when separated from other non-white females, was even higher at 53.[29]

From these data the image that emerges of the white female slave-owner is that she was generally urban, in possession of less than ten slaves, the majority of whom were females. That female slave-owners generally owned more female slaves indicates the nature of enterprises they managed and owned. It is reasonable, then, to argue that any conceptualisation of urban slavery, especially with reference to the experiences of enslaved black women, should proceed with an explicit articulation of white women as principal slave-owners. Such a departure is an analytically necessary precondition for the correct identification of white women within the slave-owning ethos, and for a more rigorous assessment of urban-rural differentiations within the slave mode of production. Furthermore, a clear conception of white matriarchy would encourage a real understanding of black women's slavery experience.

The Fenwicks' dream of accumulating a West India fortune could be realised only within the context of this slave-owning culture. For them, three related levels of engagement with slavery can be discerned: first, the need to purchase or rent slaves for their business establishment; second, the employment of slaves within the household; third, their representation of the ideology of white womanhood and its relationship to slavery as a system of race, gender and class exploitation. Their adjustments to, and working acceptance of, this culture had to be swift and practical. If private spheres of thought and action conflicted with public expectations, they had to be suppressed.

Eliza's exposure to the social economy of slavery began immediately upon arrival. She was sent to bed, and tea was brought by the 'negroes'. She was informed by her host that the governor 'is the only person on the island who has a white servant'.[30] Slaves, she recognised, were vital to the operations of propertied families, and the craft of their ownership and management had to be acquired by heads of households. After one month's residence she located her position upon the chart of pro-slavery consciousness: 'I have never yet seen any black or coloured people in the Theatre. Out of it they look queerly enough, for some of the men and women go about the streets entirely naked'.[31] She wrote to her mother:

> I think the slaves, I mean the domestic slaves, the laziest and most impertinent set of people under the Sun. They positively will do nothing but what they please .... There are always three or four to do the work of one, and they laugh in the Owner's face when reproved for not doing their duty .... I speak principally of Capn. Soaper's slaves. They take liberties that no English servant would be allowed to do; he has two who are drunk half the day, and one female Negroe who waits on Mrs. S. throws herself into fits the moment she is found fault with. They will not scour the floors that is too hard work for them, and the field Negroes are sent for to do it. By the way, I am told the condition of the field Negroes is deplorable enough, and the only way to make the domestic slaves do as they are bid is by threatening to send them to the plantations.[32]

On arrival in Barbados Mrs Fenwick reported being 'shocked at the alteration in Eliza'. She had been very ill, but much of her 'debility' had to do with the annoyances and fatigue in the management of the slaves that the 'mistress of an English family, with even the worst English servants, can form no idea of'. In spite of Eliza's physical condition, her mother found 'her heart and her principles still the same,' and we are told that Orlando 'had exactly the same impression'.[33] Like her daughter, furthermore, Mrs Fenwick found the black slaves necessary, distressing, pitiful and provoking. In a letter to Mary Hays dated 11 December 1811, she stated:

> Our domestics are Negroes, hired from their owners, and paid at what seems to me an exorbitant rate. With our small family we are obliged to keep three, or if we wash at home, four, and with that number one third of the work Eliza does herself, and another third is necessarily left undone, as she cannot do more than her strength will allow. They are a sluggish, inert, self-willed race of people, apparently inaccessible to gentle and kindly impulses. Nothing but the dread of the whip seems capable of rousing them to exertion, and not even that, as I understand, can make them honest. Pilfering seems habitual and instinctive among domestic slaves. It is said they are worse slaves and servants in this Island than in many others because there is less severity made use of. It is a horrid system, that of slavery, and the vices and mischiefs now found among the Negroes are all to be traced back to that source.[34]

Three months later, on 21 March 1815, she returned to the theme:

> It is a horrid and disgraceful system. The female slaves are really encouraged to
> prostitution because their children are the property of the owner of the mothers.
> These children are reared by the Ladies as pets, are frequently brought from the
> negro houses to their chambers to feed and sleep, and reared with every care and
> indulgence till grown up, when they are at once dismissed to labour and slave-like
> treatment. What is still more horrible, the gentlemen are greatly addicted to their
> women slaves, and give the fruit of their licentiousness to their white children as
> slaves.[35]

She strongly suspected that 'a very fine Mulatto boy about 14' who attended her school
to help 'wait on the breakfast and luncheon of two young ladies, our pupils', was their
own brother, from his resemblance to their father. It is a 'common case', she noted, and
not 'thought of as an enormity'. 'This culture', she concluded, 'gives me disgusted
antipathy and I am ready to hail the Slave and reject the Master'.[36]

Undoubtedly social values shaped by gender ideologies did affect Mrs Fenwick's
perception of slavery. She saw in the relations of slavery a clear reflection of the worse
aspects of male oppression of women, but her stifled pro-slave sentiment was confined
to the private sphere and posed no problem for the pro-slavery interests with which her
accumulation project was conceived. We see this in opinions expressed to Mary Hays
after the purchase of a male slave whom she described as one she 'could not lose': 'It
will no doubt be repugnant to your feelings to hear me talk of buying men. It was for a
long time revolting to mine, but the heavy sums we have paid for wages of hired servants, who were generally the most worthless of their kind, rendered it necessary'.

Slavery, Mrs Fenwick suggested, was about the ability of the white race to enforce
power over the black race in specific ways in order to secure greater material returns and
social advantage. The resistance to this relation of power by the enslaved, however, was
not received by her as part of an inevitable, justified political contest, but as an indication
of their possession of negative ethnic characteristics which in turn, she thought, legit-
imised their subordination. 'Poor creatures!' wrote Eliza, 'They get terribly beaten sometimes, and dare not strike a white man in their own defence even.'[37] 'An impassable
boundary', her mother noted, 'separates the white from the coloured people', which was
patrolled by laws, militias, and in the final instance, garrisoned soldiers.[38] The success of
business activities in the white community depended upon these relations of power. The
Fenwicks recognised that the fulfilment of their West India dream meant the safe negoti-
ation of a passage through the 'nightmare' of black slavery.

The contest over slavery and freedom, however, was not being waged in the public
political discourses of the white community. For some slave-owners it was a private
turbulence, ultimately suppressed by a complex perception of self-interest. Mrs Fenwick

expressed an abhorrence of slavery at three levels: first, it denied black women the ability to refuse white men access to their bodies; second, it impacted adversely on the private and public morals of white men; third, it denigrated the black race in ways that made its social morals and behaviour unacceptable to her. She had learnt, however, to live within its institutional and ideological structures, since this was the only way to advance her plans for a West India fortune. The blacks, who had never accepted their enslavement, were to present the first major rupture to the smooth implementation of her project.

Slave rebellion began on Sunday, 14 April 1816. According to Colonel Codd, Commandant of the resident imperial troops, the political attitude of slaves led by Bussa, a driver at Bayleys Plantation, was that 'the island belonged to them and not to the white men whom they proposed to destroy'. Few contemporaries, including the Fenwicks, believed that rebellion was imminent, or that a revolutionary situation existed on the island.

The rebellion began at about 8:30 p.m. in the south-eastern parish of St Philip, and quickly spread throughout most of the southern and central parishes of Christ Church, St John, St Thomas, St George, and parts of St Michael. Minor outbreaks of arson (but no skirmishes with the militia) also occurred in the northernmost parish of St Lucy. No fighting between rebel slaves and the militia forces was reported from the eastern and western parishes of St Andrew, St James, and St Peter. An attempt to spread the rebellion among the slaves in Bridgetown was put down following the deployment of a party of the Fifteenth Regiment about the streets of the town. Dwellers in the town, however, felt defenceless, and were traumatised by news of spreading arson and military combat. In geopolitical terms, more than half of the island was engulfed by the insurrection.

The rebellion was short-lived. Within four days it was effectively quashed by a joint offensive of the local militia and imperial troops. Mopping up operations continued during May and June, and martial law, imposed about 2:00 a.m. on Monday, 15 April, was lifted 89 days later on 12 July. The death toll, taken when the militia believed that the rebellious were finally eradicated, was very unevenly balanced between slaves and whites. On 21 September Governor Leith reported 144 slaves executed under martial law, 70 sentenced to death and 123 sentenced to transportation. The anonymous author of an account of the insurrection (written most probably in September) suggests that the governor's figures were a gross underestimation of the total fatalities. The author stated that 'a little short of 1,000' slaves were killed in battle and executed at law. Damage to property was estimated by the Assembly's investigative committee at £175,000. One white person was killed, a private in the Christ Church militia.[39]

Mrs Fenwick considered herself fortunate to have survived the rebellion, falling ill as she did with a 'slow fever' brought on by 'terror'.[40] Several persons, she said, 'lost their lives from their fatigues in the insurrection, and many more swept away by a fever brought hither by troops'.[41] It was damage to her business, however, that constituted the primary consideration:

> The insurrection caused us a *quarter's loss* of the *income* of the *school*, besides some delays of payment from persons who were great sufferers and who before had been rigidly punctual. My illness has, I suppose, cost £100 at least, so that we have felt a share of the general calamity and shall still feel it, as some of our debtors have died, and the accounts must wait till next year. In the end, I believe, we shall not lose, and as our pupils are returned we have still good prospects before us, and should consider the late difficulties but as dusky clouds passing over the sunshine of our prosperity.[42]

Despite her optimism for the future, the adverse effect of the rebellion upon the financial success of the school would continue to be felt.

Tensions remained within Bridgetown, and the fears of 'a second insurrection' kept the 'Militia and Regulars on the alert'.[43] The expenses of the school, Mrs Fenwick admitted, increased 'enormously' after the 'devastation committed by the Negroes.'[44] In addition, the number of students began to fall 'because so many families are removing to England' on account of the rebellion.[45] To make matters worse, the former governess of the president of the Assembly opened a school exactly upon 'the same plan as Mrs Fenwick', to which her response was that 'we shall thus destroy each other, and none of us be able to do more than barely live'.[46] She maintained, nonetheless, a positive outlook on her business venture.

These developments, however, were but precursors to a more tragic occurrence. In the years after the slave rebellion Eliza's health continued to deteriorate. Unable to maintain a fulltime career with the theatre, she decided to teach in the family school in an effort to reduce costs and increase revenues. This activity soon had to cease on account of ill health, forcing the school to hire 'a widow lady of English birth and education', who had been left in 'narrow circumstances by a dissipated Barbadian husband', at a wage of £130 per year.[47] In addition, Eliza's husband, whose 'insatiable love of company and late hours' had seduced him 'into a habit of constant intoxication', became an embarrassment to her and had to be left to himself.[48] He too, had been a teacher in the school, and his departure resulted in Mrs Fenwick hiring an 'accomplished French woman' at an 'unmentionable cost'.

The loss of both Eliza's assistance and general support from her son-in-law were charges, says Mrs Fenwick, that could be measured by the business accounts. She had no way, however, of measuring the 'heaviest calamity' of her life, the death of Orlando by 'a cruel, malignant fever which spared the aged and devoured the young'.[49]

Describing her condition as 'dark and desolate', she recognised that a prime motivation for continuing the 'Barbados project' no longer existed. Subsequently, her interest in the business declined. She considered closing the school and transferring its operations to England, but many of the parents who had promised to send their children to her reneged. This was a disappointment, especially for Eliza, now a mother of three boys and a daughter, who wished them settled in England so as to become 'right loyal subjects of Great Britain'.[50]

Mrs Fenwick also craved English society on occasions, when she would consider exchanging 'the luxuries' of her Barbados circumstance 'for a cottage and narrower means at home'.[51] A return to England, however, was not considered feasible. The Barbados success was at best moderate and unable to bear a return settlement. Such a 'removal', she said, would 'cost a little fortune', and the family would be unable to 'live in that decent and comfortable order which we think highly salutary to the habits and good taste of our children'.[52] At the same time Barbados, in spite of offering the family an opportunity to restore and advance their financial interests, could never be considered a place of final settlement. The fears of 'sudden ruin', of 'storms and hurricanes', and 'above all the fatal insurrection which we constantly dread', she observed, 'prevent the soothing consciousness of being AT HOME'.[53] 'I am pleased on this account', she informed Mary Hays, 'with our project of removal [to America] because I can look to a lasting settlement for Eliza,' as well as 'the opportunity of giving excellent educations to our boys and bringing them up to habits of industry and utility at a very moderate expense'.[54]

In 1821 Mrs Fenwick, Eliza and her four children sold their property and removed the school with six boarders to New Haven in Connecticut under the sponsorship of a gentleman from St Thomas (Virgin Islands) whom Eliza had met eight years earlier at Santa Cruz. 'I am fully persuaded', Mrs. Fenwick concluded, 'that we have done wisely. Our friends predict the most flattering success'. 'There happens to be no female school of the higher order at New Haven, though at New York', she explained, 'and it is supposed that ours would be very attractive as the principal families are now compelled to engage masters at home'.[55]

The Fenwicks' 'Barbados project', then, lasted a full ten years. It was moderately successful, in much the same way that many attempts to secure a West India fortune probably were. At the end of it, however, Mrs Fenwick could boast an ability 'to live with all the comforts of a good table, in a large and handsome house'.[56] Mother and daughter had secured a reliable income and had freed themselves from husbands considered 'a disgrace and a bother'.[57] They had taken on the West Indian world, and prepared again, as single women, to further their future on the mainland. Driven by financial motives and a desire not to fall in social status they represented the spirit of adventure, courage and determination. They both left behind husbands and broken marriages with no 'prospect of amendment', as well as a trail of decision-making and ideological markers by which it is possible to challenge the dominant historical narrative.

Neither woman concentrated energies on domestic labour, childbearing or fashioning a public reputation as the social property of a husband. Their primary concerns were with the reproduction of property and the social elevation of themselves and their children. In these roles, they functioned as part of the middling property-owning classes and forged an ideological identity that was supportive of the dominant class and race order. While they subscribed to elements of patriarchal moral ideology, such as notions of 'virtue', 'decency' and 'honour', the thrust of their autonomous accumulationist activity violated and transgressed representations in patriarchal ideology of the woman as domestic capital. It was, however, an important strength of colonial society that it could survive and be reinforced by such tensions and apparent contradictions.

It is essential, then, to refer to such 'life histories' in order to understand the varied class composition of the slave-owning community and to appreciate the significance of the white businesswoman within it. In addition, narratives of this sort are necessary in order to study the way that gender operated in society, and to give women a space and a voice with which they can challenge their historiographic exclusion. The contention of this essay, therefore, is not to demonstrate that women also dreamt of making West India fortunes. This is not an important fact to be established. That they went out in pursuit of fortunes as independent and autonomous agents is, however, of considerable importance. That they went about it with very much the same ideological and social instruments as men is hardly surprising. That their actual experiences were confined in large measure to small niches, or to the margins of areas of large-scale accumulation, however, is important to know since it has relevance to an understanding of the social relations of gender within colonialism as a violent male-managed enterprise. Furthermore, the presentation of such evidence can help us to focus on the material specificity of gender in order to break free of an ideology of gender that is assigned by an ahistorical patriarchy.

Notes

1. See Arlette Gautier, 'Les Esclaves femmes aux Antilles Francaises, 1635-1848'. *Reflexions Historiques*, 10:3 (Fall 1983), pp. 409–35; Barbara Bush, 'White "Ladies", Coloured "Favourites" and Black "Wenches": Some Considerations on Sex, Race and Class Factors in Social Relations in White Creole Society in the British Caribbean,' *Slavery and Abolition*, 2 (1981), pp. 245–62; Marietta Morrissey, 'Women's Work, Family Formations and Reproduction among Caribbean Slaves', *Review*, 9 (1986), pp. 339–67; Hilary McD. Beckles, 'White Women and Slavery in the Caribbean', *History Workshop Journal*, 36 (1993), pp. 66–82.

2. Richard Pares, *A West India Fortune* (London, 1950).

3. See Louise M. Newman, 'Critical Theory and the History of Women: What's at Stake in Deconstructing Women's History', *Journal of Women's History* 2, (1991), pp. 59–60; Mary Poovey, 'Feminism and Deconstruction' *Feminist Studies* 14 (1988), pp. 52–53; Linda Scott, 'What's New in Women's History', in Teresa de Lauretis (ed.), *Feminist Studies/ Critical Studies*, (Bloomington, 1986), pp. 22–23. Rhoda Reddock, 'Women and Slavery in the Caribbean: A Feminist Perspective', *Latin American Perspectives* 40 (1985), pp. 63–80.

4. See William Dickson, *Mitigation of Slavery* (1814. Rpt. Westport CT. 1970), pp. 439-41; Hilary McD. Beckles, *White Servitude and Black Slavery in Barbados, 1622–1715* (Knoxville, 1989), pp 115-68; 'Black Men in White Skins: The Formation of a White Proletariat in West Indian Slave Society', *Journal of Imperial and Commonwealth History*, 15 (1986), pp. 5–22.

5. For recent texts on women's gender history, see Barbara Bush, *Slave Women in Caribbean Society, 1650–1838* (Bloomington, 1990); Hilary McD. Beckles, *Natural Rebels: A Social History of Enslaved Black Women in Barbados* (New Brunswick, 1989); Marietta Morrisey, *Slave Women in the New World: Gender Stratification in the Caribbean* (Lawrence, 1989); Blanca Silvestrini, 'Women and Resistance: Herstory in Contemporary Caribbean

History' (Department of History, University of the West Indies, Mona, 1989); Lucille Mair, 'Women Field Workers in Jamaica During Slavery', (Department of History, University of the West Indies, Mona, 1989).

6. The letters of Eliza Fenwick from Barbados to her mother, Mrs Elizabeth Fenwick, in England from 1811 to 1814, and the letters of Mrs Fenwick from Barbados to her friend, Mary Hays in England, 1814–21, are reproduced in A. F. Fenwick (ed.), *The Fate of the Fenwicks: Letters to Mary Hays, 1798–1828* (London, 1927). All references to this correspondence are from this text.

7. *Ibid.*, p. 35.

8. *Ibid.*, p. 37.

9. *Ibid.*, p. 52.

10. *Ibid.*, p. 38.

11. *Ibid.*, pp. 62–65.

12. *Ibid.*, pp. 66–67.

13. *Ibid.*, p. 71.

14. *Ibid.*, pp. 71, 99.

15. *Ibid.*, pp. 97–99.

16. *Ibid.*, p. 156.

17. *Ibid.*, p. 141.

18. *Ibid.*, p. 163.

19. *Ibid.*, p. 165.

20. *Ibid.*, p. 166.

21. *Ibid.*, p. 167.

22. *Ibid.*, pp. 166–67.

23. *Ibid.*, p. 170.

24. *Ibid.*, pp. 172–73.

25. *Ibid.*, p. 177.

26. Kathleen Mary Butler, *The Economics of Emancipation: Jamaica and Barbados, 1823–1843* (Chapel Hill,1995), pp. 92–109.

27. B. W. Higman, *Slave Populations of the British Caribbean 1807–1834* (Baltimore, 1984), p. 107; *Slave Population and Economy of Jamaica, 1807–1834* (Cambridge, 1978).

28. A. F. Fenwick, p. 207.

29. Higman, *Slave Populations of the British Caribbean op. cit.*

30. A. F. Fenwick, p. 69.

31. *Ibid.*, p. 73.

32. *Ibid.*, pp. 75–76.

33. *Ibid.*, p. 163.

34. *Ibid.*, pp. 163–64.

35. *Ibid.*, p. 169.

36. *Ibid.*

37. *Ibid.*, p. 91.

38. *Ibid.*, p. 169.

39. See Hilary McD. Beckles, *Black Rebellion in Barbados: The Struggle Against Slavery, 1627–1838* (Barbados, 1987), pp. 87–110; also, 'The Slave Drivers' War: Bussa and the 1816 Barbados Slave Uprising', *Boletin de Estudios Latinoamericanos y del Caribe* no. 39 (1986). Michael Craton, 'Proto-Peasant Revolts? The Late Slave Rebellions in the British West Indies, 1816–1832', *Past and Present*, no. 85 (1979).

40. A. F. Fenwick, p. 178.

41. *Ibid.*, p. 179.

42. *Ibid.*

43. *Ibid.*, pp. 193–94.

44. *Ibid.*, p. 189.

45. *Ibid.*, p. 191.

46. *Ibid.*

47. *Ibid.*, p. 190.

48. *Ibid.*, p. 193.

49. *Ibid.*, p. 183.

50. *Ibid.*, p. 212.

51. *Ibid.*, p. 205.

52. *Ibid.*, p. 211.

53. *Ibid.*, pp. 212–13.

54. *Ibid.*, pp. 210–11.

55. *Ibid.*, p. 210.

56. *Ibid.*, p. 191.

57. *Ibid.*, p. 193.

2

Salmagundis *vs* Pumpkins: White Politics and Creole Consciousness in Barbadian Slave Society, 1800–34

KARL WATSON

> No Colony in the West Indies can boast of so many men who have acquired honored distinction, no other has produced so many publications relating to its history, in no other are there so many collections of books, and I may assert without hesitation that it surpasses every other in the number and well ordered state of its useful institutions.
>
> John Davy, *The West Indies before and since Slave Emancipation*

By the end of the eighteenth century, white Barbadian society, although numerically small, numbering slightly over 16,000 individuals, was surprisingly diversified and stratified. Differentiation was based primarily on socio-economic criteria, high status being derived from land and slave-ownership, participation in local institutions such as the militia, the Council and the House of Assembly, and through membership in one of the 120 elite families which dominated the island. The elite's status had descended largely intact from the tobacco and early sugar period of 1627-60 and was maintained through a system of inheritance based on entailment and on carefully arranged marriages. As far as the generality of the white population was concerned, earlier distinctions derived from points of origin in Europe: whether, for example, one was English,

Welsh, Scots or Irish had been nullified through the process of creolisation. The evolution of this cultural synthesis of West African and West European forms was noticed and commented on by almost every eighteenth-century traveller's account.[1] This created a strong identification with Barbados. The planter Robert Haynes thus boasted to an absentee owner in England, 'tis to me the first country in the World'.[2] As William Green notes in his discussion of the subject, 'creolization involved the identification of people, whatever their place of origin or racial composition, with the island societies in which they lived'.[3]

This proto-nationalism manifested itself in many forms, amongst which was hostility expressed by local whites towards Englishmen who were considered to be snobbish and takers of the best positions available on the island. Harassment of English naval and military officers was commonplace and often resulted in violent confrontations and duels. In 1814, J. W. Hayward complained to Earl Bathurst about the bad treatment meted out by Barbadian whites to 'my countrymen' and asked the earl to intervene, so that they 'in future may not be the sufferers at Barbadoes because they have the happiness of being Englishmen'.[4] The gradual disappearance of religious differences among the local whites also promoted social cohesion. The Quaker congregation had shrunk considerably and was no longer the force it had been in the seventeenth century. Roman Catholics were absent, and the long established Sephardic Jewish community was rapidly disappearing under the two-pronged process of conversion to Christianity and migration from the island.

Despite the emergence of a seemingly homogeneous white Anglo-Saxon Protestant group, white society was not monolithic, as much of the literature seems to indicate. Stressing as it does an erroneous and much simplified image of a population divided between rich white planters leading a garrison-like existence and oppressed black slaves confined to barracoons, this simplistic model is well entrenched. In fact, the only issue which seemed to have a unifying effect on Barbadian whites was that of race. As a minority, faced with all the attendant psychological stresses and paranoia shared by minorities everywhere, Barbadian whites felt constrained to close ranks and present a united front to the black majority, but even this unity was only apparent in times of anxiety and crisis. The reality of dependence on blacks in all spheres of activities precluded any meaningful separation of the races. Economics and the psychology of slavery created a shared space delineated by the small physical boundaries of an isolated oceanic island with a land area measuring only 166 square miles.

The slave system in Barbados functioned in a peculiarly intimate fashion. The benign topography of the island, its intricate road network which facilitated movement and communication, the intense husbandry in which more than 94 per cent of total land was cultivated, and the spatial distribution of settlement had by the eighteenth century created a shared physical and mental landscape which made Barbados unique in the West Indies. Anonymity was non-existent. In a small society of some 86,000 souls, people communicated with each other, knew each other and possessed a solid understanding of family histories and relationships which allowed them to locate each and every member of society along the socio-economic spectrum. This knowledge was not confined to either specific racial group. Both blacks and whites knew each other well. The point is clearly illustrated by the advertisements issued for runaway slaves, in which precise details of physical features, residential location and social relationships are stated. The concept of the invisible black, if at all valid for other slave societies, does not apply to the Barbadian model. Barbadian blacks could recite white genealogies with surprising accuracy and well understood the importance of lineage and its relationship to the distribution of power among the island's creole whites.

The Structure and Distribution of the White Population

Dr Coke, who visited the island towards the end of the eighteenth century, noted that 'there are more white inhabitants in Barbados than in the great Island of Jamaica, a considerable part of it being broke in very small estates of only a few acres, so that many of the whites are very poor, nay, some are even supported by the parish, a circumstance, I believe, not known in any other part of the Archipelago'.[5]

Table 1
White population (1816)[6]

Parish	Population
St Michael	5,038
Christ Church	1,618
St Philip	1,392
St John	1,246
St Joseph	1,124
St Andrew	630
St Lucy	1,058
St Peter	1,379
St James	755
St Thomas	835
St George	945
Total	16,020

As Table 1 shows, the white population was fairly well distributed, with an expected clustering in the parish of St Michael, where the capital city, Bridgetown, is located. Some 31.5 per cent of whites resided there. Other important features were the normal sex ratio characterised by a slight numerical majority of white females in all cohorts over the age of 20 and the fact that in excess of 90 per cent of whites were Barbadian born, most of whom could trace their ancestry back at least six generations, being in the main descended from families who had established themselves on the island in the period 1627-60.

As Table 2 indicates, many estates were small, a factor which deepened the creolisation process, since small estates reduced absenteeism. As late as 1838, 85 per cent of all sugar plantations belonged to resident owners.[7] The variable of size also limited the number of slaves held by individual properties, which is important for a number of interrelated reasons. Small estates forced planters to be careful with their investment in slave labour and partially explains Barbados' tendency to natural growth in the slave population since 1750, which was in marked contrast to the negative growth experienced by the other British colonies in the Caribbean. Certainly by 1817, only seven per cent of the island's black population was African born and Barbados' slave population was self-sustaining and heavily creolised.[8]

Table 2
Size of sugar plantations (1838)[9]

Numbers	Size
192	Less than 100 acres
177	Less than 100 to 200 acres
104	Less than 200 to 500 acres
16	Greater than 500 acres
489	

Because of the small size of most estates, labour needs were restricted and very few individuals owned more than 100 slaves. The surviving parish returns indicate that 50 per cent of slave holders owned ten slaves or less. Approximately 25 per cent of whites owned no slaves at all and lived a marginal existence side by side with blacks, as militia tenants on large estates, fishermen, peasant cultivators or unskilled labourers. Intimate contact with slaves on a daily basis over several generations had hastened the process of creolisation for the island's whites. George Washington visited the island in 1751 and noted in his diary what he considered to be 'Africanisms' adopted by

Barbadian whites. This reflected the changes resulting from creolisation, particularly at the level of expressive culture, where mentality, language, dietary habits, body language and musical tastes differentiated the native-born white from the expatriate. An examination of the evolving ceramic tradition of the island clearly shows that material culture too had been creolised, reflecting a synthesis of African and European potting traditions.[10] All homes, white and black, irrespective of socio-economic rank, used local forms such as the monkey jar (used for cooling and storing water) and the conaree jar (used for storing foods). The widespread use of these forms of colonoware is clearly manifest in the archaeological record of the island.

In its 31 August 1839 issue, the *Penny* magazine of the Society for the Diffusion of Useful Knowledge made the following observation directed at prospective visitors to the island, 'it is not the less pleasing to reflect that the people we shall meet on our arrival, though living in a foreign land and partaking some what of a foreign character, are fellow countrymen of our own, descended from the same ancestors'. What the *Penny* magazine perceived to be a 'foreign character' was precisely what George Washington, Pinckard and other observers regarded as Africanisms adopted by whites. Under the twin dynamics of environment and cultural inputs from Africa and Europe, Barbadians had acquired an identity, a creole consciousness with its specific world view or as Jack Greene notes, 'a coherent corporate identity, that is, a well defined sense of themselves and their society and a distinctive reputation by which they were known by the outside world'.[11]

The manipulation of power and the exercise of political rights constitute one of the most significant expressions of consciousness. Barbadian whites, although acknowledging the limiting circumstances of the small physical size of the island, the external security implications of Anglo-French rivalry in the Caribbean and the internal security concerns posed by a system of slavery, had nevertheless consistently challenged the British government for greater political participation and a control which bordered on local autonomy. These initiatives had consistently been taken by the island's major planters and had begun as early as the 1650s with the challenge to Cromwell's administration and a temporary declaration of independence. Throughout the eighteenth century, the House of Assembly (dominated by the big planters) had successfully challenged English governors for greater political control of the island, by exercising their control over money bills. During the American revolutionary period, the Assembly dominated by its speaker, the planter-aristocrat Sir John Gay Alleyne, acquired further parliamentary privileges, including liberty of speech and exemption from arrest.[12]

By the end of the eighteenth century, however, internal political changes were under way in Barbados which will now be examined in the context of conflicting levels of identity and consciousness. Barbadian white creole society had matured, but in the process, had generated levels of dissension and conflict.

The Conflict between the Salmagundi and the Pumpkins[13]

By the turn of the nineteenth century, latent class rivalries among the white population were surfacing, a result of tensions deriving from both external and internal issues. These manifested themselves in the formation of two parties which contested for control of the House of Assembly.

Undoubtedly, the precepts of the Enlightenment and the examples of the French Revolution and the Haitian Revolution played a part in heightening the political awareness and ambitions of the small planters. In a perceptive article on white Jacobins in the Caribbean (1789-1800), Anne Perotin-Dumon makes the point that it was the intermediate categories of colonial society which expressed some kind of discontent, 'a particulariste and local-oriented expression of change'.[14] Although directed at the French Caribbean, her analysis is equally applicable to Barbados. The political and social uncertainty sparked a negative reaction from large planters. This is evident in the language used by both the small planters and by their opponents, the plantocrats, who quoted or attributed French revolutionary phrases to the former group in order to discredit them.

Of even greater significance was the mounting attack on the institution of slavery by the humanitarians in England. By the 1790s this had created new stresses in what was already a stress-prone society and was responsible for fomenting reactions in Barbados, one of which was to pit the large, established landowners against the small-holders or ten-acre men. The former was a tightly-knit group whose numbers were less than four per cent of the approximately 7850 white males resident in Barbados at the time. In the Eastern Caribbean, the only comparable group were the *grands békés* of Martinique. The Barbadian planters' education, mostly at schools and universities in Britain, had conferred on them a sense of tradition and paternalism. They also enjoyed an economic well-being which permitted them to adopt a more flexible, moderate approach to the slave system, as opposed to the poorer small landholder, whose options and mobility were limited through economic constraints and whose education and experience were almost exclusively limited to Barbados.[15] This latter group was vulnerable and susceptible to many fears as its members tried to project into the future. They viewed control of the island's political institutions as the best possible means of enhancing and safeguarding their socio-economic position.

This was a proto-nationalist perspective, a natural development, bolstered by the constant attacks on West Indian whites originating from Britain at that time. In fact, a veritable cartoon war had been unleashed which portrayed local whites as sadistic, uncultured brutes. The best example this writer has seen of this genre of unbridled exaggeration and satire depicts a creole white woman looking out through an upstairs window; on becoming tired, orders her slave to instruct another slave lounging in the doorway downstairs to come upstairs immediately and take in her head. Other sources of tension came from the free coloureds, who were becoming better organised, more affluent and hence were pressing for judicial equality. Finally, pressure was being felt from the slaves who were much better informed than is customarily imagined and who constituted a significant force militating for political and social change. Marginal to all these groups was the mass of poor whites, perhaps numbering as much as 80 per cent of the white population, disenfranchised, living at subsistence level, illiterate and inarticulate but by instinct tending to support the yeomanry or ten-acre men in their challenge to the planters.

This then is the background to the emergence of the Salmagundi and Pumpkin parties. The former was made up of the middling class of Barbados. Owners of small acreages of land of more than ten acres and rarely exceeding 50 acres, they possessed the vote. Their political ideology was conservative when seen from a modern perspective, but at the turn of the nineteenth century they were considered liberal because they dared to challenge the social *status quo*. They were firmly tied to the system of slavery, but bitterly resented the socio-economic dominance of the plantocracy of Barbados. Democracy for them meant an equality which permitted them to share in the island's institutions, but their democratic visions extended no further than empowerment of whites, and their *laager* mentality closed ranks at the suggestion of the extension of political rights to the free coloured group. Even the amelioration of the living and working conditions of slaves provoked negative reactions among many members of this group. Their publications revealed that they were opposed to the 'exalted notions of the elite' and considered themselves to be democrats, 'not revolutionaries but reformers', although the opposing plantocrats considered the Salmagundis to be distinguished by an 'independence of mind' and 'levelling principles' that were divisive and dangerous to society. The Salmagundis protested against this, pointing out that they were strong supporters of church and state and anxious to preserve 'all distinctions necessary to safety'. The two operative words here, distinctions and safety were obvious references to their racial views and pro-slavery sentiments, and underscored their commitment to a doctrine of white supremacy. Schomburgk stated 'they disclaimed being classed among the richest or the greatest, but they wished to be considered as the yeomanry of Barbados'.[16]

The other party, the Pumpkins, derived much of its support from the landed elite of the island. Evidence of this is clear when one looks at surnames taken from the list of those present at a mass meeting held in Bridgetown in 1819 in support of the governor, Lord Combermere, who had been under attack for some time from the Salmagundis.[17] Of 453 signatories, 221 were members of traditional planter families. Other surnames were those of upwardly mobile families linked to the interests and values of the large planters. This group was representative of a patrician class, with vested interests to protect, powerful, conservative, and with a deep-seated feeling of class superiority. An example of their class prejudice is a manifesto which they issued to the St Philip freeholders during the 1810 vestry elections. The Pumpkins pointed out that in electing the existing vestry 'you have placed in the hands of sixteen persons possessing scarcely 300 acres of land, the concerns of this extensive parish of more than 15,000 acres'.[18] They insinuated that it would be wise to change this situation since, in their view, exercise of political power should be linked to high social status and economic well-being. Lack of economic power should thus disqualify individuals from representing the community. The St Philip smallholders' sole purpose was that of 'exhibiting power under what they term independence of mind – all this with the animosity and rancour of infatuated party politics'. The manifesto went on to mention the 'levelling principles' of the Salmagundis 'which it is their pride and utmost endeavor to distribute throughout their neighborhood'.[19] Hidden behind the rhetoric of these newspaper exchanges was a struggle for empowerment, which was the specific political agenda of the Salmugundis. This was a source of contention, in fact a threat to the elite, whose view of society was derived from medieval hierarchical concepts, the notion of allotted stations in life into which people were born, which if challenged, would upset the social order.

This static view of society and opposition to social mobility can be further illustrated by an editorial which appeared on 10 October 1809 in the island's principal conservative newspaper, the *Barbados Mercury*. This editorial discussed the recently concluded general elections, in which all former members had been returned except in St Philip, where 'a sad triumph has been gained over patriotism and public spirit: low party feud and vulgar prejudice resulted in the election of John Lord and Thomas Briggs in the place of Mr. Grasett and Mr. Barrow, the two former upright and enlightened members'.

The editor expressed the view that this development was an innovation which was sure to have a 'baneful effect': 'Those whom Nature only designed for Porters of the Lodge and never for Lords of the Manor - would take over, shunting aside men of talents, integrity and fortune causing the proud and the lofty vessel of the state, forsaken by its skilful crew and steady pilot, to drift from Pie Corner to the Cobbler's Rocks, there to founder and split into pieces.'

In the same issue the editor commented that situations to which respectable men aspired were now 'bandied' from one obscure individual to another so that even the 'Representation of the People has fallen into such contempt that from Pedlars to Pedagogues – from Cobblers to Couriers from a ci-devant shoemaker to a soi-disant printer – the legislative right passes with the Revolutionary rapidity of ca ira! ca ira!'[20]

Both parties were supported by rival newspapers. The Pumpkin party used the *Western Intelligencer* and their opposition, the Salmagundis, the *Globe* to express their views and to mount attacks 'on a set of men who were sacrificing the good of their country'.[21] The island's major newspaper, the *Barbados Mercury*, did not adopt a neutral posture but sided with the plantocracy.

The first three decades of the nineteenth century were marked by acrimony and bitterness. There were frequent references in the local press to the disturbed state of the island, which was seen as destructive to 'domestic peace, social concord and national prosperity'.[22] The challenge issued by the white middle class to the planter-controlled establishment caused worry in several quarters. Lord Seaforth in 1809 reported in a dispatch to London 'that if no opposition is made to such violent encroachments ... the Government of the Colony would be soon purely Democratic'.[23] In 1817, before sailing for Barbados to assume the governorship of the island, Lord Combermere was warned by Lord Bathurst of the situation and he was given names of individuals 'who invariably opposed every measure of the home government and its representative, the governor'.[24] The British government was aware of the internal political problems of Barbados and linked these to nascent nationalism and that pride and awareness of self which separated the Barbadian white Creole from the Englishman.

The enslaved population did not sit by idly with the island in political uproar. They also had a political agenda with freedom as their main objective. Among the contributory factors to the 1816 revolt was the politically disturbed condition of the island, which created an opportunity for the slaves to take action. It is no coincidence that St Philip's parish was the focus and starting point of slave revolutionary activity. This parish was one of the more economically diversified, with cotton, aloe and ginger cultivation in addition to sugar cane, and had a large poor-white, ten-acre man population. From 1796-1816 it had been marked by frequent, rowdy political meetings attended not only by whites, but also by free coloureds and slaves, who witnessed confrontations of one white group with another, underscoring their divisions and destroying the myth of a white monolithic social structure. The point is made even more forcefully if this is compared with the early situation in St Domingue/Haiti in which the rivalry between *grand blancs* and *petit blancs* during the 1790s created conditions favourable for the slaves to revolt.

During Lord Combermere's administration events came to a head and the

Salmagundis triumphed, taking control of the House of Assembly. As in the eighteenth century, the issue which precipitated this dispute was the role of the governor. The newspaper of the Salmagundis, the *Globe*, criticised the governor for calling out the local militia for a parade. The editorial of 25 February 1819 suggested that the governor merely wanted to add pomp to the special service organised to fund the Barbados Society for Promoting Christian Knowledge, but argued that this went beyond the bounds of the governor's power, since he could only call out the militia on extraordinary occasions. It was necessary to 'oppose oppression and resist a system of tyranny which according to our interpretation, is not sanctioned by custom or law'.[25] The editor, Michael Ryan, was prosecuted for seditious libel on the Colonial Government and offered bail of £10,000, which he refused. While he was in prison awaiting trial, numerous public meetings were held throughout the island to express support for him. A Salmagundi body was formed on 18 May 1819 which called themselves 'The Friends to Liberty and a Free Press'. The date chosen was symbolic and deliberate since on the same day in 1805 the then governor, Lord Seaforth, had declared martial law, fearing a French attack. He had been heavily criticised for this action, which the House of Assembly claimed, 'was highly unconstitutional, contrary to law and subversive of the dearest rights of the people'. Ryan's eventual acquittal evoked great joy from thousands who had flocked to Bridgetown. Viscountess Combermere in her memoirs mockingly wrote: 'The Chief Justice tried to check the enthusiasm, but the joy of a *nation* – even though a very small one – celebrating the discomfiture of its tyrants will make itself heard'.[26] Lord Combermere himself noted that 'a spirit of insubordination has been planted, the fruit of which may one day be gathered with sorrow and repentance'.[27]

Two Salmagundi magistrates, John Lane and Cheeseman Moe, took part in the celebrations and were struck from the Commission of Peace by Combermere, on the grounds that their actions constituted 'dereliction of duty'. Both men vigorously protested against their dismissal. Lane is reported to have told the governor: 'As the chief magistrate you command my respect, you yet are but a man and so am I; and while I keep within the pale of the laws, I fear not your frowns – your smiles I never courted'.[28] Further meetings were held to condemn the governor. To counter these, the Pumpkin party held a mass rally in Bridgetown in support of Combermere at which resolutions were passed praising the good work of the governor and circulated for signatures. These were later published in the *Barbados Mercury*. One in particular criticised 'the principles of unbounded licentiousness which have gained a dangerous ascendancy over the Press of certain Newspapers published in this island'. Such developments were 'incompatible with the exercise of improved civilization and enlightened manners, destructive of domestic peace, social concord and national prosperity'.[29]

The clergy took the unprecedented step of publishing an open letter to the governor, in which they stated that 'with the most painful sensation we contemplate the unhappy divisions now existing throughout the island, tending to foment all those malignant passions which are most at variance with the true temper and genius of Christianity'.[30]

For his part, the governor replied: 'All classes of His Majesty's subjects in this community enjoy the privileges and blessings of our glorious constitution – they know that their just grievances will be attended to provided the proper and legitimate mode of seeking redress be adopted. I have therefore the more sincerely to lament with you the unhappy differences now prevailing amongst the white inhabitants of this colony.'[31]

The general elections of 1819 were bitterly fought. Individuals such as John Beckles (Pumpkin) who had never before placed advertisements in papers soliciting voters' support were now doing so. Beckles stated that he had been elected for nearly 37 years, but 'I am not so silly as to suppose that it gave me a right to your votes in all events'. He reminded voters that they could trust him since he was a man of integrity. Somewhat arrogantly, he added 'I am not actuated by any interested motives, for I stand in need of no emoluments.'[32] In the parish of St Thomas, N. Forte (Pumpkin) declared to his electorate that he was committed to the 'general welfare of the country and the particular interests of my constituents'. His opponent John Carew (Salmagundi) declared in a competing advertisement: 'I will never suffer your rights to be infringed nor will I be led away by the eloquence of any man.'[33] Voters were offered a choice between solid Pumpkin tradition and continuity, a philosophy similar to that which says that 'your social superiors know what is best for you in these turbulent times', as opposed to the Salmagundi platform that the very existence of white Barbadian society was threatened by the humanitarian propaganda emanating from Britain and that the island could only be saved by a strident defence of white political and economic privileges. The results were a landslide for the Salmagundis. Thirteen of the incumbents, including Beckles, Speaker of the House, lost their seats. All the losers were from old planter families and only five of the elite retained their seats, so that the composition of the House now consisted of seventeen seats for Salmagundis, five seats for Pumpkins.

Among those elected to the Assembly were Cheeseman Moe and John Lane. Responding to their prodding, the House of Assembly appointed a committee 'to inquire into the causes which had led to (their) dismissal from the Commission of the Peace'. This committee solicited evidence from the governor, who testily replied that as the committee 'was an officious interference with his prerogative, he shall certainly not lay any evidence whatever before them'. Lord Combermere dissolved the House, fresh elections were called, and the Salmagundis again won, this time with a majority of two.

Lord Combermere's tenure was, however, at an end. In his farewell address of 30 May 1820, he lamented the fact that he had 'not been able to accomplish much'. This he attributed directly to 'those mischievous and vulgar squabbles which have of late disgraced this island in the eyes of the mother country'. Yet the polarity existing on the island, which Combermere referred to as 'squabbles', masked even deeper issues.

In the period 1820-26 (the year of passage of the Slave Consolidated Act which reformed existing slave laws) there were stormy sessions within the House of Assembly and between that body and the planter-dominated Council. The amelioration proposals coming from the British parliament and the pressure brought to bear on the island by the humanitarian movement created considerable apprehension. Fear was evident and in this charged atmosphere clashes were inevitable. In 1823, an enraged white mob completely destroyed the Methodist chapel in Bridgetown, because it had opened its doors to slaves.

The House of Assembly minutes for 1821 and 1822 contain quite strong, even radical, language which confirms the class conflict, but also reflects the extent to which Barbadians had evolved a separate identity and community awareness or Barbadian *mentalité*. The Salmagundis pointed out that they had grouped to break the plantocracy's hold on society and to correct 'numberless abuses': 'They were no longer prepared to suffer tamely the insults of the large planters – a set of men who were sacrificing the good of their country to the gratification of their private resentment.' Despite the fact that their principles were not congenial to the elite, they were resolved 'not to desist in their efforts until they had been freed from injustice and oppression'.[34]

It is ironic that despite these claims of opposition to 'injustice and oppression' the Salmagundis resisted the amelioration proposals emanating from Britain. The world view/*mentalité* of the small planters seemed unable to comprehend that change was inevitable and that the system of slavery was itself doomed. Victims themselves of the system, their vision and consciousness was warped by the peculiar circumstances of their very society. The Council (the organ of the old plantocracy) was prepared to adopt the proposals, thus confirming a flexibility and pragmatism which their class and economic status permitted – patrimonial politics at its best. However, the Assembly resisted incorporating the changes requested on the grounds that slavery was a local system operating in a local environment, and raised the old cry that as a Barbadian body it would enact the appropriate legislation in time, and that any attempt to enforce the amelioration proposals was unconstitutional and would constitute interference in local matters.

This point was discussed and accepted by the Colonial Office, but after delays and half-hearted attempts by the Assembly to introduce measures to improve the lot of the slaves, a frustrated Colonial Office in 1826, in a punitive strike designed to force the Assembly to act, appropriated the duties paid on American and foreign goods which had previously been paid into the Colonial Treasure and used for the purposes of the island. Protests were immediately sent to Britain, but to no avail.[35] This 'bigstick diplomacy' had its desired effect: after considerable debate in the House of Assembly, the consensus was that Britain had other harsher ways of imposing her will, and so compliance was the wisest choice. The Slave Consolidated Act, deficient as it was, passed the House. This marked a decline in the class divisions which, as Governor Warde had commented, were so pronounced that 'never was a colony in a more disturbed state ... the House of Assembly are at open war with the Council'.[36]

It was now evident that emancipation was on its way and as this loomed, old divisions died down and new alliances were forged. Abolition made obsolete the 1721 Act which established race as the principal barrier to democratic participation. Suffrage was still limited however, by gender and property qualifications.

On 13 June 1843 a new chapter opened in the history of the House of Assembly. Samuel Jackman Prescod, the first elected non-white to the House, took his seat as a member representing the new constituency of Bridgetown. A new challenge manifested itself to white Barbadians, that of non-racial democracy. For over 100 years, whites fought a persistent rearguard action with the obvious intention of delaying full black political participation. In a perverse but understandable way, their successful retention of political power until the 1930s demonstrates the extent to which they as a group were committed, albeit selfishly, to their island home. The economic, sociological and psychological dimensions of white unwillingness to share or concede empowerment in no way detracts from the fact that they too belonged and were part of the complex fabric of island society. The events described in this paper confirm the complexity of white Barbadian society and the extent to which the creolisation process had transformed them from Englishmen and women – not into 'foreign characters' as the *Penny* magazine suggested, but into native Barbadians, secure in their identity, proud and conscious of their achievements and traditions.

Notes

1. William Dickson, *Letters on Slavery* (London, 1814), p. 322; George Pinckard, *Notes on the West Indies; Written During the Expedition under the Command of the late General Sir Ralph Abercromby; including Observations on the Island of Barbadoes*, Vol. 1, p. 294; J. M. Toner (ed.), *The Daily Journal of Major George Washington in 1751/2. Kept while on a Tour from Virginia to the Island of Barbadoes with his Invalid Brother Major Laurence Washington* (Albany, 1982), p. 61; Robert Poole, MD, *The Beneficient Bee or Travellers Companion* (London, 1753), p. 288.

2. Robert Haynes to T. Lane, 20 January 1816. Newton Estate Papers, 523/760. Palaeography Department, University of London.

3. William A. Green, 'The Creolization of Caribbean History: The Emancipation Era and a Critique of Dialectical Analysis' in Hilary Beckles and Verene Shepherd (eds), *Caribbean Freedom: Economy and Society from Emancipation to the Present* (Kingston, 1993), p. 28.

4. J. W. Hayward to Earl Bathurst, 10 January 1814. CO28/85, f. 107.

5. *An Extract of the Journals of the Rev. Dr. Cokes Five Visits to America* (London, 1793), p. 182.

6. CO 28/86.

7. Bentley Gibbs, 'White Power in 1836', Department of History, University of the West Indies, Cave Hill, unpublished seminar paper, (1989/90), p. 4.

8. For an authoritative discussion of Barbadian slave demography see B. W. Higman, *Slave Populations of the British Caribbean 1802-34* (Baltimore, 1984).

9. Gibbs, *op. cit.* pp. 2–4.

10. See Jerome Handler, 'An Archaeological Investigation of the Domestic Lives of Plantation Slaves in Barbados', *Journal of the Barbados Museum and Historical Society* 34 (1972), pp. 64-72. Personal communication with Dr Tom Loftfield.

11. Jack P. Greene, 'Changing Identity in the British Caribbean: Barbados as a Case Study' in Nicholas Canny and Anthony Pagden (eds), *Colonial Identity in the Atlantic World, 1500-1800* (Princeton, 1987), p. 214.

12. See Selwyn H. H. Carrington, 'West Indian Opposition to British Policy: Barbadian Politics 1774-82', *Journal of Caribbean History* 17 (1982), pp. 26-49; N.A.T. Hall, 'Fragments of Empire: A Study of Constitutional and Political Developments in Barbados and Jamaica, 1783-1815', unpublished manuscript (1971), pp. 147-256; Karl Watson, *The Civilised Island Barbados: A Social History 1750-1816* (Barbados, 1979), pp. 15-25; Andrew J. O'Shaughnessy, 'The Stamp Act Crisis in the British Caribbean', *William and Mary Quarterly*, 3rd series, 51 (1994), pp. 203-26.

13. Richard Schomburgk, *The History of Barbados* (London, 1848), pp. 401-10. Lord Combermere noted that on his arrival, 'The white population of Barbados was divided into two parties, whose political differences, as must ever be the case in small communities were carried to the extent of personal virulence. The Liberals assumed the name of "Salmagundi" while their opponents were branded by them with the sobriquet of "Pumpkins"'. Colloquial usage equated pumpkins with important people. It also had the connotation of a pompous, puffed-up individual. Salmagundi, on the other hand, was used to denote a general mixture/miscellaneous collection, hence the association with common/ordinary folk as opposed to the plantocracy.

14. Anne Perotin-Dumon, 'Ambiguous Revolution in the Caribbean: The White Jacobins, 1789-1800', paper presented at the Sixteenth Annual Conference of Caribbean Historians, Cave Hill, Barbados (1984), p. 3.

15. The distinction between big planter and small planter was based primarily on economic considerations: to qualify as a big planter, one had to own more than 100 acres of land. Of course, there were other status considerations such as family and educational background and member-

ship in the island's institutions. But the principal criterion establishing class was land ownership, preferably inherited land.

16. Schomburgk, *op. cit.,* p. 405.

17. *Barbados Mercury*, 21 August 1819.

18. *Barbados Mercury*, 24 November 1810.

19. Ibid.

20. Editorial, *Barbados Mercury*, 10 October 1809.

21. Schomburgk, *op. cit.,* p. 404.

22. *Barbados Mercury*, 21 August 1819

23. Minutes of a meeting of the inhabitants of the island at Free Masons Hall, 16 August 1819.

24. Mary, Viscountess Combermere, *Memoirs and Correspondence of Field Marshall Viscount Combermere* (London, 1866), vol. 1, p. 340.

25. Schomburgk, *op. cit.,* p. 404.

26. Viscountess Combermere, *op. cit.,* p. 365.

27. Schomburgk, *op. cit.,* p. 409.

28. Schomburgk, *op. cit.,* p. 406.

29. *Barbados Mercury*, 21 August 1819.

30. *Ibid.*

31. *Ibid.*

32. *Barbados Mercury*, 6 November 1819.

33. *Ibid.*

34. Minutes of House of Assembly 27 August 1822, Department of Archives, Barbados.

35. A. N. Wiltshire, 'The Reaction of the Barbadian Plantocracy to Amelioration, 1823–1833', University of the West Indies, Cave Hill, MA thesis (1983), p. 42.

36, 'Warde Letters - 1' *Journal of the Barbados Museum and Historical Society* 34 (1974), p. 205.

3

The White Elite of Trinidad, 1838-1950

BRIDGET BRERETON

Although Trinidad was late to develop as a slave society, by the 1830s, when slavery was abolished in the British empire, the island possessed the classic three-tier social structure typical of the Caribbean sugar colonies. At the top was the white minority, people of European birth or ancestry. This small group, always less than 10 per cent of the total population in the period under consideration, and only 1.9 per cent by 1960, was a true elite for this whole period: it was dominant in the economic, social and political life of the island. But it was far from being a homogeneous or monolithic group. Indeed, because the island had been under Spanish rule, with a large French community since the 1780s, its white elite was more diverse than that of any other nineteenth-century British Caribbean territory.

The origins of the white community

The white community consisted of people born in Europe and the Creoles born in the island (or perhaps elsewhere in the Caribbean). Most of the former were British: the officials, plantation owners, managers and overseers, businessmen and professional men who came out to Trinidad to work and to make money. Some, especially the career colonial officials, were true 'birds of passage' who stayed for only a short time and then moved on, but others established homes and families in the island, often intermarrying with the white Creoles and identifying with them. Nevertheless, a certain tension between the British-born and the Creoles was inherent in the colonial situation.

Inevitably European birth and upbringing conferred special status, and the Creoles often complained of the arrogance and the unjustified sense of superiority displayed by the newcomers, especially the officials.

Apart from the distinction between those born in Europe and the Creoles, the white community was further divided along what might loosely be described as 'class' lines. At the top was the undoubted elite: the owners of plantations and substantial businesses, the executives of major concerns (including the sugar corporations and the oil companies), the wealthy professional men and the top officials. A 'middle' group consisted of estate overseers and employees in the stores and commercial firms, small businessmen and minor professionals and civil servants, a few teachers, clergymen and missionaries, governesses, a few French or British artisans, officers in the police force, skilled workers in the oil industry (mostly Americans). People in this group were often upwardly mobile; an overseer might possibly acquire landed property, a Scottish shop clerk might be helped to set up his own firm, a fortunate marriage might mean assimilation into the elite group. Trinidad had no real 'poor white' community, but in the nineteenth century there were a few whites who might be described as constituting a 'lowerclass' group. Portuguese gardeners and small shopkeepers might be included here, along with a few whites employed as domestics and valets by wealthy creole families, some of them probably from 'poor white' communities in Barbados and St Vincent, or from Cayenne. These 'class' lines intersected with divisions related to ethnicity and national origins. Unlike Barbados or Jamaica, with their homogeneous white communities, Trinidad's white Creoles consisted of people of Spanish, French, British, German, Corsican and Venezuelan ancestry, and those of British origins were in the minority. The largest group consisted of the 'French Creoles', families of mostly French descent, but the term was (and is) generally understood to include those of English, Irish, Spanish, Corsican and German origins, born in the island and almost invariably Roman Catholic.[1] The most prominent of the 'French Creole' families (the 'capitulants') were established by French, Spanish, Irish and Corsican immigrants who had arrived in Trinidad before the British conquest in 1797 or soon after. Although a few mostly Catholic families of English origins assimilated with the French Creoles, the 'English Creoles' came to constitute a distinct enclave. These were people of English or Scottish origins, born in the island, Protestant (mostly Anglican or Presbyterian) in religion. Not surprisingly, they had close links to the expatriate British residents, with whom they often intermarried.

The established creole elite, the 'old families', was augmented by people coming from Europe or North America after 1838, who settled in the island and intermarried with Creoles. White Venezuelan immigrants might also be assimilated into this group.

The Siegerts, a Venezuelan family of German origin, came to Trinidad in the 1870s; the de Limas, Venezuelans descended from Portuguese Jews, arrived in the following decade. Both families were part of the commercial elite in the twentieth century.

In the decades after emancipation Portuguese immigrants from Madeira were brought to the island as indentured labourers. Coming from a peasant or labouring background, working in Trinidad as gardeners, butchers and village shopkeepers, the Portuguese were clearly not part of the white elite in the nineteenth century, despite their ethnicity. But by the 1880s and 1890s several Portuguese families, becoming prosperous through shopkeeping, acquiring landed property and educating their children up to secondary school, were upwardly mobile. By the 1920s or 1930s many families of Portuguese origin, affluent and educated, were entering the elite; the career of Errol dos Santos (1890-1992) exemplifies this trend.

Immigrants from the Middle East began to come to Trinidad in small numbers after 1890 and by 1950 Trinidad had a tiny but distinct 'Syrian/Lebanese' community, known locally as the Syrians. Many were Maronite Christians, others adopted Catholicism in Trinidad. In terms of the island's ethnic scheme, the Syrians could be regarded as 'white', and by the middle of the twentieth century they were challenging the established commercial families with their success in the retailing sector. But they remained a closed 'trader minority', strictly endogamous, and still unassimilated into the white elite.

This ethnically and culturally diverse white community played a major role in shaping Trinidad's development in the century after emancipation. First the economic base will be examined, for it was control of the island's resources that enabled the whites to exercise social and political hegemony. Second, the evolution of inter-ethnic relations within the white community will be analysed. Lastly the social development of the white elite – its traditions and claims, cultural and associational life, domestic relations and sense of identity – will be considered.

The economic base

The plantation sector

Trinidad's white elite was historically a landowning group based on plantation agriculture, and at least until the 1920s or 1930s most of its members probably derived their incomes chiefly from the land. Sugar was the traditional staple, pioneered by the first generation of the French creoles in the late eighteenth and early nineteenth centuries. By the 1890s, however, the French Creoles – and, in fact, white Creoles in general – had lost ground to British companies or individual British proprietors in the ownership of the sugar industry. In 1871, out of 129 sugar estates, 43 were owned by British companies or individuals resident in Britain, 43 by English Creoles or British living in the island, and about 40 by French Creoles – an almost equal division between the three categories. But by 1895, out of only 59 estates (reflecting a process of amalgamation and consolidation over the previous decades), 34 were owned by British companies, 20 by resident Englishmen or English Creoles, and only three by French Creoles; no estate producing over 1,000 hogsheads a year was in French Creole hands by then. The situation by the end of the century was that British concerns controlled most of the large estates, French Creoles were no longer significant owners of sugar property, and resident Englishmen and English Creoles continued to hold a number of plantations, including some large ones.[2]

Some French Creoles had been forced out of sugar during the prolonged crises of the 1840s, caused by labour difficulties and the loss of the protected British market, and had often sold out to larger and more heavily capitalised British planters. Others continued to own important estates into the 1870s, like Paul Guiseppi with the Valsayn and Caroni estates. But the smaller, under-capitalised estates, still producing muscovado sugar, became increasingly unprofitable after 1874, when preferential duties in favour of muscovado sugar entering Britain were abolished, and still more so during the period of very low sugar prices in the 1880s and 1890s. These decades saw most of the French Creole sugar planters losing their estates. Louis Julien de Verteuil, for instance, owned and managed three estates near San Fernando (Cupar Grange, Union Hall and Concorde). The first two were sold to British concerns in the early 1870s; Concorde, heavily mortgaged, was sold soon after his death in 1879. Other French Creoles managed to hold on to their land, but gave up sugar cultivation as the industry was increasingly concentrated in the Naparimas and central Trinidad: by the 1880s, for instance, sugar had been abandoned at the Champs Elysées estate in Maraval, owned by the de Boissières.[3]

Several prominent French creole families fell on 'hard times' during this squeezing-out process: Louis Julien de Verteuil's widow had to help educate her numerous children, after the loss of the family sugar estates, by making and selling jellies and preserves, quilts and rag dolls; she had to sell her Port-of-Spain house. A French priest, visiting in 1879 the country house of the Kernahan family (French Creoles of Irish origin), commented on their 'straightened circumstances': the ladies of the house had to do the cooking and housekeeping, and packing cases and barrels served as seats.[4]

British companies or individual capitalists resident in Britain bought out the local whites. The Colonial Company, for instance, bought de Verteuil's Union Hall estate in

the 1870s, along with several others; John Cumming, the largest resident sugar proprietor around the turn of the century, sold three estates to the company in 1911. The
Scottish Lamont family was active in this process; John Lamont, who arrived in Trinidad
in 1802, had accumulated several estates in the Naparima area by the time of his death
in 1850. His nephew, James Lamont, systematically bought up small estates in the district during the 1860s and 1870s (mostly from French Creoles, including de Verteuil),
ending up with two large, adjacent conglomerations, Phillipine and Palmiste. He
scrapped the small muscovado factories and erected a central factory at Palmiste in the
early 1880s. Although the Lamonts were well capitalised, with substantial investments
in Britain as well as Trinidad, they found it difficult to make steady profits from their
sugar properties, and after 1917 Norman Lamont (James's son) gradually abandoned
sugar, though he remained a substantial landowner up to his death in 1949. By the early
years of the twentieth century very few local whites were involved in the sugar industry
as estate owners, but many found positions as managers, overseers and engineers with
the large sugar firms; in 1933, for instance, the Usine St Madeleine employed about 100
whites in managerial or supervisory positions. The large, locally owned firm of Gordon
Grant & Co acquired and managed sugar properties in the first half of the twentieth century; in 1949 it sold its Reform estates to one of the two major British corporations then
active in the local sugar industry.[5]

Largely squeezed out of the sugar industry by around 1880, the French Creoles
found the basis for their recovery in cocoa, which expanded rapidly in the 50 years after
1870. In the late 1860s the more far-sighted French Creoles, recognising that they were
losing ground in sugar, began to focus on the extensive Crown lands and their potential
use for establishing cocoa estates. In 1866 a group of them petitioned for the opening up
of the Crown lands so that they could set up cocoa plantations cheaply. Louis de
Verteuil, by then the acknowledged spokesman of his community, made it clear that the
petitioners' aim was to create opportunities for 'white youths belonging to respectable
families . . . descendants of the first settlers of the island', who were being squeezed out
of sugar, or had failed as managers or clerks.[6] With the opening of the Crown lands in
1868-69, and rising demand for cocoa and chocolate in Europe and the United States the
cocoa boom began. Many French Creoles who had sold their sugar estates used the pro-
ceeds to purchase land and establish cocoa estates; others, who had held on to their
lands, switched to cocoa, like the de Boissières at Champs Elysées. By the 1880s cocoa
was clearly profitable, and the capital needed to buy Crown lands and purchase small
cocoa plots was willingly extended by merchants, often French Creoles themselves.

Most of the owners of large cocoa estates between 1870 and 1920 were French
Creoles. In 1895, of the 375 cocoa estates listed in the Annual Register for that year, at

least 270 were owned by them. In 1887, of the 14 largest properties in the Montserrat Ward Union (a major new centre of cocoa cultivation), 13 were owned by French Creoles, including prominent families such as the de Verteuils, d'Abadies, Agostinis, de Labastides and Ciprianis. After 1880 cocoa became the backbone of the community's recovery and then of its prosperity. With prices generally good until 1920, with capital easily available on the security of the land and the trees, planters developed estates even in marginal areas, and many owned several properties, all heavily mortgaged. Planters active around the turn of the century, like Carl de Verteuil, founder of the Cocoa Planters Association, could live lavishly in great country houses as well as town mansions, with frequent trips to Europe and sons and daughters being educated in Britain or France. The great house La Chance near Arima, established in the 1880s by J. G. de Gannes, symbolised the French Creole renaissance based on cocoa. One of the patriarch's grandchildren, P. E. T. O'Connor, remembers great gatherings of the extended family at La Chance; the New Year's Day reunion in 1912 involved 54 grandchildren, and each family brought its quota of nannies and nurses. The cocoa planters around Arima used to play polo every Sunday on the Santa Rosa savanna.[7]

Although French creoles dominated the cocoa industry up to and beyond the great crash in the early 1920s, other local whites invested extensively too, especially in the first two decades of the twentieth century when prices were high. Norman Lamont switched from sugar to cocoa on some of his properties, like La Resource; Sir Joseph Needham, the English chief justice between 1870 and 1885, owned a large, flourishing estate in Santa Cruz. A few Portuguese families invested in cocoa, such as Alfred Mendes, who owned several valuable estates by 1914 in both Trinidad (Manzanilla) and in Tobago. The de Limas, of Venezuelan origin, whose main business was their jewellery store, bought a Santa Cruz cocoa estate, L'Esperance, in the 1920s. Local import-export firms, often owned by French Creoles, acquired cocoa estates by foreclosing on small landowners who were heavily indebted to them for credit and supplies. Gordon Grant & Co, founded by a Scot, owned numerous cocoa properties in many parts of Trinidad and Tobago in the first half of the twentieth century. Indeed, by 1920, most well-to-do Trinidadians were interested in cocoa.[8]

The collapse of cocoa prices in 1920-21, the persistently depressed market in the succeeding two decades and the ravages of witchbroom disease after 1928 combined to plunge the industry into a prolonged depression. Since so many white Trinidadians were involved, the colonial government made extraordinary efforts to shore up the industry and help the large planters with various kinds of financial aid. Of course, while depressed prices and disease were beyond the planters' control, their situation had been worsened by mismanagement, high living and heavy debts; as A. A. Cipriani pointed out in 1930, they were 'bon vivants, they had lived off the fat of the land, and they wished to continue living off the fat of the land in spite of the depression'. The cocoa industry never recovered its former prosperity, but it had formed the base of the French creoles' 'comeback' between 1870 and 1920; and after the 1920s, still the owners of substantial landed wealth, they were able to diversify into commerce, finance, real estate and manufacturing. The land they had amassed during the days of the 'golden pod' was a critical resource in this exercise.[9]

As a landowning elite whose economic base was plantation agriculture, the white Creoles came into close contact with the rural labour force, both the blacks (the ex-slaves and their descendants) and the Indians. This was especially true of the French Creoles, whose ancestors had been the pioneers of plantation settlement and the first significant slave-owners in the island. They preserved many of the paternalist attitudes towards 'their people' long after emancipation. A. H. Gordon, the governor between 1866 and 1870, wrote of the French creoles that 'their influence with the lower classes is considerable, and in the country almost paramount, the English proprietors never having acquired or indeed attempted to acquire it to the same degree'. On the death in 1876 of Philip Maingot, a substantial proprietor in the Santa Cruz valley, an obituary commented: 'It was amusing to see with what pleasure he was received, by Creoles and Coolies alike, when he visited his estates .... Like his father before him, he seemed invested with a sort of patriarchal character in the quarter; and it was pleasant to see with what readiness and confidence the poor people submitted their differences to his decision.'

Of course, this paternalism was usually accompanied by a determination to exact all the customary dues and services from 'their people'. Poleska de Boissière, who managed the Champs Elysées estate between 1870 and 1927, letting much of it to labourers and peasants in small lots, always knew exactly which tenants – and there were hundreds – owed rent, and 'on spotting them, would call out to remind them when driving past in her carriage'. Her son Arnauld de Boissière had a powerful telescope on the porch of his hillside home, with which he surveyed his domain; he would then descend on horseback to surprise 'unsuspecting trespassers grazing their animals or cutting grass, impounding the former and confiscating the grass knives of the latter'.[10]

The commercial sector and the oil industry

White Creoles and resident Europeans dominated Trinidad's commercial sector throughout the period, owning nearly all the major import-export agencies and retailing firms. The most prominent commercial agency up to the 1880s was A. Ambard & Son, founded by Andre Ambard, a Frenchman who came to Trinidad in 1820. On his death in 1870 it was carried on by his son Lucien, and by his two sons-in-law, Leon Agostini (first president of the Chamber of Commerce, founded in 1878) and John Bell Smythe, who were both unofficial members of the Legislative Council. In the 1870s the firm greatly extended its cocoa business, becoming the leading buyer and seller of cocoa in Trinidad. It also conducted an import trade in lumber, provisions and stock, and manufactured goods in general, from North America and Europe. In 1878 the partners were able to buy a group of estates for over £80,000 cash, which they raised in 14 days. Their profits were mainly derived from the cocoa trade and the import business, as suppliers for many large estates and as agents for large British and American firms. They were in fact the 'recognised leaders of Trinidad's commercial world'; hence the consternation when the firm went bankrupt in 1886, due to difficulties with their main creditors in Britain. French Creoles were also prominent in many other import-export agencies and firms dealing mainly in the cocoa trade right up to the mid-twentieth century.[11]

Scottish businessmen by the middle of the nineteenth century were establishing a strong presence in the commercial world, especially the 'dry goods' sector (stores selling everything except foodstuffs and drink). Scottish merchants sent out young men to Trinidad to work as shop assistants or clerks, often in stores owned by relatives. If they did well they would, after a few years, set up businesses themselves, or be admitted as partners with established Scottish merchants. For instance, James Miller arrived from Glasgow in the late 1860s. In 1880 he opened Miller's Public Supply Stores, a pioneering shop catering for low-income customers, and by 1914 he had branches in Princes Town, Arima and Tobago. W. S. Robertson, born in Glasgow in 1849, came to Trinidad in 1869 to work with his brother-in-law's firm in San Fernando. Later he took over the business, and by 1890 he was considered the leading merchant of San Fernando, symbolised by his nomination to the Legislative Council in 1894. Wilson & Co, described in 1914 as the largest dry goods business in the West Indies, was founded by James Wilson, another Scottish immigrant.[12]

One of Trinidad's largest commercial firms in the first half of the twentieth century, Gordon Grant & Co, was established by William Gordon. He came to Trinidad from Scotland as a young man in 1864 or 1865, and joined Campbell Hannay & Co of Port-of-Spain. In 1884 he set up Gordon Grant & Co, taking another Scot, George Grant, as his partner. By 1900 the firm was well established in a wide range of business activities: the cocoa trade, agencies for metropolitan banks, insurance companies, manufacturers and steamship lines, and real estate. After 1900 it acquired many cocoa, coconut and sugar estates in both Trinidad and Tobago. It frequently expropriated cocoa estates, often owned by black or brown families and mortgaged to the hilt, sometimes using

Chinese or Indian local shopkeepers as intermediaries; this was one of the main ways in which this firm (like others) amassed land. It also developed a motor car agency and went into the wine and spirits business. By 1950 Gordon Grant & Co was the largest commercial firm in Trinidad; it was involved in banking and finance, import-export business, plantation agriculture, manufacturing and dealerships in lumber, cement and hardware. It held agencies for exporting and manufacturing firms, insurance companies, airlines and shipping lines; it owned plantation properties comprising some 100,000 acres in both islands. Gordon Gordon (who built the splendid Port-of-Spain mansion Knowsley, now the Ministry of External Affairs) headed the firm he had founded for 36 years until his death in 1923. After his death family members continued to own and manage the company until after national independence.[13]

Another important commercial firm was founded in 1901 by Thomas Geddes Grant, the son of a Canadian Presbyterian missionary of Scottish ancestry, Kenneth Grant. After working as a young man for Charles Tennant of San Fernando, he set up on his own in Port-of-Spain as a commission agent and manufacturer's representative. In 1917 T. Geddes Grant was established as a limited liability company. By that time it was the largest commercial shipping agency in the island, with its business founded on the trade with Canada. Branches were set up in Guyana, Barbados and Jamaica between 1916 and 1920. Despite difficulties during the depression years of 1929-31, the firm continued to expand; by 1954, it was representative for over 100 manufacturing firms, distributing a very wide range of goods. T. Geddes Grant remained a tightly controlled family firm up to the 1980s, with every managing director and chairman a family member until 1987; in 1963, all its directors and managers were white men, the majority related to the Grants.[14]

German immigrants arriving in Trinidad during the course of the nineteenth century also became a strong element in the commercial elite, among them Hugo Hoffman, Adolf Wuppermann, J. F. Urich, Fritz Zurcher, K. G. Boos and Conrad Stollmeyer. Many of these German families intermarried with the French Creoles and were assimilated into the group. Perhaps the most important firm established by the Germans was J. N. Harriman & Co. After 1828 it was owned or managed by members of several German families – the Gerolds, Urichs, Wuppermanns, Zurchers – but in 1885 it was bought by K. G. Boos, and it remained in the Boos family for the next 100 years. Between 1921 and 1975 J. N. Harriman was run by Carl Boos and E. Herman Boos, the son and grandson of K. G. Boos respectively. A few Venezuelan immigrants also entered the commercial sector. Yldefonso de Lima set up Y. de Lima in 1885. This was a family jewellery store in Port-of-Spain, which did well enough (along with a pawnbroking business) to make the de Limas prosperous and well established by the 1930s. By the 1950s several Syrian businessmen had 'graduated' from itinerant peddling to opening dry goods stores in Port-of-Spain and other towns; in the following decades they mounted a serious challenge to the established white mercantile elite.[15]

The oil industry became the dominant sector of Trinidad's economy in the twentieth century, and from the start it was mainly controlled by British and American capital and management; the financial outlays and technological sophistication it required were beyond the reach of the local white elite. Nevertheless, many local whites profited from their ownership of oil-bearing properties or worked for the oil companies in managerial and supervisory positions. The pioneers of the oil industry, Charles Darwent in the 1860s and Randoph Rust in the early 1900s, were both Englishmen resident in Trinidad. Rust began drilling on his Aripero estate in 1900 and then, with Canadian capital, at Guayaguayare in 1902. This was the effective beginning of the industry.

Although he and his Chinese-Trinidadian partner John Lee Lum both lost money in the venture, Rust continued to promote the island's oil prospects at home and abroad. Other local whites had interests in the early oil industry. A. F. Mathison was the part owner of La Fortunée estate, Point Fortin, where Trinidad Oilfields had most of their wells in 1914; Edgar Agostini, QC, retired Attorney-General, served in 1914 as general counsel to and director of the Trinidad Oil Company. T. Geddes Grant bought up oil-bearing lands around Fyzabad, and became a substantial shareholder in Apex Trinidad Oilfields, which found oil on his properties, later serving as an Apex director. Conrad Stollmeyer invested in Kern Trinidad Oilfields, which began operations in 1920.[16]

Nearly all the managerial and technical staff were expatriates during the first decades of oil in Trinidad; even the skilled workers (the rigmen) were Americans. But by the 1920s a few white Creoles had entered the industry as managers or supervisors. P. E. T. O'Connor was the first local graduate (in petroleum engineering) to work in the industry when he joined Kern at Brighton in 1923. He joined the 'bachelors' mess' where all his colleagues were British engineers or American drillers. When O'Connor returned to Trinidad in 1937 after a stint abroad and joined the Antilles Petroleum Co, the senior staff in the industry was still exclusively white and mostly expatriate, although a few more local whites had followed his lead; this situation was not to change until the 1950s.[17]

The diversification of economic activities after 1920

Plantation agriculture and import-export trade were the main economic bases of the white elite in Trinidad to the mid-twentieth century. But increasingly after about 1920 – with the cocoa depression and the growing domination of British corporations in sugar

– they diversified their activities by entering real estate development, manufacturing and finance, which were often fairly easy extensions of their commercial and plantation enterprises. This diversification ensured that local whites remained solidly entrenched in the island's economic life at the time of independence in 1962.

As a landowning group, local whites were able to invest heavily in real estate development, especially suburban housing, in the middle of the twentieth century, selling off those estates which had been cultivated in cocoa and other crops and were strategically situated close to the major towns. For instance, the de Boissières sold off their large property in Maraval between the 1920s and the 1940s; the advent of the car had made this district an ideal suburb for Port-of-Spain. Large blocks were sold to property speculators or to organisations like Maraval Lands, to build a golf course, and smaller house lots were sold to affluent buyers. After 1949 Norman Lamont's heirs sold much of his land around San Fernando for suburban estates like Bel Air, La Romain, La Resource and Phillipine. In the 1950s the de Limas turned their cocoa estate in Santa Cruz into a housing development (Sun Valley); the Stollmeyer family sold some of their extensive properties in the same valley for suburban housing between the Second World War and the 1970s. In the 1960s and 1970s T. Geddes Grant & Co invested heavily in construction and real estate development, especially in Diego Martin and Petit Valley, booming suburbs to the west of Port-of-Spain.[18] This successful 'monetarisation' of their land assets, at a time when plantation agriculture was becoming problematic but suburban development was increasingly promising, like the earlier shift from sugar to cocoa, suggests a pragmatic flexibility on the part of these white families.

In much the same way, when prospects opened up for local manufacturing enterprises after the Second World War, several white-owned import-export firms adjusted, either by becoming distributors for locally produced goods, or by entering production themselves, or both. Both strategies were followed by T. Geddes Grant, for instance, between the 1960s and the 1970s. Up to 1945 the de Lima jewelry store sold mainly imported products, although some pieces made by traditional East Indian craftsmen sold well, especially to tourists. But after the war, under the leadership of Jack Y. de Lima, the firm expanded into factory production for both the local and the Caribbean markets. Y. de Lima had a staff of 50–60 by the 1950s. The Siegerts had been manufacturing their famous Angostura bitters in the island since Carlos and Alfredo arrived from Venezuela in 1875. By 1900 they had entered the rum trade, buying bulk rum and blending and bottling it under their firm's name. The family lost control of the business for a time, but after 1936, led by Robert Siegert (great-grandson of the original founder), the plant became modernised and as Trinidad Distillers it became by the 1950s the major distiller of fine spirits in the island, in addition to producing the original bitters. By the

1960s, moreover, a few successful Syrians, owners of dry goods stores, had opened factories making ready-made garments.[19]

Local white businessmen became involved in finance, at first often as agents or managers for British, Canadian or American banks and insurance companies. Both Gordon Grant & Co and T. Geddes Grant acted as agents for banks and insurance firms, and the former firm had a considerable business lending money on mortgages held on estates and houses. Although until 1962 much of the financial sector was foreign-owned, local insurance companies were established by white businessmen (in 1905 A. F. Mathison founded a fire insurance company), and the Trinidad Building and Loan Association was owned by resident whites. The white monopoly of the life insurance industry was challenged in the 1930s by CLICO, owned by two mixed-race businessmen; the colonial government refused to let CLICO policy-holders pay their premiums through salary deductions, a privilege that had been granted to Standard Life of Canada. No locally-owned bank existed before 1970, but several local whites served on the boards of the foreign banks (such as Jeffrey Stollmeyer at Barclays Bank in the 1960s), and many worked for them in managerial and supervisory positions.[20]

Whites were still solidly entrenched in business by the time of independence. In the year before, 1961, the black-dominated, nationalist government led by Eric Williams had issued a rhetorical challenge to their control of local business in his famous 'Massa Day Done' speech. But little was actually done before the Black Power movement of 1970-71 and the oil boom starting in 1973, to erode that control. A study of the island's business elite conducted in 1969-70 suggested that some 68 per cent of the directors of major locally-owned firms were white or 'off-white' (a category that included persons of Portuguese and Syrian ancestry). This study also confirmed that 95 per cent of the persons with low educational qualifications who had been hired for top positions were white or off-white; persons of European or Syrian ancestry were also typically hired to top or middle-level posts at younger ages than others, and were promoted more rapidly. The evidence suggested that despite the decline in plantation agriculture by 1970, distribution, manufacturing, construction, real estate and finance remained substantially in the hands of local whites, except for the foreign-owned concerns.[21]

The civil service and the professions

White creoles entrenched themselves in professions useful to their economic enterprises. Several practised as medical men; the two leading spokesmen for the French Creole community in the Legislative Council between the 1860s and the 1890s, Louis de Verteuil and J. V. de Boissière, were both doctors. But surveying and the law were even more important. Many white creoles were solicitors and barristers. The more distinguished of the latter often entered government service. Two French Creoles of Irish origin, George Knox and Henry Court, served respectively as Chief Justice and Puisne Judge between 1849 and 1887. Charles Warner, from a leading English Creole family, was a formidable Attorney-General between 1844 and 1870; opponents and allies alike acknowledged that he often seemed more powerful than the governors for much of that period. George Garcia, of Spanish and Venezuelan ancestry, succeeded him as Attorney-General in the early 1870s, and his son, G. L. Garcia, was appointed to the same office in 1892. Most, however, remained in private practice. Surveying was dominated almost entirely by French Creoles. The doyen of the nineteenth-century surveyors was Sylvester Devenish, from a French Creole family of Irish descent. In practice from 1842 until the end of the century, he played a key role in surveying and opening up the interior and the hill ranges of the island, as well as being a gifted amateur scientist and collector and a famous hunter. Other French Creoles followed his lead. For a group bent on the steady acquisition of land, control of surveying was a sound move; since they also practised as lawyers, they were able to save on expenses related to conveyancing and land transactions generally. Thus functioning as planters, solicitors and surveyors, the French Creoles further entrenched themselves in the business of exploiting the land.[22]

It was not unusual for white Creoles to embark on careers in the government service, although the top posts were generally reserved for Britons for nearly the entire period of colonialism. The most prominent nineteenth-century example was probably John Scott Bushe, an English Creole who held for many years the second highest post in the government, that of colonial secretary. He was the son of an English planter who had settled in Trinidad early in the century, and rose to prominence after he married the sister-in-law of Lord Harris, governor between 1846 and 1854. Though considered an able and 'popular' civil servant, the Colonial Office doubted his suitability for higher office, and a local commentator remarked caustically that 'he provided comfortably in the Government service for such of his connections as needed it'. Many French Creoles of Irish ancestry also served in the civil service in the nineteenth century, proportionately far more than Creoles of French descent; no doubt their greater fluency in English was one reason for this.[23]

The tradition of white Creoles serving in the government service continued in the next century. Arnauld de Boissière entered the service straight out of public school in England, in 1891, and rose to the post of Protector of Immigrants (1914-30). His son also joined the service as a teenager and was appointed in 1926, at the age of 19, private secretary to the governor, subsequently serving as ADC to several governors. He became a career colonial official and served in Trinidad and Nigeria until his retirement. Three

white Creoles with distinguished service careers in the first half of the twentieth century were Errol dos Santos, Alan Reece and Werner Boos, all knighted for their achievements. Dos Santos, born in 1890 to a fairly humble family descended from a Madeiran
immigrant, joined the service straight from St Mary's College and rose steadily up the
ranks, becoming in succession colonial treasurer and financial secretary, and retiring as
colonial secretary in 1948, when he became a prominent businessman. He was the formidable boss for nearly 40 years of the Queen's Park Cricket Club, and was president
of the West Indies Cricket Board of Control for most of the 1950s. Werner Boos and
Alan Reece joined the civil service in 1928, straight out of St Mary's and Queen's Royal
College respectively. Both rose through the ranks. Boos retired in 1959 as deputy chief
(formerly colonial) secretary; he acted as governor-general in 1964. Reece's career continued after independence; he retired in 1963 as permanent secretary to the prime minister and head of the civil service. Both Boos and Reece served after their retirement in
prominent public positions in the 1960s.[24] This trio of civil service knights might be
seen as symbolising the end of an era; after the 1950s, very few local whites sought a
career in government service. In any case the private sector, especially estate agriculture
and commerce, was always far more important as an economic base for the white elite.

Very few white women engaged in salaried work in the nineteenth century. A handful of women from 'good' families, unmarried or perhaps widowed and inadequately
provided for, ran private kindergartens and schools for elite children, or gave lessons in
their own homes, especially music. A few 'lower-order' women were employed as
domestics, and some affluent creole families had British or French governesses. By the
early decades of the twentieth century, however, it was becoming acceptable for young
white girls to work in clerical positions in the private sector, at least before marriage.
For example, Grace Norman, the daughter of an inspector of police, worked as a secretary in the Port-of-Spain office of an oil company between 1917 and 1923, before her
marriage to Lindsay Grant, a son of T. Geddes Grant. But the professional or career
woman from the white elite was a distinct rarity before the 1950s. Olga Boos
(Mavrogordato) was unusual in taking an active part as a director in the management of
the Boos family firm, J. N. Harriman, after 1940. Jocelyn Urich was one of a group of
three pupils at St Joseph Convent, Port-of-Spain, who were the first girls to take the
Higher School Certificate examinations, in 1932. She went on to take degrees (BA, MA,
Dip Ed) from Oxford, returned to the convent to teach as Sister Francis Xavier and
became the first Trinidadian principal early in the 1950s. But marriage and motherhood
remained the normal destiny of elite white women in this period, and little emphasis was
placed on the higher education of girls among the group, as compared with the black and
brown middle stratum at the same time.[25]

Inter-ethnic relations within the white elite

Trinidad's white community was divided along lines of ethnicity – national origins, culture, language and religion – and 'class'. These divisions, especially the ethnic ones, were quite salient in the first part of our period, but they became distinctly more muted towards the start of the twentieth century. At the risk of over-simplification, we might suggest that between 1838 and about 1880, divisions were sharp and tensions between the factions, particularly between 'French' and 'English', were high. The years between 1880 and 1920 saw considerable rapprochement, a reduction of tensions and a gradual erosion of the distinct 'French' culture of the French Creoles. Finally, the decades after 1920 were characterised by solidarity within the white community, which closed ranks against challenges from both the middle stratum and the working people, and by the incorporation of some Portuguese and even Syrian families previously outside the traditional elite.

In the 40 years after 1838, French Creoles felt, justifiably, that their position as the island's native aristocracy and their distinctive culture were under threat from a hostile colonial government bent on making the colony completely English. The 'anglicisation' campaign, led by a succession of governors and generally backed by the English Creoles (Charles Warner as attorney-general between 1844 and 1870 was probably its main instigator and ideologue), swept away several institutions cherished by the French Creoles, including Spanish legal traditions, the old *cabildo* and the militia. The Catholic Church came under attack and the Anglican Church, with few adherents, was given privileged status. In education the Catholics were discouraged from opening schools and when they did, they were denied state aid. Every effort was made to spread the English language at the expense of both French and Créole. French Creoles were generally excluded from government posts and seats in the Legislative Council, while many of them were squeezed out of the sugar industry in the crises of the 1840s. These decades formed the lowest point in the fortunes and status of the French creole community.[26]

During these years, feeling themselves to be under attack, the French Creoles stressed their distinctive cultural traditions and their differences from the English. French remained the first language of the group. For instance, Elisa de Verteuil (née Le Cadre), who was born in 1830, spoke English badly right up to her death in 1917. She used French in all her family correspondence. In these decades there was a flourishing literary tradition carried on by a few French Creoles; they wrote and circulated among themselves, poems, songs, skits and speeches, all in French. Most children from the more affluent families were educated at least in part in France, and instruction at St Mary's College (founded in 1863) and at St Joseph Convent was in French. The group was strictly endogamous, and marriages even to whites of good family who were not French Creole were quite rare.[27]

The acute tensions between 'French' and 'English', the sense of French Creole isolation and difference, began to be gradually eroded from the mid-1860s. The decisions and actions of A. H. Gordon, governor between 1866 and 1870, removed some of the chief grievances of the French and Catholic 'party', and overt anglicisation ceased to be government policy. French Creoles were appointed to more posts in the government service, and in 1864-65 two prominent spokesmen, Louis de Verteuil and J. V. de Boissière, were given seats in the Legislative Council. The expansion of the cocoa industry after 1870 provided a solid economic base for the French Creole recovery. By the late 1870, a period of rapprochement between the major factions of the white community had begun, and the distinctive culture of the French Creoles was gradually weakened in the following decades.[28]

Of course, the tensions and resentments did not disappear overnight, and there is clear evidence that they continued to exist in the 1880s and 1890s. The local historian L. M. Fraser, writing around 1890, thought that 'the elements of discord were always in existence, nor have they even yet entirely disappeared. The lines of demarcation between . . . the French and the English sections of the community are certainly not so clearly and rigidly drawn as they were fifty or even five and twenty years ago, but they still exist.'

Father Massé, a French priest serving in the island who kept a copious private journal, reported in 1882 that 'one of the top employees of the Queen in Trinidad' had stated 'we must . . . destroy at any price the French influence'. Anthony de Verteuil is correct in his view that one major element in the 'Reform Movement' of the 1880s, a campaign to gain elected members on the Legislative Council in which several French Creoles participated, was resentment of British officialdom and its hostility (real and alleged) towards the 'foreign' Creoles. Philip Rostant, the main leader of the Reform Movement in the 1880s, exemplified this resentment; he was strongly anti-British, even anti-colonialist in a limited sense. As late as 1894, the white elite was considerably agitated by an incident connected to the reception of a visiting Russian fleet which seemed to have revived 'party feeling' between 'French' and 'English'.[29]

But in general, as the century drew to its close, the differences between the French and English Creole whites became blurred. One sign of this was the gradual erosion of French as the first language of the former. The shift from French to English seems to have occurred between 1880 and 1910. Poleska de Boissière (1836-1927) habitually spoke and wrote in English, using French as a private language with her husband, although at times she switched to French to heighten her image as a *grande dame* of the ancien régime or to put down visitors she considered vulgar. Frederick de Verteuil

(Elisa's grandson) was born in 1887, and as a child spoke both languages at home; by the time he went to school in England at the age of 14 he was completely fluent in French. But P. E. T. O'Connor, born in 1899, did not learn French at home. His parents' generation, born around 1860, were nearly all bilingual and used French as their 'home' language. But they did not pass it on to the children born around the turn of the century, like himself, the first generation of French Creoles for whom English was their first language. By about 1880 French had virtually disappeared from the local newspapers, and the tradition of composing and circulating poems, skits and songs in that language gradually died out between 1880 and 1900.[30]

In the later decades of the century, moreover, it became more common for affluent French Creoles to send their children to Britain, not France, for schooling. Many French Creole boys born after about 1850 went to leading English Catholic public schools, such as Stonyhurst, Ushaw, Oscott and Beaumont College; many of the girls attended convent schools in England. For instance, René de Verteuil, Louis' eldest surviving son, went to Stonyhurst, and as a result, according to Louis' biographer, 'he did not share the grand manner, Parisian culture and wide interests of his father, so that with Louis was to die out in large measure the French aristocratic tradition of the family'. Carl de Verteuil, Louis's nephew, born in 1857, went to Ushaw, and according to his son was 'very English in sympathies, with the outlook of an eighteenth-century English squire.'[31]

The erosion of the French language and culture was accelerated by the 'anglicisation' of the Catholic Church, always dominated by the French Creoles, and its schools, St Mary's College and St Joseph Convent, which were attended by most of their children even if they were subsequently sent off to Europe. The Church had been so identified with them that it was universally known as the 'French Church'. Father Massé reported this anecdote in 1881: 'Abbé Donelli, Parish Priest of Couva, Scotsman by origin, receiving at his home the Governor of Trinidad told him: "I am a French priest (Catholic) but English by nationality" '. But in the 1890s the Catholic authorities bowed to the inevitable and started to replace French Dominicans (like Massé) with Irish Dominicans and to phase out the use of French for sermons. This transition was presided over by the Irish Archbishop Flood, who came to Trinidad in 1887; by about 1910 the country parishes were largely in the hands of Irish Dominicans. Naturally this was resented, both by the French priests who were superseded and by many French Creoles who regarded the Irish clerics as uncultivated peasants. Father Massé complained in 1883:

> the antipathy of the Coadjutor who is English, in regard to the French priests, an
> antipathy which is felt more and more, forces us to keep ourselves on guard, more
> again because the Archbishop allows the Coadjutor to do what he wants. To judge

by his manner of acting he would like a wholly English clergy, but necessarily, for
many more years still, he will be obliged to have French priests, because although
Trinidad may be English, French is spoken just as much as English.

But Rome decreed that English-speaking clergy should replace the French priests, and
by about 1900 the French Creoles had more or less accepted the change.[32]

Up to 1870 St Mary's was essentially a French school, staffed by French Fathers of
the Congregation of the Holy Ghost; English was taught as a foreign language. But in
that year the school was granted state aid, and its pupils began to compete with those of
the government Queen's Royal College (QRC) in the Junior and Senior Cambridge
examinations. Of course this required that English be the language of instruction and
that curricula and texts be speedily anglicised. Irish clerics of the Holy Ghost Order soon
replaced Frenchmen; by the time Frederick de Verteuil got there (around 1898) nearly
all the staff were Irish and the school's distinctively French character had disappeared.
A similar process took place at St Joseph Convent some 20 years later. French was the
language of instruction well into the 1890s, but under the Irish Superioress, Mother
Milburge Walton, English replaced French in the mid-1890s, and the programme of
study was thoroughly anglicised, despite considerable opposition.[33] Since most French
Creole children attended either St Mary's or St Joseph Convent, their transformation
into essentially 'English' schools by the 1890s made a major contribution to eroding the
distinct cultural practices of the group.

As the differences between the ethnic factions of the white community lessened,
the whites closed ranks in the first half of the twentieth century against the challenges
posed by the black and brown middle stratum and the working class. The white Creole
resentment of the expatriate British, although still present, became less salient. As C. L.
R. James noted, writing in the 1930s, the white Creoles made 'common cause' with the
'colonial Englishman' in order to preserve white hegemony and blunt any liberal
impulses from the Colonial Office. In the 1880s and even 1890s several prominent white
Creoles, like Louis de Verteuil, had supported the campaign for constitutional reform;
by the 1920s the white community was nearly monolithic in its advocacy of the *status
quo*. By then, too, the French Creoles had ceased to be a culturally distinct group. The
death in 1927 of Poleska de Boissière of Champs Elysées, for decades the acknowledged social leader of the French creole community, symbolised the end of an era. Her
grandson, the writer Jean (Tony) de Boissière, wrote of her funeral 'it was not only the
passing of Poleska de Boissière they were mourning. They were assisting at the obse-
quies of a class; as such the French had passed from the scene'. Their 'Frenchness' survived only in sentiment and memory, as in a somewhat comic episode of around 1950.
At that time creole whites organised Carnival bands which paraded at the Trinidad

Country Club, occupying the old de Boissière mansion, Champs Elysées. The chairman of the Club was the 'venerable head of one of the old French families'. When a band leader (ironically a de Gannes) proposed a band of sans-culottes singing the 'Marseillaise', the old gentleman persuaded the committee to ban it as an insult to the memory of their royalist ancestors, especially in the former home of two French Creole families.[34]

By the early 1900s Trinidad's white community had by and large solved the ethnic difficulties of earlier times. Many 'foreign' Creoles served in the British forces during the first World War, along with Creoles of British descent, often (but not invariably) as commissioned officers. No fewer than 17 men of the Maingot family saw active service, 11 of them as commissioned officers. Two young de Verteuils enlisted in a British cavalry regiment, refusing to seek the commissions to which their social background right 'entitled' them. Both Arnauld de Boissière and A. A. Cipriani served as officers in the British West Indian (BWI) regiments, and each fought hard to defend their black troops against the racism of the British military authorities.[35] Around this time, too, French Creole families seem to have started to abandon their practice of strict endogamy, marrying more freely with whites of British descent or foreigners (Europeans or Americans). For instance, nearly all of the 14 grandchildren of J. V. de Boissière (1830-1906) married British people.[36]

Although this 'closing of the ranks' was a reality, some of the old Creole resentment of the colonial Englishman naturally persisted. Arnauld de Boissière (1872-1947) was said to have been strongly imbued with pride in his French ancestry; 'every inch a grand seigneur', he had deeply resented British attitudes towards his troops during the war, and was often engaged in skirmishes with British officials during his service as Protector of Immigrants. He refused to let his daughter dance with the Prince of Wales during his 1920 visit to Trinidad, though whether this stemmed from anti-British feeling or concern for her moral welfare is not clear.) Yet this kind of ambivalence about British officialdom was only a feeble echo of earlier tensions; Arnauld's children married Britons and his eldest son was a career colonial official all his working life, having been made private secretary to the governor at the age of 19.[37]

In general, as C. L. R. James had noted, the politics of the white Creoles was solidly conservative in the first half of the twentieth century, hostile to movements for self-government and for improvements in working-class conditions. Granted that Crown Colony government served their interests more than adequately, and that they were the main employer class, this is hardly surprising. But there were, of course, exceptions, men who broke ranks with their class and supported or led popular movements. Easily the most prominent of these was A. A. Cipriani (1875-1945), known universally as 'the

Captain'. Cipriani came from a land-owning French Creole family of Corsican descent. He became interested in politics mainly because of his experiences during the First World War, when as a captain in the BWI Regiment he had defended his troops against ill-treatment by the Army authorities. On his return to Trinidad, he involved himself in the incipient labour movement, becoming president of the Trinidad Workingmen's Association (TWA) in 1923. Cipriani operated from three bases: the TWA, which was by far the most important popular organisation between 1923 and 1936; the Legislative Council, to which he was elected in 1925, retaining his seat until his death 20 years later; and the Port-of-Spain City Council, on which he sat continuously between 1926 and 1941, serving as Mayor for eight terms. There is no doubt that the Captain was the most important popular leader of the 1920s and early 1930s, or that TWA under his leadership played a major role in politicising the working class, especially the urban blacks. After the mid-1930s he lost control of the labour movement and became increasingly conservative in his politics, but his achievements in leading and organising the 'barefooted man' (a favourite phrase of his) were significant. A white man from a planter family, he became an authentic popular hero to the Trinidadian workers.[38]

A few other members of elite white families broke away from the conservative world view and limited interests of their group. In the 1930s a small group of young men with literary and artistic interests organised themselves around the *Beacon* magazine; they were self-consciously anti-bourgeois and iconoclastic. Alfred Mendes, son of a wealthy Portuguese businessman and landowner, published two novels in 1934 and 1935 which portrayed the working classes in a sympathetic light, and contributed to the magazine. He participated in leftist politics in the 1930s and 1940s. Jean (Tony) de Boissière, Poleska's grandson, also a writer, was a member of the *Beacon* group and later brought out two other magazines, *Picong* and *Callaloo*; he was strongly critical of his class and distinctly Bohemian in his lifestyle. As a contemporary recalled much later, 'when, one busy morning, Hugh Stollmeyer [an artist from a well-known white family] and Jean de Boissière strolled down Frederick Street [Port-of-Spain's main shopping street] sparsely clad in open-neck shirt, creaseless trousers, sockless and sandalled ... it seemed to one and all that the decadent years of an empire had begun'. The leader of these *enfants terribles* in the *Beacon* group was Albert Gomes, son of a Portuguese shopkeeper. He was involved in radical and labour movements in the 1930s and 1940s, though by 1950-56, when he held ministerial office under a transitional constitutional arrangement, his politics had become much more conservative. By the 1950s, with adult suffrage and the consequent emergence of parties based firmly on the African or Indian middle and working classes, there was little scope for white Creole leadership in political organisations.[39]

Despite the activities of Captain Cipriani and the young iconoclasts of the *Beacon* group, the Trinidad white community was generally united in defence of white hegemony at least up to the end of the Second World War. The challenge from black and brown leaders of the middle stratum, and after 1937 increasingly from labour leaders too, brought about a large degree of inter-ethnic solidarity. The passage of time, of course, helped this process by dimming memories of distinct ancestral cultures. In the first half of the twentieth century the whites were by and large both ruling class and ruling race; the tensions and divisions of the previous century had been resolved in the interest of the whole community.

The Whites and Society

White Creole views on race and social status

The members of Trinidad's white elite, especially the French Creoles, saw themselves as constituting a genuine native aristocracy through their descent from the pioneers of settlement who had opened up the island in the late eighteenth and early nineteenth centuries. A preoccupation with aristocratic traditions, family connections, birth and breeding was characteristic of the group. The 'old families' cherished the memory of their ancestors, some of whom certainly were members of the pre-1789 French *petite noblesse*; others were descended from noble Spanish families such as the Farfans, settled in St Joseph since the seventeenth century. They recalled with pride their ancestors' service to the ancien régime and the Bourbons, often at immense sacrifice, like the Chevalier de Verteuil. The persistence of the royalist tradition was shown in the 1890s by the enthusiastic welcome extended to a visiting Bourbon prince by the 'old' families. Pride in family traditions was an article of quasi-religious faith. As Anthony de Verteuil writes of his ancestor Louis de Verteuil (1807-97), leader of his group for much of the century:

> If he had any fault it was excessive pride in his family and his aristocratic back-
> ground .... He was a great gentleman with something of that grand manner about
> him that perished for the most part on the guillotine .... On one famous occasion,
> shortly after the Queen had conferred the knighthood on him, it is related that
> Governor Broome addressed him as 'Sir Louis'. Louis answered 'Do not call me
> Sir. Call me Count. The British Government made me a knight, but I was born a
> Count.[40]

Pride in birth, breeding, and family traditions remained important to the white creoles well into the twentieth century. Poleska de Boissière, born a Roget de Belloquet, was fanatically devoted to the traditions of her own and her husband's families. She used to exaggerate the prestige of her own ancestors, carefully giving out misinformation which later appeared in her obituaries, such as the claim that the Rogets descended from Hugh Capet. Another example was Frederick de Verteuil, born in 1887; although he starts his 1938 autobiography with the assertion 'I would much rather have been born of good middle-class stock' and claims that the de Verteuil blood was 'too blue to be quite normal', pride in his ancestry runs all through his account of his chequered life. 'An authentic pedigree is one of the only things in the world that rich men cannot buy', he wrote; 'I am a believer in the old blood'. He cherished his aristocratic 'contempt for money', a de Verteuil tradition, and his ability to mix easily with all men, another legacy (he believed) of the old *noblesse*. These aristocratic families formed a closed circle at least up to the end of the nineteenth century; in 1887, when Frederick was born, 'about a dozen families were intimate, the others just did not exist'.[41]

These white Creoles were extremely sensitive on all points of family honour. P. G. L. Borde, the local historian of Trinidad, noted that the French Creoles were hot-tempered, preoccupied with their honour and prone to take offence at the slightest 'insult' or 'equivocal glance'. A duelling tradition was part of their aristocratic legacy. Father Massé noted in 1883: 'At a certain time duels were very frequent in Trinidad and quite close to here (Oropouche) there is a little rise where the duelists gave their rendez-vous. There have been many men killed in this spot'. On several occasions in the late nineteenth century, newspaper editors who insulted leading Creole families in their papers were attacked and assaulted in public. Arnauld de Boissière engaged in a twentieth-century version of a duel when he took on a British officer, with whom he had a disagreement, in a boxing match on the street. Creole families were careful to conceal any hint of scandal in their midst, especially if it involved a woman's reputation.[42]

Above all, creole whites had an extremely strong sense of the absolute need for 'racial purity'. Much more than the resident Europeans, they were open to the suspicion of having 'Negro blood'. Legal marriage to anyone known or reputed to have non-white ancestors would have meant automatic loss of membership in the Creole elite. Such marriages were extremely rare throughout the period. Philip Rostant, the radical French Creole journalist, married a young East Indian teacher in 1891, at the age of 69; but he was something of a maverick, generally disapproved of by his class; indeed, his niece Yseult Bridges recalled that there was a family legend that he was the son of a liaison between a Rostant woman and a coloured man, although perhaps this was a ploy to distance the family from this black sheep.[43] 'Outside' liaisons between white Creole men and black, mixed-race or East Indian women were a well-established convention, but even long-standing mistresses could not be married. Charles le Cadre, having lived with his mistress for 23 years, told his priest in the 1880s that marriage to her was impossible; his sister Elisa was a respected de Verteuil matriarch and her relatives would suffer disgrace if he did such a thing.[44]

Needless to say, the offspring of such 'illicit' liaisons could not move in French creole society, even though they often bore the 'respected' names. The numerous brown Boissières, many affluent and well educated, were not admitted to Champs Elysées during Poleska's lifetime, though she did borrow money from one of them. The de Verteuils were enraged when a son of the old Chevalier, the family patriarch, and his mixed-race mistress obstinately insisted on using the 'de' as part of his name. Acting as head of the family, Louis de Verteuil declared that the Chevalier had expressly ordered his illegitimate children not to use the 'de', a distinction to which only the legitimate offspring of the *noblesse* were entitled, and threatened 'to take steps' if Ludovic de Verteuil persisted in his 'pretensions'. This family quarrel became public; no doubt it reflected a widespread phenomenon. There was much gossip about well-known creole families having non-white ancestors. In 1912 a visitor was told that the Garcias, a prominent local family of Venezuelan origin, were 'very nice people, but they are said to be touched – with Negro blood, you know. It may not be so. It is fashionable here to blacken people's skins as well as their reputations'.[45]

Fear of the taint of 'Negro blood', and exaggerated deference to aristocratic traditions and family connections, ensured that the French Creoles' endogamy continued, even if marriage to whites outside the narrow ethnic community became more thinkable by the early twentieth century. On the whole, though, inbreeding was the safest way to avoid undesirable connections. In a 1934 novel, Evelyn Waugh describes a fictional French Creole girl going home from her school in Paris to get married. She explains to the hero that she is not yet engaged, 'but you see there are so few young men I can marry. They must be Catholic and of an island family. . . . There are two or three other rich families and I shall marry into one of them'.

She was limited to seven possible candidates, and one of them was eliminated because although very rich 'he isn't really a Trinidadian. His grandfather came from Dominica and they say he has coloured blood'. For the French Creoles, intermarriage and inbreeding, social and familial incest, were both a virtue and a necessity. In the words of the Trinidadian writer Lawrence Scott, himself born into a French Creole family:

> There is something a little sad
> Certainly predictable still,
> in the Maingot who marries a d'Abadie,

the de Verteuil who marries an Agostini:
the fear of miscegenation
supersedes mongolism.[46]

Pride in aristocratic traditions, preoccupation with family honour and concern for racial 'purity' were most characteristic of the French Creoles, though they were not absent among the Creoles of British ancestry. The Irish Creoles by and large assimilated with the French Creoles. P. E. T. O'Connor demonstrated his own family's complete assimilation by noting that his grandfather had married a Ganteaume, his father a de Gannes de la Chancellerie, and he himself had been delivered by Dr Ferdinand de Verteuil! Most saw themselves as an integral part of French Creole society rather than as a separate group, though Anthony de Verteuil thinks that they were important in the nineteenth century as a bridge between the Protestant English and the Catholic, French-speaking Creoles, along with the few Protestant French families like the de Boissières and the Germans, who were both Protestant and Catholic though most eventually intermarried with the French Creoles. Their greater familiarity with the English language and with British ways gave them an advantage with respect to careers in law and the civil service. It is no coincidence that the two white Creoles appointed to the Supreme Court in the nineteenth century, George Knox and Henry Court, were both of Irish origin.[47]

Few Creoles of English and Scottish ancestry cherished aristocratic traditions in quite the same way as the French Creoles, and most of them, descended from immigrants who came to Trinidad in the course of the nineteenth century, could not claim to have ancestors who had pioneered the settlement and 'civilisation' of the island. On the whole their roots in the Caribbean were more shallow than those of the French Creoles, and they were descended from Englishmen or Scotsmen from the middle class rather than the gentry. (An exception was probably the Warners, the leading family among the English Creoles; they were proud of their descent from Sir Thomas Warner, the seventeenth-century pioneer of English settlement in the Caribbean.) On the other hand, their British ancestry, in a British colony and at a time of British greatness as a world power, conferred a certain prestige. White Creoles of English and Scottish ancestry married freely with each other and with British-born whites; Charles Warner's son Aucher married the governor's daughter in 1886; William Gordon, Scottish-born founder of Gordon Grant & Co, married Maude Bushe from a prominent English Creole family. Marriages between French and English Creoles were not common because of the religious divide, but they did occur; Lechmere Guppy, son of a prominent English-born lawyer and politician, married into the Rostant family. Marriage to a non-white was probably as unthinkable for the English Creoles as for the French.[48]

The education of a white elite

White children in Trinidad were educated in private, religious and government schools, and the more affluent ones also attended institutions in Europe or (more rarely) North America. Early schooling was usually carried on in private kindergartens and elementary schools typically run by unmarried white ladies. Young children on the country estates might be taught by a planter's wife at home. It would have been unusual for elite white children to have attended the ordinary government or assisted elementary schools in this period, although a few did go to the Boys and Girls Model Schools in Woodbrook, Port-of-Spain, later known as the Tranquillity schools. After primary schooling, elite girls generally proceeded to St Joseph Convent if they were Catholics. Nearly all the daughters of the French Creole elite spent a few years here. Country girls could board. As we have noted, the school was thoroughly anglicised from the mid-1890s, but it remained an elite French Creole stronghold well into the 1940s, with most of its pupils white or fair-complexioned, and retaining its strongly ecclesiastical character. Girls from Protestant families generally avoided the Convent, although it was open to all creeds. Some of them attended private secondary schools for white girls. Yseult Bridges, for instance, whose strongly anti-Catholic father probably objected to the Convent, went to Miss Buncle's school for young ladies in Port-of-Spain, around the turn of the century. Miss Buncle was English. She employed a few young women, white Creoles, as teachers; Bridges recalled them as undereducated and with little notion of how to teach or keep order. The school had some 60 pupils while she was there, all white. Around 1910, P. E. T. O'Connor's sister attended an 'exclusive school for young ladies' in Port-of-Spain, run by the Misses Scott. White Protestant girls might also attend the 'higher classes' conducted by the Tranquillity Girls' School in the early years of the twentieth century, which offered a few years of secondary instruction; Bishop Anstey's College, an Anglican secondary school for girls, opened in the 1920s.[49]

Upper-class boys usually attended either Queen's Royal College (QRC) or St Mary's; normally, Protestants went to the former, Catholics to the latter. Both were fee-paying colleges, though a handful of exhibitions were offered after 1870. All the sons of T. Geddes Grant, for instance, went to QRC; Lindsay Grant won an exhibition there from Tranquillity Boys' School in 1911, the same year that C. L. R. James won his scholarship. Jeffrey Stollmeyer and his four brothers went to QRC in the 1920s and 1930s. St Mary's was very much a French Creole school well into the middle of the twentieth century, though from the first non-white boys also attended it. Boys from the elite families routinely spent a few years there before going on to a college in Europe. Frederick de Verteuil, entering the school around 1898, described the boys as 'polyglot',

French Creoles, 'half-castes', Venezuelans, Indians, 'and here and there an honest-to-goodness negro'. Some were vicious, some stupid, most were lazy, he recalled; 'I learnt little or nothing'.[50]

It was an article of faith among the elite white Creoles that both their boy and girl children must be sent off to school in Europe at the age of 13 or 14; it was common for children to spend a few years at St Mary's or St Joseph Convent and then complete secondary schooling abroad. This was sometimes rationalised on climatic grounds: Frederick de Verteuil asserted that in the tropics boys became unduly precocious; the sun 'caused a sort of moral miasma in the young' and 'the only salvation for a European child is to be sent to Europe'. Yseult Bridges thought it was mainly to prepare elite girls for the marriage market. Two or three years in England were necessary to 'finish' a girl, to prepare her to enter 'Society' and to 'eradicate the insidious singsong Creole accent and acquire that poise and complexion, that cachet, which would enhance her change of making a good match . . . the whole object of a woman's existence'.[51]

Amelia Gomez, the wife of a prominent Venezuelan lawyer, Antonio Gomez, sent her son off to school in England at the age of 11, in the care of a ship's captain and his wife. This was in the 1840s. Elite French Creole boys were sent either to colleges in France or Belgium or, increasingly after about 1860, to Catholic public schools in England or Ireland. The leading Catholic colleges in England were Stonyhurst (where Louis de Verteuil's son René went), Ushaw (attended, for instance, by Carl de Verteuil and his son Frederick), and Beaumont College where the sons of J. V. de Boissière were educated after a stint at St Mary's P. E. T. O'Connor went to a public shcool in Ireland. Young ladies might go to finishing schools in Paris, convent schools in England (like the Sacred Heart Convent in Kensington) or private boarding schools in England or Ireland. On the whole, few elite Creole boys attended university, unless they were entering medicine or law. Frederick de Verteuil thought that a lingering Catholic prejudice against Oxford and Cambridge was one reason. An unusual choice was made in the 1920s by A. V. Stollmeyer when he sent his first three sons to American universities because he thought they might get a 'more useful' education there; and Jeffrey Stollmeyer opted to go to the locally based Imperial College of Tropical Agriculture to read for the Diploma in Tropical Agriculture, which he obtained in 1941.[52]

Trinidad's white upper class was influential in shaping and (to a considerable extent) controlling the island's cultural, associational and social life in this period. The dominant culture was essentially European, and many of the patterns of British upper-middle-class life were recreated in Trinidad, though the French sentiments and aristocratic traditions of the French Creole elite modified those patterns at times, or at least provided an alternative model. Though many white families lived on country estates,

Port-of-Spain was clearly the centre of upper-class life.

The white elite established and controlled various associations for its social activities, particularly clubs. The Union Club became the premier association for the commercial elite; most of its members at first were English Creoles or Englishmen, but by the early twentieth century many French Creoles were also included. Acton Camejo found that in 1969-70, 36 per cent of the country's business elite belonged to the Union Club, still in the post-independence period very much an exclusive enclave. The Union Club was a businessman's group, but the Trinidad Country Club, established in the 1930s, became the most important social centre for the white elite in general. The club's premises became the grand Champs Elysées mansion in Maraval, formerly the de Boissière home. In 1969-70, 67 per cent of the business elite belonged to the Trinidad Country Club.[53]

Sports provided another arena for elite social life. Golf and cricket, both quintessentially British, were the main upper-class sports. St Andrew's Golf Club was founded in 1891 by a few enthusiastic Scots; by 1897 it had over 100 members, all white, and a nine-hole course on the savanna just outside the city. In the 1930s it purchased part of the Champs Elysées estate in Maraval and laid down a fine course there. St Andrew's was still an important club for the business elite in 1969-70. Cricket in Trinidad was controlled by the Queen's Park Cricket Club (QPCC). Although most of its members were white throughout the period, it always included some mixed-race or black professional men, at least from the 1880s. Until the 1890s most of the teams fielded by the QPCC were all white, and the cricketers were definitely 'gentlemen players' from the 'respected' white families. Upper-class whites dominated Trinidad cricket until the mid-twentieth century. Among the prominent white cricketing families were the Grants (sons and grandsons of T. Geddes Grant) and the Stollmeyers. The formidable Errol dos Santos ran the QPCC almost as a personal fief between 1941 and 1980, as vice-president in the period 1941-62, during which period the governors were nominal presidents, and as president from 1962 to 1980. He fiercely resisted the movement to replace the QPCC, which after all was a private club, with a national governing body to control the country's cricket. It was only when this step was finally taken, in 1980-81, that dos Santos resigned as QPCC president at the age of 90. Dos Santos also served as president of the West Indies Cricket Board of Control for most of the 1950s, where he is said to have obstructed the appointment of Frank Worrell as the first black captain of the West Indies Test side. Incidentally, dos Santos at different times also served as president of the Union Club and chairman of the Trinidad Country Club, and as president of the Portuguese Association and the Portuguese Club, organisations run by the country's Portuguese community.[54]

Charitable societies, run by upper-class men and women, were another part of the elite's social life. Anglican women ran the Daily Meal Society to provide meals for Port-of-Spain paupers, the Anglican bishop chaired the Trinidad Purity Alliance to combat illicit unions and illegitimate births, the Temperance Movement was active from the 1870s (though one suspects that few white Creole men subscribed), and Catholic women in Les Amantes de Jesus organised charitable activities. In 1901, upper-class women established the Trinidad Home Industries Association to enable gentlewomen in reduced circumstances to earn money through home and cottage industries and to aid distressed working women. Freemasonry was a long-established tradition in Trinidad. Many elite men, both Catholics and Protestants, were masons. The de Limas, for instance, belonged to the United Brothers Lodge, the oldest in the island (established in 1795 as Les Frères Unis).[55]

Trinidad's white elite was not noted for its intellectualism, nor were literary or scientific matters high on its agenda. Charles Day, who lived in Trinidad in the late 1840s, was appalled by the ignorance and lack of culture he found among the island's whites, both men and women. To speak of literature, science or art was to be charged with 'showing off'; only a few professional men, Day thought, retained a trace of their European education. Decent society, intelligent conversation, were rare; nearly all white men drank too much, partly because alcohol was needed to participate in the inane conversations of the social round. Most white women, in Day's experience, were undereducated and ignorant. By the 1870s spokesmen for the coloured and black intelligentsia often boasted of being more 'cultured', more interested in the life of the mind, than the local whites who were accused of crass materialism. Nevertheless, several local whites were involved in scientific and literary activities by the late nineteenth century, and this small circle of men established institutions like the Trinidad Public Library, the Trinidad Field Naturalists Club and the Victoria Institute, which set up the nucleus of a museum and sponsored scientific and similar events. The two leading amateur scientists of the later nineteenth century were Sylvester Devenish, the Irish-French Creole surveyor, and R. L. Guppy, a scholarly student of natural history.[56]

A handful of whites devoted themselves to literature. We have noted that a lively tradition of writing (and performing) poems, songs and skits in French flourished in a small circle of French Creoles in the second half of the nineteenth century, although it gradually disappeared after 1880. Louis de Verteuil wrote a valuable and generally perceptive general account of Trinidad's geography, history and social development. Both of the two historians of Trinidad writing in the 1880s and 1890s were white. P. G. L. Borde, a French Creole, published an important and scholarly history of Trinidad between 1498 and 1797; significantly, he chose to write in French and to publish in Paris. As a historian, Borde ranks high among nineteenth-century writers on the West

Indies for his scholarship and his balanced perspective. L. M. Fraser, author of a two-volume history of Trinidad between 1783 and 1840, published in the 1890s, was an Englishman who married into the French Creole elite. His book is less scholarly than Borde's, but it still ranks as one of the better local histories published on the region before the mid-twentieth century. In the 1930s and 1940s, as noted earlier, a few young white men participated in the literary movement associated with the *Beacon* magazine. At least one of them, Alfred Mendes, was an important writer, and Albert Gomes and Jean (Tony de Boissière were not without talent. Two French Creoles born in the 1880s achieved some success as novelists, although both lived outside Trinidad for most of their adult lives: Yseult Bridges, née Guppy, wrote several novels under a pseudonym, and Frederick de Verteuil published 15 novels (some commercially successful) under three different names. Both Bridges and de Verteuil wrote autobiographies which are full of valuable testimony about white Creole society at the turn of the century.[57]

The sphere of white elite women

Upper-class social life revolved around private visits and parties. The men had their clubs, but women were largely confined to domesticity (apart from church and charitable activities). The sun was dangerous to the complexion, and there was always the risk of offensive remarks, or worse, from the lower orders. Limited to domestic management and family affairs, often poorly educated, Trinidad's white women can rarely have developed wider interests. A chivalrous local author, writing in the 1860s, thought that they were 'extremely courteous and lady-like, superb musicians and dancers, with well informed minds'. Though free from pretensions or airs, they maintained a necessary pride: 'instructed from infancy to entertain a high opinion of their own consequence, they are cautious of doing an act which may lessen their consciousness of their proper dignity'. Day, observing the ladies in the late 1840s, was much more caustic. He considered that most of the Creole women were ignorant and ill-bred, reading nothing but light novels and unable to converse except on local or domestic trivia. Educated, elegant women were rare, to be found among the French Creoles if at all; the most 'vulgar' women, in Day's view, were Scottish or English. But Day acknowledged the restrictions and monotony of the average plantation woman's life, stuck on inaccessible estates, virtual prisoners in the great house (so-called: Day said they were mostly 'mere Scotch farm-houses, subject to all the inconveniences of a rude state of society').[58]

Marriage at quite an early age, to a suitable man, was the only acceptable destiny for the elite girl (except for those who took the veil). Failure in the marriage sweepstakes meant that the girl, after two or three unsuccessful seasons, would be 'relegated to the background of the home, there to live parasitically or to eke out a genteel existence in some ladylike way'. For the careful French Creole *mère de famille*, securing proper marriages for her teenaged daughters was a critically important duty. Alice Rostant Guppy, Yseult Bridges' mother, was probably quite typical. She believed that a good marriage was the only object for a daughter, one that was socially and financially desirable. The 'finishing' in England was essential to prepare a girl for a good catch, so elite girls were usually sent to British or French boarding schools at around 13 or 14. On their return at 17 or 18, they 'came out', often at the annual Debutantes' Ball at Government House. Yseult Bridges vividly describes the drama surrounding the preparation of her sister Ruth for this great event, involving a horde of relatives, domestics and retainers, two of whom were detailed to fan the girl during the elaborate dressing ritual. Her mother monitored available white bachelors with great care. The man's age was unimportant – in fact someone much older was far more likely to be financially secure – and Alice was happy to look outside the French Creole circle, since she herself had married an Englishman, in a rare 'mixed marriage' (that is, Catholic-Protestant). Thus Ruth was married at the age of 18 to an Englishman 17 years her senior. The family knew Ruth was not 'in love', but her groom was from a good family, had private means and was well established in the colonial service. Alice was sure love would come, especially with babies; for her, children and domesticity were the 'very foundation of life' for a woman.[59]

Elisa de Verteuil (1830-1917) would have agreed; she wrote 'family life is for me the only true happiness'. The mother of 12 children (the last born when she was forty-five), Elisa was utterly devoted to them and to her grandchildren. Her family life had its share of tragedies. Two of her sons were stricken with leprosy and had to be sent away to a country house near Arima where they were nursed by Elisa's mother until they both died in 1887. Her husband's death in 1879, and the loss of the family's sugar estates at around the same time, meant poverty when Elisa still had several young children to raise and educate. She and her two daughters (neither married) made jellies, jams, preserves, quilts and rag dolls to sell through relatives and friends, but she had to sell her Port-of-Spain house and live with her married sons. The two unmarried, adult daughters moved with her from house to house, dependent on their brothers, illustrating the truth of Yseult Bridges' comment about the fate of girls who failed in the marriage game. Elisa exemplified the values of French Creole womanhood: utter devotion to family, rigid Catholicism, hard work, social conformism.[60]

Domestic management, along with child care, was the focus of the white woman's day-to-day life. Although only those whose circumstances were seriously 'reduced' did much housework themselves, they all directed their servants, who were plentiful and cheap. Yseult Bridges gives an excellent portrayal of her mother's domestic round in Port-of-Spain around the turn of the century. Alice Guppy was something of a 'despot' over her large staff, whose work she supervised meticulously and criticised freely. Besides the live-in servants, a number of old retainers, pensioners of either the Rostants or the Guppys, drifted in and out, and there were other important personages like the 'mulatto' Mrs Laycock, who made and mended the linen and sewed, and Mary Hodge, the laundress who operated from her own house. Mrs Laycock's husband was the handyman, their son was his assistant. When the son seduced Alice's maid, she was instantly dismissed, pregnant and penniless; so much for paternalism. When the family moved to a cocoa estate in the country, Alice unilaterally decided the fate of the servants: who would go with the family, who would be pensioned off, who would be handed over to relatives. She freely intervened in the personal and family lives of the servants and the plantation employees, forcing an overseer, for instance, to get married to his long-time common law wife, with disastrous results.[61]

Yseult Bridges recalled most of the servants of her childhood home as loyal and devoted domestics of the 'old school', who identified fully with their employers' families. But the local newspapers of the late nineteenth century were full of complaints about the difficulty of getting decent, clean, civil servants; the old type of family retainers had disappeared, and most of those available were 'greedy and dishonest Barbadians, who did nothing right and demanded exorbitant wages'. In 1884-85 there was a series of court cases in which servants brought actions against employers for assault. 'Insolence' by the servant 'provoked' the employer to strike him, or her. In most of these cases the plaintiffs were awarded damages, to the great indignation of the elite; this was only 50 years after the end of slavery. Poleska de Boissière's 'grand manner' towards her servants reminds us that she was a slave-owner's daughter. When she appeared on her daily inspections of the extensive Champs Elysées gardens, the gardeners (some 20 of them) all sprang to life, and she often (according to her grandson) 'dug the tip of her sunshade into the buttocks of the Indian garden boys'. According to another grandchild, as her maid knelt at her feet to put on her stockings and shoes, she would sometimes push the servant over with her foot, then 'fling her a shilling' to make up for it. Still, Poleska was gracious to her numerous tenants, if they paid all their dues and knew their place; she chatted with the men about the crops, with the women about the babies, and she gave a few pennies each to the boys who arrived at the great house each month with the family rent.[62]

For elite women, social life consisted mainly of private visits and occasional large parties and balls. Alice Guppy visited, or was visited, nearly every afternoon after about four, gossiping away while her scholarly husband stayed in his study. She was immensely aware of social differences among her visitors, all of whom were white. Should she kiss them? If yes, what kind of kiss? What part of the house should they be received in? Ladies went on carriage drives in the afternoon but rarely walked; young women might play tennis. Red-letter days were the races on the Port-of-Spain savanna, the governor's balls, the occasional musical or theatrical events and large private parties and dances. Coblenz, a grand mansion in St Ann, near the city, was the centre of many splendid parties hosted by Leon Agostini and his son-in-law Leon Centeno in the late nineteenth century, which were described with gushing adulation in the local papers. In the early years of the twentieth century, Poleska de Boissière made Champs Elysées the most outstanding social centre for the white elite and herself the unchallenged doyenne of French Creole society. She held Sunday afternoon receptions attended by most of the island's prominent people from the governor down, and a great annual ball which became the most conspicuous social event outside Government House. It was said that she left home only to go to church or to visit Government House. Women were careful in their social relations, and generally abstemious: Poleska refused to serve whiskey, saying it was fast and definitely not for ladies, though her rum cocktails were famous.

But the men were less inhibited. Poleska's brother Henry Roget was a well-known city drunkard whom she barred from Champs Elysées and cut in the streets. Charles Day was astonished at the amount they consumed; on the French Creole estates, he said, the morning drink was rum and sugar, while breakfast (that is, lunch) featured claret, punch and champagne. Few men drank water without mixing it with strong white rum (maybe to kill the germs). Even doctors and priests drank too much. Young British immigrants were soon ruined in this dissolute, hard-drinking society; few of them were without one or two 'half-caste children, a discredit to them here and a burden to them in after-life'.[63]

Social relations with non-whites

Day was speaking of the late 1840s; probably the hard-drinking tradition was modified later in the century as Victorian values permeated the elite, even the French Creoles. As Donald Wood puts it, 'the temper of the age was decorous . . . the unashamed whoring of the eighteenth century was now furtively hidden under the cloak of respectability'. But liaisons between elite men of the leading families and black or brown women remained common. Although probably most of these men provided decently for their mistresses and illegitimate children, this was by no means always so. Father Massé noted in 1882: 'I cannot tell you what painful sentiments I experience every day when I see passing in front of my door a little boy, three quarters of the time wearing nothing but a shirt. He is the bastard son of one of the richest businessmen of Port-of-Spain, one of the highest men in the colony, an Honourable as they call them. He basely abandoned in the greatest misery the fruit of his debauchery'.[64] This kind of situation helps to explain why men of the white elite strongly opposed the so-called 'Bastardy Ordinance' of 1888, a measure to compel the fathers of illegitimate children to contribute to their support. The unofficial members of the Council voted solidly against it, and it was carried only by the Administrator's casting vote. Their reaction must surely have stemmed from the habit of upper-class men of maintaining mistresses and illegitimate children, and the fear that such arrangements would be exposed in court, undermining the very basis of their 'respectability'and revealing the double standard of morality which the upper class maintained.[64]

In a few cases white fathers provided generously for their illegitimate coloured children. A good example is J. B. Brunton, who had a coloured son, Nicholas Brunton, born in 1836. When he turned 18, his father set him up with a small sugar estate in Chaguanas, and father and son also became partners in the purchase of Woodford Lodge Estate. When J. B. Brunton died around 1859, he left all his Diego Martin estates to Nicholas, who was the wealthiest coloured landowner in the island by the 1860s. Significantly, though, Brunton's white neighbours in Diego Martin refused to visit him. In the 1840s Amelia and Antonio Gomez, definitely members of the elite, were on 'visiting' terms with St Luce Philip and his family. St. Luce belonged to an affluent coloured family and was himself a doctor; his wife was 'a white person well educated and very agreeable'.

Amelia's diary makes it clear that the Philips were part of her inner social circle, and she also visited St Luce's mother ('a respectable coloured lady') and sister. On the other hand, she described a supper at Government House in 1841: 'The Novelty of the night was the introduction of the coloured class. The Intention was good but many persons absented themselves from the amusement rather than meet these individuals'.[65] No doubt these 'persons' reflected the general white attitude to social relations even with elite coloureds. A military officer who served in Trinidad around the same time commented that only those with 'an undoubted pedigree of three generations of WHITE ancestry' could be admitted to 'what is designated as GOOD SOCIETY' in the island. A man with any trace of 'African blood' could never hope to mix with 'the illustrious gentry', however rich, educated or polished he was. White Creole youth were trained to perceive at a glance 'shades of complexion, utterly imperceptible to a stranger', otherwise they (especially the girls) might at any time 'commit serious errors'.[66]

In general, despite exceptions such as St Luce Philip, elite whites did not socialise with anyone known to have non-white ancestry in this period, though they (mainly the men) did have many contacts with brown and black persons at school and in public, business and professional life. Other contacts were in stereotyped class relationships: planter and labourer, mistress and servant, JP and offender. Intimate social relations based on equality were confined to the white community, and, before about 1900, mainly to one's particular ethnic faction. Non-whites were inevitably excluded, even if – or especially if? – they were relatives. We noted earlier the de Verteuils' public quarrel with their coloured kin over using the 'de' in their surname. The de Boissières also had many coloured relatives; they did not presume to use the 'de', and they were definitely not admitted to Champs Elysées, though most of them were both affluent and well-educated (Poleska borrowed money from at least one of them). Indeed, Poleska was of the old school in her social attitudes. In the 1920s, she refused to permit an English woman of 'good family' to take a short cut across a corner of the Champs Elysées property on her morning rides 'because Madame de Boissière would not allow the facility to someone married to a coloured gentleman', in fact a de Boissière relative. A perceptive British visitor reported in 1933 that educated coloureds in Trinidad rarely mixed socially with the local whites, 'through fear of insult'. Not much had changed, in this respect, since the Government House supper attended in 1841 by Amelia Gomez.[67]

A noted scholar has commented that white Creoles were (and are) an integral element of Caribbean society, 'natives' just as much as the majority non-white population, sociologically marginal not to their own society, but to the metropolitan one. Nevertheless, the white Creole's sense of identity, his perception that Trinidad, not France or Britain, was 'home', was always ambivalent. Anthony de Verteuil, who has done more than any other historian to enrich our understanding of the history of Trinidad's French Creoles, believes that they clearly and unequivocally regarded the island as their home, much more so than the English Creoles. Their ancestors, often Caribbean Creoles of other islands, had arrived earlier; their identification with France had been weakened by revolutions and republican regimes; as planters they were less mobile than the English Creole merchants, professionals and managers. De Verteuil convincingly points to many heart-felt expressions of patriotism and love for the island contained in the poems and songs written by French Creoles in the second half of the nineteenth century. Writers such as Louis de Verteuil and P. G. L. Borde combined pride in their ancestors and in French civilisation with a genuine island patriotism. Borde says that he wrote his history so that Trinidad's youth could know and love their country; he was the first Trinidad historian to express 'nationalist' sentiments. At times, for instance in the 1880s, French Creoles defended the cultural traditions of Trinidadians in general, such as Carnival, Creole music and dance. While marriages between English Creoles and British people were common, the French Creoles were much less likely to marry people not born in the island, at least before about 1900, and less likely to leave Trinidad for good as adults. For de Verteuil, the French Creoles were clearly Trinidadian in self-identification.[68]

Yet the ambivalence was real. Amelia Gomez was born in Grenada of English descent and had lived all her life in Grenada or Trinidad; she was married to a Venezuelan who had lived in the island for about 30 years. Yet she wrote in he diary in 1843 that she and her husband 'are some time thinking of going home'– England. Yseult Bridges was the child of a French Creole mother whose ancestors had been in Trinidad since the 1790s, and an English-born father who had lived there all his adult life. When she first visited England as a child of nine, she recalls that she knew it was 'her country' much as she loved her native island, her home could only be England, where the 'roots of her being' were implanted. With their part-English ancestry, perhaps neither Gomez nor Bridges were truly representative of the French Creole attitude. Yet Frederick de Verteuil, born in 1888 into Trinidad's leading French Creole family, had an almost identical reaction when he first went to England to attend school at the age of 14: 'To the European born abroad there is something mystic about his arrival in Europe. He realises quite suddenly that he has come home'. England was home, 'not the glare and shameless growth of the tropics but the half tones of an old and cultured land. I suppose France would have had the same effect on me'. For him, 'the glittering island. . . indeed was not my home'.[69]

Frederick de Verteuil was something of a maverick. He had a distinctly jaundiced view of his native island and its population, which he described as mostly 'half-baked barbarians'. Noting that the de Verteuils had lived in Trinidad from 1797 to 1909 – the year in which he decided not to return to the island to live, he wrote: 'I do not think that Europeans can live more than three generations in a hot climate and not degenerate, especially living in a small island, inter-marrying inevitably and having interests so circumscribed that only the strongest mind can fail to addle'. In fact, he lived for the rest of his life in India and England. This was not a common decision on the part of Trinidad French Creoles, at least before the 1950s or 1960s; most seem to have stayed in the island. An exception is the de Boissière family. After 1900 most of them married non-Trinidadians, generally British, and ended up living in England. By 1930 most of the white de Boissières were there; in 1993 only two still lived in Trinidad.[70] Many English Creoles, often marrying British or North American spouses, migrated to England, but few French Creoles left their island for good, until the loss of white hegemony and the social upheavals of the independence and post-independence period drove many away.

Trinidad's white Creoles had a double self-identification, with their island and with their ancestral Europe. Identification with Britain and France conferred status in a colonial society in a period when few challenged the superiority of Western culture and 'white' civilisation. Yet the sense of belonging to the island was also real and deep, especially for the French Creoles. Despite the upheavals of the second half of the twentieth century, Trinidad's white community is still here, still playing an important, often privileged and at times controversial role in the nation's affairs. Perhaps we can leave the subject with the words of Ian McDonald, Trinidad-born white West Indian.

> I have no harbouring-place but this [the Anglophone West Indies]. I have no other homeland and I want no other .... I have always felt confident about my West Indian credentials. I have never felt the white colour of my skin or my European ancestry might preclude me from complete status as a West Indian. More remarkably, I have never felt in the new dispensation of political independence, with white authority broken on all sides, any pressure of rejection or even resentment from the huge majority of West Indians with different skin colour and different ancestries now in a position to dictate complete marginalisation for people like myself. I have been able to play a full part in the drama of our West Indian life without let or hindrance or any seeming resentment or prejudice that I have ever noticed.[71]

Notes

1. Throughout this essay, the term 'French Creoles' will be used in this broad sense.

2. *Trinidad Annual Registers and Almanacks,* 1871-1895; Bridget Brereton, *Race Relations in Colonial Trinidad,* 1870-1900 (Cambridge, 1979), pp. 47-48.

3. *Port of Spain Gazette* (POSG) 18 September 1873; A. de Verteuil, *And Then There Were None: A History of the Le Cadre Family in the West Indies* (Port-of-Spain, 1974), chapter 5; M. Pocock, *Out of the Shadows of the Past: The 'Great House' of Champs Elysées, Trinidad, and the Families Who Lived There, 1780-1932* (Hastings, 1993), p. 449.

4. A. de Verteuil, chapter 5; *The Diaries of Abbé Armand Massé 1878-1883.* Translated and edited by M. L. de Verteuil, 4 Vols. (Port of Spain, 1988; privately printed), pp. 111, 216-17, entry for 11 August 1879.

5. Norman Lamont, *Problems of Trinidad* (London, 1933) and 'The Life of a West Indian Planter 100 Years Ago'. Public lectures delivered under the auspices of the Trinidad Historical Society, 1933-36; O. Rudder, *A Traveller in the West Indies* (London, 1933), chapter 4. For the development of the sugar industry in the 20th century, see Brereton, *A History of Modern Trinidad, 1783-1962* (London, 1981), pp. 205-207, 211-13, 217.

6. CO 295/235 Rushworth to Cardwell 19 June 1866 no. 71 & enclosures; 295/239 Gordon to Buckingham 8 June 1867 no. 80.

7. Brereton, *Race Relations,* pp. 49-51; A. de Verteuil, *And Then There Were None,* pp. 68-99; A. de Verteuil, *Sir Louis de Verteuil, his Life and Times* (Port-of-Spain, 1973), p. 88; P. E. T. OConnor, *Some Trinidad Yesterdays* (Port-of-Spain, 1978), chapter XI.

8. A. Burkett, *Trinidad, a Jewel of the West* (London, 1914), p. 54; A. de Lima, *The De Limas of Frederick Street* (Port-of-Spain, 1981); D. Harrison, 'The changing fortunes of a Trinidad peasantry: a case study' in *Peasants, Plantations and Rural Communities in the Caribbean,* M. Cross and A. Marks, (eds) (Leiden, 1979), pp. 28-32.

9. For the cocoa industry in the twentieth century, see Brereton, *History,* pp. 207-210, 213, 218; also C. Y. Shepherd, *The Cacao Industry in Trinidad* (Port-of-Spain, 1932).

10. CO 295/247 Gordon to Granville 24 May1869 (Secret); *Palladium* 2 December 1876; Pocock, pp. 392, 454.

11. Brereton, *Race Relations,* p. 51.

12. *Ibid.* pp. 51-52; Burkett, p. 10.

13. Harrison, pp. 28-32; R. Sebastien, 'The development of capitalism in Trinidad, 1845-1917', Ph.D. thesis, Howard University, 1978, pp. 197-203.

14. S. Hill, *To Live Twice Over to Live Forever: Memoirs of Sir Lindsay Grant,* (Port-of-Spain, 1988); C. Nicol, 'The Strength of Enterprise: Geddes Grant', *Sunday Express* (Trinidad), 21 August 1983.

15. O. Mavrogordato, *Voices in the Street,* (Port-of-Spain, 1977), pp. 148-50; de Lima, *The De Limas;* L. A. Barclay, 'The Syrian/Lebanese Community in Trinidad: a case study of a commercial elite', *Caribbean Affairs,* 5 (1992), pp. 129-46.

16. Burkett, pp. 2, 22, 28-30; *Trinidad Guardian,* 6 September 1971: Letter from H.B. Bayne; Hill, pp. 41-42.

17. O'Connor, chapters XIV and XV.

18. Pocock, pp. 449, 520-28; *Sunday Guardian,* 11 December 1988; De Lima; J. Stollmeyer, *Everything Under the Sun* (London, 1983), pp. 14, 170-72; Nicol, *Sunday Express,* 21 August 1983.

19. De Lima; Mavrogordato, pp. 104-105; *Sunday Guardian* (Trinidad).

20. Burkett, pp. 28-30; S. Ryan and L. A. Barclay, *Sharks and Sardines* (St Augustine, 1992), p. 66; Stollmeyer, pp. 170, 190-01.

21. Ryan and Barclay, pp. 51-52; A. Camejo, 'Racial Discrimination in Employment in the Private Sector in Trinidad and Tobago', *Social and Economic Studies,* 20 (1971), pp. 294-318.

22. I. Bodu, *Trinidadiana* (Port-of-Spain, 1890), pp. 29, 71.

23. Brereton, *Race Relations*, 54; de Verteuil, *Sylvester Devenish*, chapter 2.

24. Pocock, pp. 416-20; *Sunday Express* (Trinidad), 2 September 1990, *Trinidad Guardian*, 9 December 92, *Trinidad Express*, 9 December 1992; C. N. Comma, (ed), *Who's Who in Trinidad* (Port-of-Spain 1966), pp. 56, 201.

25. Hill, pp. 46-47; *150 Years of Witness and Worship. The Sisters of St. Joseph of Cluny in the Caribbean, 1836-1986* (Port-of-Spain, 1986), pp. 76-89.

26. D. Wood, *Trinidad in Transition* (Oxford, 1968), especially chapters 9, 10 and 14.

27. A. de Verteuil, *And Then There Were None*, p. 99; A. de Verteuil, *Trinidad's French Verse 1850-1900* (Port-of-Spain, 1978).

28. Wood, especially chapter 14.

29. L. M. Fraser, *History of Trinidad* (Port-of-Spain, 1891, 1896), Vol. 1, p. 291; *Mass Diaries*, IV, p. 210, entry of 6 February 1882; A. de Verteuil, *The Years of Revolt: Trinidad 1881-1888* (Port-of-Spain, 1984), chapter 4; Brereton, *Race Relations*, pp. 46-47.

30. A. de Verteuil, *And Then There Were None*, p. 99; Pocock, p. 399; Frederick de Verteuil, *Fifty Wasted Years* (London, 1938), p. 23; O'Connor, p. 61; A. de Verteuil, *French Verse*, p. 149.

31. A. de Verteuil, *Sir Louis*, p. 57; F. de Verteuil, p. 6.

32. *Massé Diaries*, IV, p. 238, entry of 13 May 1881; A. de Verteuil, *Sylvester Devenish*, chapter 5; *Massé Diaries*, pp. 11, 238-39, entry of 30 September 1883.

33. A. de Verteuil, *Sylvester Devenish*, chapter 5; F. de Verteuil, p. 12; *150 Years of Witness and Worship*, pp. 76-89.

34. C. L. R. James, *Life of A. A. Cipriani* (Lanceshire, 1938), pp. 8-9; Pocock, pp. 403, 150.

35. Ellis Maingot, 'The Saga of the Maingot Family in World War I', *Trinidad Guardian*, 27 February 1984; F. de Verteuil, p. 156; Pocock, p. 421.

36. Pocock, pp. 388-89.

37. Pocock, pp. 421, 441, 447, 466.

38. James, *Life of Cipriani*; Brereton, *History*, chapter 9.

39 . R. Sander, *The Trinidad Awakening: West Indian Literature of the 1930s* (New York, 1988); D. Archibald, 'Alfred Mendes – an appreciation', *Trinidad Guardian* 27 January 1972; Pocock, pp. 475-77; A. Gomes, *Through a Maze of Colour* (Port-of-Spain, 1974).

40. Brereton, *Race Relations*, pp. 35-41; A. de Verteuil, *Sir Louis*, pp. 84-85.

41. Pocock, pp. 392, 397-98; F. de Verteuil, pp. 1, 3, 4, 21, 56, 280.

42. P. G. L. Borde, *Histoire de la Trinidad sous le governement espagnol* (Paris, 1876, 1882) vol. ii, p. 270; *Massé Diaries*, iv, p. 164, entry of 12 July 1883; Brereton, *Race Relations*, pp. 39-40; Y. Bridges, *Child of the Tropics: Victorian Memoirs* (London, 1980) pp. 91-92.

43. *Public Opinion*, 25 August 1891; A. de Verteuil, *The Years of Revolt*, p. 235; Bridges, p. 89.

44. A. de Verteuil, *Years of Revolt*, p. 17.

45. Pocock, pp. 390-405; Brereton, *Race Relations*, p. 40.

46. Evelyn Waugh, *A Handful of Dust* (New York, 1945; first published 1934), pp. 163, 166; Lawrence Scott, Poem, *Trinidad and Tobago Review*, (1993), p. 45. Scott's 1992 novel *Witchbroom* is a brilliant fictional portrayal of a Trinidadian French Creole family.

47. O'Connor, chapter VI; A. de Verteuil, *Sylvester Devenish*, pp. 57-58.

48. Brereton, *Race Relations*, pp. 42-44. For two jaundiced views of English and Scottish immigrants in Trinidad in the 1830s and 1840s, see Charles Day, *Five Years Residence in the West Indies* 2 vols (London, 1852), pp. 1, 174, 204, 208-09 and S. Hodgson, *Truths from the West Indies* (London, 1838), pp. 63-73, 103-05.

49. F. de Verteuil, pp. 8-9; O'Connor, chapters IX, X; Bridges, pp. 97, 116-20; *150 Years of Witness and Worship*, pp. 91-93.

50. Hill, *To Live Twice Over*, Stollmeyer, chapter 1; A. de Verteuil, *And Then There Were None*, chapter 5; F. de Verteuil, pp. 12-13.

51. F. de Verteuil, p. 14; Bridges, p. 157.

52. Unpublished diary of Amelia Gomez, 1841-43 (typescript and notes by M. Pocock), entries of April-May 1843; A. de Verteuil, *And Then There Were None*, chapter 5; F. de Verteuil, pp. 16, 25, 48; Pocock, p. 388; O'Connor, chapter IX; Stollmeyer, chapters 1 and 2.

53. Brereton, *Race Relations*, p. 57; Camejo, pp. 294-318.

54. Brereton, *Race Relations*, p. 57; Camejo, pp. 294-318; articles on dos Santos in *Sunday Express*, 2 September 1990, *Trinidad Guardian*, 9 December 1992; *Trinidad Express*, 9 December 1992.

55. Brereton, *Race Relations*, pp. 57-58; De Lima.

56. Day, II, pp. 100-102; Brereton, *Race Relations*, p. 58; A. de Verteuil, *Sylvester Devenish*, chapter 3.

57. A. de Verteuil, *French Verse*; Louis de Verteuil, *Trinidad* (London, 1858, revised edn, 1884); Brereton, *Race Relations*, pp. 58-59; Fraser, History; Borde, *Histoire de la Trinidad*; Sander, *The Trinidad Awakening*; Bridges, *Child of the Tropics*; F. de Verteuil, *Fifty Wasted Years*.

58. Daniel Hart, *Trinidad and the other West Indian Islands and Colonies* (Port-of-Spain, 1866), pp. 169-70; Day, I, pp. 223-24, 253-55, 261.

59. Bridges, pp. 157-66.

60. A. de Verteuil, *And Then There Were None*, chapter 5.

61. Bridges, pp. 27-64, 181, 188-91.

62. Brereton, *Race Relations*, p. 60; Pocock, pp. 395-97.

63. Bridges, pp. 31-32; Brereton, *Race Relations*, pp. 61-62; Pocock, pp. 392-94; Day, II, pp. 66, 87, 100-02.

64. Wood, pp. 171-72; Brereton, *Race Relations*, pp. 60-61; *Massé Diaries*, II, p. 115, entry of 19 June 1882.

65. A. de Verteuil, *A History of Diego Martin, 1784-1884* (Port-of-Spain, 1987), pp. 126-28, 134; Gomez Diary, several entries May-September 1841; quotation 26 May 1841.

66. Hodgson, pp. 58-60.

67. Pocock, p. 251; Rudder, chapter 4.

68. H. Hoetink, *The Two Variants in Caribbean Race Relations* (Oxford, 1967), p. 66; A. de Verteuil, *Years of Revolt*, pp. 215-24; Brereton, *Race Relations*, pp. 58-59.

69. Gomez Diary, 24 March 1843; Bridges, p. 172; F. de Verteuil, pp. 18-20.

70. F. de Verteuil, p. 73; Pocock, pp. 406-08.

71. Ian McDonald, 'No Other Home', *Trinidad and Tobago Review* (1993) p. 7. McDonald is a novelist, poet, editor, publisher, cricketer and sugar executive who has lived in Guyana for 37 years. He was born and educated in Trinidad. His novel, *The Humming-Bird Tree*, is a sensitive evocation of a white boy's childhood and adolescence in Trinidad of the 1930s and 1940s.

4

Bay Street, Black Power and the Conchy Joes: Race and Class in the Colony and Commonwealth of the Bahamas, 1850-2000

MICHAEL CRATON

Only three British West Indian colonies had sufficiently large and politically well-organised white minorities to ensure the uninterrupted continuation of self-legislation after the emancipation of their slave majorities in the 1830s: Bermuda, Barbados and the Bahamas. Proportionately smaller than the white maritime oligarchy of Bermuda but larger than the white plantocracy of Barbados, what Howard Johnson has called the white agro-commercial bourgeoisie of the Bahamas[1] exhibited features found in both, including the dependence on a subordinate and ultra-racist sub-category of poor whites and a small intermediate buffer group of non-whites who carried on the ambivalent roles of the coloured and black freedmen of slavery days. Yet of the three socio-political systems, that of the Bahamas was and has remained much the most complex.

As this essay will briefly show, the story of the Bahamian white minority has been complicated temporally and spatially; by radically different socio-economic phases since colonial and slavery days, by a wider range of both whites and non-whites than elsewhere in the region and by great variations in interactions between them, and, above all, by the unique diversity of an archipelago that extends hundreds of miles outwards on a NW–SE axis from the metropolitan hub of Nassau on New Providence island. In the twentieth century, with an acceleration since mid-century, have been added the effects of the great differential in the demography of the different groups and the limited but subtly varied effects of racial mixing, and of the influence of immigrants and external cultures (black as well as white) in the face of rapid economic changes and the emergence of a proud national consciousness.

As the Commonwealth of the Bahamas approaches the twenty-first century, officially, and to a large degree in reality, the issues of race and of the distinctive role of the white minority have declined in importance, after polarisations and much tension during the 1950s, 1960s and 1970s. Yet to claim that differences of race and ethnicity have been entirely subsumed by the categorical imperatives of class and to deny the continuing vitality of subtle sectional variations within the Bahamian mosaic, is only one degree removed from the tendency, understandable during the years of euphoria following the triumph of the underprivileged black majority, to consign the Bahamian white minority to history's dustbin.

Slavery – with 'slave' and 'black' virtually synonymous – was coeval with the colony of the Bahamas, which had been founded in 1648 and taken over by the Crown in 1718. But it was not until the eve of the American Revolution that 'reputed blacks' edged ahead of white settlers in numbers, in a total population of scarcely 4,000, of whom three-quarters lived in Nassau's island of New Providence and almost all the remainder in nearby Harbour Island and Eleuthera. Already there were perceptible disparities in the race ratios, with whites constituting 82 per cent of the population of Harbour Island, 68 per cent in Eleuthera, and only 36 per cent in New Providence. With very little agriculture and no sizeable plantations, all of the slaves in small groups, and most slaves either mariners or domestics, the colony of the Bahamas in 1775 was merely a poorer and more scattered version of Bermuda.[2]

This situation radically altered with the coming of the Loyalists and their slaves after the Treaty of Versailles. Put most simply, the influx during the 1780s 'trebled the colony's population, raised the proportion of slaves and other blacks from one-half to three-quarters of the whole, and increased the number of permanently settled islands from three (or five) to a dozen'.[3] Yet the Loyalist migration was in fact much more complex. Numerically, the largest components were would-be cotton planters and their considerable gangs of slaves, who developed the agriculture of Eleuthera, Exuma and Cat Island, and initiated that of Abaco, Long Island, Watling's Island, Rum Cay, Crooked Island and Acklin's Island (as well as the Turks and Caicos Islands, then under Bahamian jurisdiction). The Out Island planters regarded Nassau as their metropole and preferred residence, but the Bahamian capital was more obviously the home of a new wave of professionals and would-be merchants, who vigorously competed with the established whites, and whom Governor Maxwell termed 'the most tormenting, dissatisfied people on earth'.[4]

Keeping much lower profiles but almost equally important were two further classes of Loyalist immigrant. An uncertain number of free coloured and black Loyalists, most of them freed during the recent war, helped to raise to 15 per cent the non-slave non-white component of the total Bahamian population. Of these non-white free persons, 74 per cent lived in Nassau. Rather more numerous and with greater prospects of practical freedom and economic opportunity were the hundreds of poor white Loyalists relocated by the British. Arriving mainly from New York, with little money and very few slaves, the most independent of these formed scattered small plantations and stock farms in Long Island, while the majority settled on the offshore cays of Abaco and northern Eleuthera. There they soon melded with and were subsumed in the lifestyle of the old-established white inhabitants, living off the sea and a subsistence agriculture based on the nearby mainlands and the labour of their few black slaves.

By 1807 whites comprised 22 per cent, and free non-whites 9 per cent, of the total Bahamian population (including the Turks and Caicos Islands) of 16,000, but the variations in racial proportions were significant. In New Providence, where 37 per cent of the total population lived, the whites made up 29 per cent of the people and slaves 54 per cent, with coloured and black free persons constituting the remaining 17 per cent. At opposite ends of the scale, whites made up 65 per cent and free non-whites only 3 per cent of the combined populations of Harbour Island, Spanish Wells and Abaco, while slaves constituted 91 per cent and whites less than 5 per cent of the population of the newly settled plantation islands, where 44 per cent of the total Bahamian population now lived. The figures for Eleuthera were 32 per cent whites, 61 per cent slaves and 7 per cent free non-whites; and for Long Island, 15, 78 and 7 per cent, respectively.[5]

The white Loyalists confidently expected to transform the Bahamas; but in the event they were more changed by local conditions than vice versa. Moreover, subsequent developments, especially the failure of the cotton plantations, the emancipation of the slaves, and the settlement of thousands of liberated Africans in the Bahamas, substantially altered the context in which the Bahamian white minority sustained its hegemony for a further century and a half.

Defeated by the sparse soil, pests and the declining world market price of cotton in their attempt to replicate and match the expansion of the plantation economy of the American South, those Loyalist planters who could not forsake the Bahamas altogether (by remigrating to England or even returning to the United States) left on their decayed Out Island estates the slaves they could not shift to the salt-pans or the West Indian plantation colonies, and concentrated in Nassau, where they gradually converted themselves into a component of that bourgeois oligarchy – controlling commerce, land and politics – which in due course was accorded the generic nickname Bay Street. The always poor white Out Islanders, without the resources or will either to forsake the islands or diversify, became progressively more isolated while following one of three options: to maintain an almost heroic absolute ethnic separation (as in the settlements of Spanish Wells, Cherokee Sound, Hopetown, Man-o-War Cay and Guana Cay); to constitute the dominant half of bifurcated settlements (notably Harbour Island and Green Turtle Cay); or (as in Long Island, Ragged Island, Acklin's and parts of Eleuthera) gradually to meld genetically with their slaves to form poor but vigorous communities of near-whites.[6]

Left more or less to their own devices, the slave gangs of the failed cotton plantations turned themselves into what have been termed proto-peasants, while healthily multiplying. Increasingly aware of allies in the imperial metropole, the slaves resisted their owners' attempts to work them hard, split them up for sale, or even shift them. Over the same decades, the imperial government's determination to improve slave conditions (particularly in respect of food and clothing issues and punishments), prevent the slaveowners' capitalising on their chief remaining resources through sale and transfers, and to move inexorably towards slave emancipation, intensified the traditional animosities and distrust between local whites and the representatives of the Crown from the governor downwards.[7] This, indeed, led to a lasting dichotomy in which not just appointed officials but all expatriate whites saw themselves as a super-elite and tended to equate and treat with equal contempt the comparatively rich and poor local whites alike, terming them all 'Conchy Joes'. At its most offensive, this metropolitan attitude not only ignorantly oversimplified the complex racial composition of the Bahamas but cast aspersions on the local whites' most prized attribute, their sense of the distinctiveness and superiority of being white.

> God bless the white folks one and all, though hark ye,
> I see no harm in blessing too the darky!
> But which is the darky and which the white?
> God bless us all! That is beyond me quite![8]

Despite its disparagement by most expatriate officials, Bay Street was cannily able to turn British actions and policies to its own advantage after slavery and the transitional period of Apprenticeship ended in 1838. The relocation in the Bahamas of some 6,000 Africans captured from illicit foreign slavers between 1811 and 1861 not only widened the gap between Bahamian whites and blacks, but divided the blacks themselves by providing an unacculturated (and thus easily despised) element that competed for the available land and employment. At the same time, the legacies of slavery were perpetuated as those non-whites who had been freed before general slave emancipation continued to regard themselves as a subaltern elite, grateful for the token and limited concessions which distinguished them from the black majority, while for its part, the mass of the newly freed continued to exhibit some of the symptoms of dependency on their former owners.[9]

Table 1
Bahamas: categories of race from 1851 census[10]

	Whites	%	'Coloured population'	%
All Bahamas	5,499	19.98	22,020	80.02
New Providence	1,534	18.80	6,625	81.20
Eleuthera & Spanish Wells	1,211	26.27	3,399	73.73
Harbour Island	953	51.79	887	48.21
Abaco & Cays	1,178	58.58	833	41.42
Bimini	103	62.80	61	37.20
Long Island	194	13.13	1,283	86.87
Ragged Island	16	4.61	331	95.39
Inagua & Mayaguana	61	11.51	469	88.49
Grand Bahama	1	0.01	921	99.99
Exuma	144	7.10	1,883	92.90
Cat Island	30	1.64	1,798	98.35
Watling's Island	13	3.39	371	96.61
Rum Cay	37	4.31	821	95.69
Crooked Isl., Long Cay & Acklin's	12	1.10	1,080	98.90
Andros	1	0.01	1,029	99.99

Though ostensibly liberal, the prevailing imperial policies of laisser faire, free trade and fiscal self-sufficiency almost entirely favoured the white ruling class. The key factor was the continued control of the legislative process. The franchise was nominally widened, but property qualifications, the commodity value of the vote in a desperately poor colony, the systems of multiple votes and double and triple member constituencies, and the over-representation of Out Islands for which relatively wealthy Nassau-based candidates had a campaigning advantage, ensured that non-whites never made up more than a third of the members of the Assembly before the mid-twentieth century, and in any case were scarcely of the class or temperament to rock the socio-political boat.

Predictably, the regime was much concerned with matters of law and order and the fear that the black majority would be educated beyond its station. Following British liberal principles, and with much the same hegemonic purposes, an efficient workhouse, prison and police system was developed despite financial stringencies though by the end of the nineteenth century the constabulary was recruited in Barbados and Jamaica in preference to the Bahamas itself. Similarly made a purely local responsibility after the removal of the Negro Education Grant in 1846, the education system was not just underfunded but skewed, so that only the wealthy or urban middle class (of all colours) achieved more than mere literacy before the 1950s.[11]

With the Bahamas on the impoverished margins of a modernising world, however, it was chiefly through the control of the local economy that Bay Street sustained its hegemony. Banking was rudimentary, but what capital there was was in the hands of the white Nassau merchants. Likewise, Out Island land was generally of such low value that it was rarely traded (at least until the twentieth century), and most Out Islanders were allowed to subsist where they could, though not encouraged towards freehold possession. The control of the salt-pans, however, remained in Bay Street hands and in some of the more fertile islands whites capitalised on their formal ownership through share-cropping arrangements. Much more insidious, as Howard Johnson has cogently demonstrated, was the development of systems of truck and virtual debt peonage in all Bahamian industries, which were related to and exacerbated by the Bay Street merchants' almost absolute monopoly of the export and wholesale import trades.[12]

The payment of wages through retail goods supplied on credit under very disadvantageous terms probably originated in the employment of liberated Africans at the salt-pans before the end of slavery, and similar methods of paying black stevedores and migrant workers lasted down to World War One. The truck system was exacerbated where agricultural industries needed factory processes (as with pineapple canning or rope-making), but in a predominantly maritime economy probably reached its apogee in the sponge industry of the 1880s, where the mercantile class dominated boat building and boat ownership as well as the purchase, processing and export of the product.[13] To a degree, even the poor white Out Island sponge fishermen suffered from Bay Street's exploitation, though compared with black mariners they had two advantages besides the colour that made upward mobility at least theoretically possible. These were a long-standing boat building industry using only materials culled from the islands or from wrecks, and that enterprising mobility (albeit born of a desire to escape from black competition to a country where slavery existed until 1865) that had led them to colonise Key West, off Florida's southern tip, from the 1840s. It is also possible to argue that the economies of racially bifurcated Out Island settlements, chiefly Harbour Island and Green Turtle Cay, Abaco, were simply subordinate versions of the vertical exploitation by Nassau of the Out Islands at large.[14]

As the Bahamas belatedly entered the world mainstream in the twentieth century, Bay Street was threatened by the larger capitalist pressures represented by international banking, world trade networks and large-scale foreign investment, mostly emanating from the United States and initiated by Henry Flagler's huge Hotel Colonial (1899), the giant Bahamas Timber Company operation at Wilson City, Abaco (1906), and the opening of the first branch of a metropolitan bank (1908). Nassau slowly modernised, but the all-white Out Island settlements seemed to some to be lingering on in an economic and sociological time warp, culturally interesting perhaps, but in most respects desperately backward. This view was proposed by T. Wesley Mills in his 1887 study of Green Turtle Cay, but most forcefully propounded in the notorious study of Hope Town, Abaco, made by Dr Clement Penrose and other members of the Baltimore Geographical Society in 1902.[15]

Penrose and his helpers drew up a genealogical chart which showed that the thousand whites of Hope Town were all descended from a Loyalist widow, Wyannie Malone, and her four children, and claimed that five generations of resolute endogamy had resulted in the worst effects of genetic inbreeding. Adding features that were simply the product of poverty, overcrowding, poor hygiene and lack of education including leprosy, syphilis, TB or even cholera, to the few genuine cases of congenital blindness, deafness and idiocy, Penrose wrote of 'hopeless degeneracy' and implied that Hope Town was an affront to progressive white America. Without breaking out from their self-imposed isolation and more particularly, without an expansion of the genetic pool, Hope Town and similar Bahamian settlements were condemned to total retardation, if not extinction.

Such pessimism sprang from the arrogant Social Darwinism that was a corollary of the new-found imperialistic self-confidence of the United States, and it proved grossly exaggerated. Though the isolated all-white northern settlements changed most slowly (retaining aspects of archaic charm well into the era of tourism), Bahamian whites ingeniously adapted to the twentieth century, taking advantage of their traditional sociopolitical dominance, and harnessing to their own benefit the surges of prosperity that followed the two world wars. Mills, Penrose and similar Social Darwinians, indeed, would have been gratified by the way in which the different elements within the Bahamian white minority gradually drew closer together and reinforced each other, seized their opportunities and thereby seemed to prove an inherent superiority.

The First World War during which Bahamian whites served in the United States, Canadian and British forces rather than the colonially subordinate British West India

Regiment, did indeed open new horizons, and while more and more white Bahamians sought education and marriage partners abroad, others steered the difficult middle course between taking advantage of the opportunities of the rum-running era and the flood of American investment in the 1920s, and keeping the profits in Bahamian, and what they regarded as the right Bahamian, hands. The ending of American Prohibition and the Great Depression were major but temporary setbacks, and the flood of airborne tourism, offshore banking and investment in Bahamian land and resources that followed the Second World War produced a glittering, if not entirely honourable, heyday for Bay Street and its white Bahamian leaders and beneficiaries.[16]

Three key figures epitomised the great era for the white Bahamian minority between 1919 and 1967; Roland Symonette, Harold Christie and Stafford Sands, all of ancient if not pre-Loyalist lineage, but, significantly, emerging from poor Out Island 'Conchy Joe' families rather than the established nineteenth-century Bay Street elite. A barefoot seaman with a rudimentary education, born at The Current, Eleuthera in 1898, Symonette first forced his way into the Bay Street oligarchy and then rose to its head by parlaying rum-running profits made in his early 20s into a business empire based on liquor wholesaling and shipbuilding, and extending into hotel ownership, food merchandising, construction and road building by the time he was knighted and became the first Bahamian Premier in 1964.

A Bahamian Citizen Kane, Symonette throughout his career exhibited an uncomfortable combination of ruthless business enterprise, racial sensitivity, and Bahamian nationalism, with the unlocking psychic key (his subliminal 'Rosebud') being, perhaps, his own well-attested but never publicly acknowledged mixed ancestry. Early on excluded from the snobbish Royal Sailing Club (dominated by the old Bay Street families, officials, and white expatriates), he was one of the founders of the rival Nassau Yacht Club, which soon excelled in the traditional Bahamian sport, but practised the even more extreme Conchy Joe form of racial exclusiveness. Symonette always condemned what he considered the prevailing Afro-Bahamian characteristics of laziness, improvidence and superstition. On one occasion he called black Bahamian workers 'the worst class of labour it is possible to have', though in his later years he used the rhetoric of paternalism and relished his nickname, 'Pop'. It is unlikely, though, that he appreciated the addition by a graffiti artist of the adjective 'Black' on a poster proudly proclaiming him 'Our First Premier' in the 1960s.[17]

Though also self-made magnates, Harold Christie and Stafford Sands were less ambiguous figures than Roland Symonette, and with fewer pretensions to statesmanship; but they were at least equally influential, in distinctive ways. Far more than Symonette they were attracted to the profits to be made by attracting foreign tourists, settlers and investors, favouring those from North America. Christie was the second chairman of the Development Board, which the rather younger Sands later transformed into one of the best-funded government departments and a quasi-ministry. Christie made his personal fortune by recognising the unexploited potential of Bahamian land. Starting in New Providence in 1922, he gradually acquired a huge portfolio of freeholds, leaseholds and options on tracts and cays throughout the archipelago hitherto regarded as almost worthless, planned luxurious developments, travelled widely, and applied his considerable charm to attract foreign buyers. His most famous coup was to persuade the American-Canadian mining tycoon Harry Oakes to purchase 10,000 acres of New Providence and settle there in 1934.[18]

Originally so poor that he was one of the few white students in the only government high school, Stafford Sands was a locally qualified lawyer and a naturally brilliant financier who at the peak of his career during the 1960s combined the all-powerful ministerial posts of tourism and finance. Open-endedly ambitious and never very discriminating, he exploited the potential of the Bahamas to rival Batista's Cuba (and to replace it after Castro's revolution in 1959) and demonstrated the mutual attractions to foreign investors and local business partners of setting up offshore 'suitcase' companies. More subtly, at a time when Britain was gradually devolving power, he and his political associates took advantage of complaisant governors to assume the control and disposition of Crown Lands from a colonial administration traditionally disdainful of Conchy Joes and distrustful of Bay Street operators.[19]

Sands' greatest achievement was to facilitate the creation of the almost independent enclave of Freeport-Lucaya in Grand Bahama, though it was also to prove his nemesis and virtually that of his class. From his earliest days as a Bay Street lawyer, Sands had been engaged in plans to include casinos among the attractions for foreign visitors and investors, and as the numbers of foreign businesses nominally located in Nassau gradually rose into the thousands and the annual flow of tourists approached a million, so the stakes rose, and more discreditable and dangerous elements, including Mafiosi, became involved.[20]

In August 1955, the innocent-sounding Hawksbill Creek Agreement granted 50,000 acres of Grand Bahama, with immunity from taxes, duties and immigration restrictions, to a company headed by a developer, Wallace Groves, who had left his native United States after serving a prison term. After initial requirements had been fulfilled, the Agreement was augmented even more generously in 1960. A year later, after an alleged meeting in Miami between Freeport company officials, Bay Street representatives and underworld figures, casino licenses were granted, which were extended to Paradise Island off New Providence in 1966 (despite the opposition, it was said, of 'Pop'

Symonette). With the dredging of a harbour for ocean liners, the building of an international airport, oil refinery and bunkering facilities, cement and chemical factories, major hotels, two casinos, four golf courses, a giant International Bazaar and an excellent network of roads, water and electricity facilities, as well as house-lot sales worth up to $30 million a year, Freeport-Lucaya for a decade seemed a boom town to out-rival Nassau. The chief beneficiaries besides the developers themselves were the Bay Street politicians, headed by Stafford Sands, who received a payment of $500,000 and a retainer of $10,000 a month from the Freeport company, besides his innumerable other fees and personal investment profits.[21]

But the 1950s and most of the 1960s were the pinnacle of opportunity, the last and greatest days, not just for the Bay Street oligarchy but for the white Bahamian minority as a whole. The most obnoxious effect of the flood of American tourists and investors, traceable since the 1920s or even earlier and reaching an apogee in the first phases of the development of Freeport, was the substitution of American patterns of racism and residential apartheid for the relaxed and pragmatic Bahamian tradition of coexistence and interdependence. Both in over-tender deference to their American clients and because they were increasingly dependent on the political support of all resident whites, Bay Street resolutely favoured Out Island whites in filling jobs and also gave more encouragement than ever before to white employee immigrants, inventing mainly for them the ingenious new status of Bahamian Belonger in 1964. By that time, though native-born whites had fallen well below 10 per cent of the Bahamian total, those residents born in the United States, Canada and the UK amounted to more than 5 per cent, while within the boundaries of burgeoning Freeport-Lucaya probably 80 per cent of residents were white, the majority either from the American South or from segregationist Abaco.[22]

An anti-discrimination resolution was tactically adopted by the regime in 1956, but this did not seriously dent the whites' advantages or slow their advance.[23] In a rapidly expanding economy there were much improved chances for middle-class non-whites, but even better employment and business opportunities for all Bahamian whites, including those from the poorest and traditionally most isolated settlements. While thousands of poor black Out Islanders continued to look for their best opportunities as migrant labourers in the United States (a system popularly called the project or the contract, which lasted from 1943 to 1965)[24] and many retained the habit of dependency on the patronage of their white Bay Street representatives in the legislature, Out Island whites flocked to Nassau and Freeport and surged ahead of their non-white competitors in employment and business; the most able and best connected, indeed, vaulted at dizzying speed from shop counter and workshop to front office and boardroom. Even those who stayed behind in the islands used their privileged access to Bay Street money to take advantage of expanding opportunities in Out Island tourism, real estate development, fishing and large-scale agriculture. As a result, almost within the decade of the 1960s, the white Out Island settlements were transformed and modernised; the traditional wooden homes were piped, electrified and brightly painted, and many brand-new concrete bungalows were the homes of prosperous absentees.[25]

Table 2
Bahamas: categories of race from 1953 census[26]

	'European (White)'	%	'African (Black)'	%	'Mixed'	%
All Bahamas	10,709	12.62	61,627	72.64	12,024	14.17
New Providence	6,742	14.62	32,144	68.89	6,784	14.71
Eleuthera	665	10.96	4,331	71.35	1,060	17.46
Spanish Wells	662	96.50	21	3.06	3	0.44
Harbour Island	198	23.57	591	70.36	51	6.07
Abaco & Cays	1,045	33.61	2,039	59.85	224	6.57
Bimini	147	11.09	903	68.15	174	13.13
Long Island	564	15.02	1,330	35.42	1,861	49.56
Ragged Island	–	0.00	110	34.38	211	65.63
Inagua	58	5.81	845	84.58	94	9.41
Mayaguana	2	0.33	603	98.05	1	0.16
Grand Bahama	305	7.45	3,343	81.63	447	10.91
Exuma	58	1.99	2,799	95.89	62	2.12
Cat Island	13	0.41	3,102	96.91	86	2.69
Watling's Island	46	6.63	597	86.02	51	7.35
Rum Cay	–	0.00	133	100.0	–	0.00
Crooked Island	7	0.74	755	90.31	74	8.85
Long Cay	–	0.00	54	67.50	26	32.50
Acklin's Island	–	0.00	860	67.56	413	32.44
Andros	78	1.09	6,809	95.42	247	3.46

The inevitable result of these developments was racial polarisation and rapidly escalating political tension. There had been a time (especially during the Great Depression) when Bay Street's exploitation of the black majority and the indifference of the imperial regime inspired opposition among the more idealist of non-black

Bahamians. The most remarkable instance of this was the unsuccessful attempt by Percy Christie, the 'black sheep' brother of Harold Christie, to emulate Trinidad's Captain A. A. Cipriani and set up a labour union in 1935. The newspaper opposition to Bay Street from the 1920s to the 1960s was led by Etienne Dupuch, who never really came to terms with the fact that he was not a white. Significantly too, when the political opposition coalesced into a formal party with the formation of the Progressive Liberal Party (PLP) in 1953, its leaders and propagandists were a dynamic quartet of poor near-whites with Out Island roots: William Cartwright, Holly Brown, Cyril Stevenson and Henry Taylor.[27]

Bay Street's reaction to the PLP's gains in the 1956 election, the resurgence of the labour movement and the General Strike of 1958 was to constitute itself as the United Bahamian Party (UBP), which cannily combined gerrymandering, electoral corruption, astute patronage and scare journalism, with a campaign of minimal liberal concessions that Antonio Gramsci would have recognised as hegemonic tactics. When the UBP rode the economic boom and the black people's lack of self-confidence (especially that of the recently enfranchised women) to win a stunning victory in the 1962 general election, the response of the PLP was to turn itself unequivocally into the party of the black majority, adopting the extreme rhetoric and tactics of the Black Power movement in the United States. Concurrently and as a consequence, a power struggle within the PLP led to the excision of all non-whites and the emergence of Lynden Pindling as paramount leader, while moderates like Taylor and Dupuch came close to defecting to the UBP regime.[28]

The tumultuous political events of 1967-68 had a climactic simplicity. Concentrating for the first time on the over-represented Out Islands, the PLP achieved a majority of one in the general election of October 1967 by making deals with the single labour victor and a maverick white from Roland Symonette's district in Eleuthera who was appointed Speaker of the House. Less than a year later, after the revelation of the UBP's Freeport deals and other scandals, a second general election produced a landslide for Lynden Pindling and the PLP. Before the next election in 1972, Stafford Sands had died in exile, the UBP had been disbanded, the opposition reconstituted as the multiracial Free National Movement, and the number of whites in the legislature reduced to four out of 38, compared with 21 out of 29 in 1956 and 21 out of 33 in 1962.[29]

The collapse of Bay Street's power and the political marginalisation of the Bahamian white minority were phenomena almost as complete as they were sudden, although they did not occur entirely without resistance, and the attitudes of the victors were not as unambiguous, and certainly not as vindictive, as might have been expected or historically justified. As soon as it was entrenched, the PLP government, besides making improvements in social services that, incidentally, gave the Bahamas its first foretaste of a national debt, introduced substantial constitutional and sweeping electoral changes. Waving the banner of Bahamianisation, the PLP amended the immigration law virtually to eradicate the ambiguous Belonger status and made threatening moves in the direction of Freeport. Some Bay Street magnates followed Stafford Sands' lead, sold up their commercial interests and migrated; the remainder kept a low profile or cannily widened the composition of their boards. A white long-term Canadian resident, D'Arcy Ryan, made a determined test case of his Belonger status that went all the way to the Judicial Committee of the Privy Council in London and brought a PLP minister close to arrest for contempt of court, before its almost inevitable failure. But the chief resistance, predictably, came not from New Providence, where the heterogeneous raft of 'white' candidates had won only two of the 20 seats in 1968 and polled a mere 14 per cent of the vote altogether, but from the northern Out Islands where the result had been much more equivocal, and as late as 1967 white UBP candidates had obtained a substantial majority in the polls.[30]

At Freeport early in 1969 the white licensees (who themselves had only recently won concessions from the corporate autocracy) staged what Peter Barratt has exaggeratedly termed a revolt by protesting against the PLP government's infringements of the Hawksbill Creek Agreements. But the complainants were cowed by Pindling's fiery speech at Pinder's Point in September 1969, in which he threatened that if Freeport did not bend to the winds of change it would be broken. A 1970 Royal Commission headed by the black West Indians Sir Hugh Wooding and Sir Fred Phillips was fairly moderate in its recommendations. But these were followed by the retirement of Wallace Groves, the 'flight' of many foreign investors and white residents, and the steadily increased participation in Freeport by Bahamians, especially blacks. By the end of the decade, Freeport had been essentially Bahamianised, though the positive aspects of the change were clouded by the general recession in the world economy during the 1970s.[31]

Potentially much more serious was the reaction of the more obdurate Abaconians. As the PLP tightened its grip on the Abaco mainland, the recession deepened, and the government moved inexorably towards the final breaking of colonial ties with the UK, the beleaguered white minority (in alliance with a few conservative blacks) complained bitterly of Nassau's neglect and underdevelopment of their homeland, talked of Abaco separating and remaining a British dependency, and formed the Greater Abaco Council to promote these aims. Loyalist petitions and delegations were sent to London, but rejected on the Catch-22 grounds that they were not authorised by the elected government in Nassau. When even the opposition FNM accepted Bahamian Independence on principle, denied the right of Abaco to separate and expelled the black separatist Abaconian MP from the party, a minority of hotheads formed the Abaco Independence

Movement (AIM), secretly negotiated with shady American backers and arms dealers, sent young men to Georgia for guerrilla training and invited the infamous British mercenary 'Mad Mitch' Mitchell to lead them in a war of independence.[32]

These sinister and essentially un-Bahamian plans were thwarted by a combination of the will of the Abaconian majority, the calculated magnanimity of the PLP regime, and the decision of wiser heads among the whites to make the best accommodation possible in the circumstances. In telling contrast to his 'bend or break' speech in Grand Bahama in 1969, Lynden Pindling reassured white Abaconians in July 1973 that they had nothing to fear from Bahamian independence. 'I believe it will be a while before the white community will be enthusiastic [about Bahamian independence]', he was quoted as saying. 'However, the place of Abaconians in history is somewhat different from the other white or black Bahamians. They felt that as loyalists they had a special niche and there were many of us that appreciated that. But what we didn't understand were those that tried to exploit this'.[33]

Adjustment, indeed, was slow and never complete. As late as 1977 the representative of the Abaco Home Rule Movement (successor to the discredited AIM) was elected MP, if by a mere four votes. But at the following general election in 1982, he was decisively defeated by the first white Abaconian PLP candidate, an opportunistic farmer of unimpeachable Loyalist stock called Edison Key. Even more remarkably, when prominent Green Turtle Cay whites planned a Loyalists' Memorial Garden in 1983, with as its central icon a heroic Loyalist woman waving the union flag and a loyal slave woman a suitable step or two behind, among the persons who accepted an invitation to self-commemoration in the surrounding pantheon of paid-for busts, was Pindling's wife Marguerite, presumably more on the grounds of her descent from a Major McKenzie, white Loyalist planter settled in Long Island, than because of her black and slave ancestors.[34]

Having won six successive general elections and ruled for a quarter-century, Lynden Pindling and the PLP fell from power in August 1992, the month of Hurricane Andrew and the year of the Columbus Quincentennial. Even the leader's political astuteness and genuine charisma were unable to disguise any longer the erosion of those qualities that had made the PLP seem indispensable to the Bahamian majority; above all, the notion that it alone could bring an economic prosperity shared by all. The rhetoric of Black Power and the prestige of having overturned Bay Street and created an independent Bahamian nation were no longer compelling to a people awakened to the reality that they were effectively ruled by a new black elite that outdid old Bay Street in its acquisitiveness and indifference to corruption, and in a declining world economy that had saddled the new nation with a national debt of more than $1 billion.[35]

A more equitable electoral system, Bahamianisation and two decades of national independence had certainly led to greater self-confidence among those able to take economic advantage; but by the same token these changes made the redistribution of wealth and the restructuring of classes more important and divisive issues than racial distinctions. Racial crossovers occurred commonly at every level. With citizenship much more strictly defined and controlled, expatriates were no longer feared as potential recruits for a racist regime. White residents and contract employees, in fact, were welcomed for the money and expertise they brought, while black illegal migrants from Haiti and the West Indies were almost universally resented, despised and repatriated whenever possible. If in proportion to their wealth, pretensions, or will to integrate, rather than to their demographic preponderance, blacks were found alongside whites in the most prestigious clubs, schools and residential areas. Lynden Pindling and his most favoured ministers, for example, were fêted wherever they chose to go, sent their children to the most exclusive private schools and lived in some of the most splendid houses in the best places.

In all types, and at all levels, of private employment, positions only went to expatriates in the absence of qualified Bahamians, and opportunities were equal for all Bahamians depending upon their qualifications, with hugely improved opportunities for education and training than before 1967. Simply by the continuation of family traditions, whites tended to train their children towards the professions and mercantile jobs, although they no longer predominated in these occupations more than their proportion in the overall population warranted. By a continuation of the same tradition, blacks remained the overwhelming majority of those working in the all-important tourist industry, though now filling many of the supervisory and management posts too. Lower down the scale of tourist employment, there had been a time when current ideology and memories of former discriminatory working conditions led to a feeling that such jobs were demeaning, and service accordingly suffered. But the new national self-confidence, as well as the prime minister's well-publicised stint as a waiter (as well as the worsening economic situation that revalued all steady employment), showed that good service need not necessarily require servility, so that standards improved.[36]

Only in government jobs was there arguably a degree of practical discrimination, and this was the reverse of the traditional, in that it represented the fruits of 25 years of dominance and political patronage by the party whose members were almost exclusively black. Outside the realm of politics and government employment, however, and to the great credit of the PLP regime, there was no active discrimination, let alone persecution, of the former white commercial and professional elite. During the 1970s and 1980s some non-Bahamian licensees in Freeport complained of harassment by Bahamian rivals. Yet, for the most part, those white Bay Streeters who had weathered the political storm continued to flourish, if more discreetly than before. Many of them, indeed, although politically neutered, continued to live in their accustomed smart locations and style on Prospect Ridge or Nassau's Eastern Road, being dubbed, without rancour, the White Knights by one political columnist. It might also be argued that elements of the non-white middle class, including the so-called 'Long Island Whites' also more or less marginalised during the PLP's heyday, actually enjoyed a period of unprecedented economic prosperity.[37]

What then, if anything, has the long delayed victory of the FNM signified for the white Bahamian minority, and what residues, if any, are there of previous forms of distinctiveness? Led by Hubert Ingraham, a black Abaconian former member of the PLP, the FNM contemptuously dismissed the campaign charge that it was the old UBP revived, pointing out that it had fewer millionaire lawyers and businessmen among its candidates, and scarcely more whites, than had the PLP. The historic symbols of race and class that, according to Colin Hughes, had for a generation dominated partisan discourse in the absence of real ideological differences, were clearly moribund, if not entirely dead.[38] Coming to power in the second phase of national independence, however, the FNM has had not only the predictable tasks of reform, reconstruction and reconciliation, but also the tasks of projecting a new and distinct ideology. In this it seems to have followed the trend throughout the Western world, and inclined towards the 'liberal, laisser faire' principles of reducing government spending, promoting private enterprise, and returning to traditional values generally associated with Margaret Thatcher's Conservatives in the UK and Ronald Reagan's Republicans in the United States. Although emphatically not a return to UBP values, this undoubtedly is a shift that encourages the fuller participation of the native white minority in the Commonwealth of the Bahamas, while at the same time it does not threaten its cherished sub-ethnic identity.

The extreme example of the new dispensation is the recent history and present state of what was once the most notoriously isolationist and racist all-white settlement; Spanish Wells, on St George's Cay, off Northern Eleuthera. A model of opportunistic Thatcherite prosperity, the settlement is admired for retaining so many of its traditional values, including its spirit of self-sufficiency. In recent years it has become the richest Family Island community by developing the most efficient fishing operation, annually harvesting hundreds of tons of Bahamian lobster for sale to Florida at $10 per lb. From its own resources it has filled the available land space on its original St George's Cay with modern homes, spilling over on to adjacent Russell Island. Its community-owned electricity and water services are said to be the best in the Bahamas, and its locally-owned supermarket draws shoppers from the entire mainland of Eleuthera. Along with

Freeport, Grand Bahama and Marsh Harbour on the Abaco mainland, it is one of the few Family Island settlements whose population has grown in the last decades. Yet except for a handful of government officials (and, anomalously, the black wife of a white Methodist minister), the entire population of the original settlement remains 'Conchy Joe' white, the majority are blood relations and more than one-quarter rejoice in the single surname Pinder.[39]

The only reprehensible feature of the transformation of Spanish Wells (apart from the embarrassing involvement of one 'Sigillian' in drug running during the 1980s) has been that in place of the traditional exploitation of black labourers from Eleuthera, it now obtains its necessary manual labour from Haitians, many of them illegal immigrants. In this respect, the Sigillians are no worse than many other modern Bahamian employers, irrespective of colour, and far better than some. Just as former Sigillian whites kept their slaves on the nearby mainland, and by tradition as late as the 1960s all blacks were constrained to be 'off the Cay by nightfall', so the modern Haitian labourers are as far as possible segregated. Those with sound immigration papers or guaranteed employment live in rent-tied huts in the interior of Russell Island (paternalistically claimed to be happier and better housed than any other Bahamian Haitians), and the illegally landed or casually employed are forced to make shift as squatters in the shanty settlements of Blackwood and Gene's Bay, on the mainland opposite St George's Cay.[40]

On the wider national canvas, as it looks towards rescuing the Commonwealth of the Bahamas from its economic woes and lead it towards the twenty-first century, the FNM government of Hubert Ingraham enrols the sons and daughters of Bay Street and the Conchy Joes alongside the variegated native middling classes and the black majority while being far more guarded about foreign white expatriates and distinctly unfriendly towards non-invited blacks from Haiti and other parts of the West Indies. Far more than proved possible to Lynden Pindling and the PLP even at the desperate end of their long regime, Hubert Ingraham's government comfortably includes representatives of all types of Bahamian, neatly (although, of course, without a formal quota system) in their due proportions. In complexion, naturally, the great majority are blacks or browns. But beside them are a son of Sir Etienne Dupuch, a white businessman from Long Island, a Conchy Joe from the Abaco Cays and the son (victor in a recount over the PLP's white candidate for North Eleuthera) of a former Bay Street grandee who was Chairman of the Senate under the UBP. Most remarkably, Ingraham has appointed to the Senate and his Cabinet the son of Roland 'Pop' Symonette, awarding him the tourism portfolio once held by Stafford Sands. What more forthright subscription to the Bahamian motto of 'Forward, Onward, Upward, Together' could there be than this?[41]

Finally, what are the chances of the Conchy Joes surviving as a distinct ethnic and cultural group? More important questions are what do they, can they, will they, contribute economically and culturally to the Commonwealth of the Bahamas and its people as a whole? At present numbering no more than 10,000, the Bahamian white minority will almost certainly continue to decline in numbers, more rapidly in relative than absolute terms. Miscegenation has not notably increased (most of that occurring being between Bahamian non-whites and foreign whites), and for the whites of the northern cays it continues to be almost non-existent. An important demographic factor is that with greater prosperity, the white communities more obviously than others exhibit the 'middle-class' and 'modern' tendency to a slower rate of natural increase. This is clearly borne out by the case of Spanish Wells, the nearest to an all-white settlement remaining and the only one for which sufficient demographic statistics are available. The population of Spanish Wells rose from 686 in 1953 to 1,372 in 1990, but the latter total included up to 400 Haitians, non-white Bahamians and non-Bahamian white residents. Partly as a consequence of these newcomers, but also because of the true Sigillians' low average fertility and small family sizes, only 7.5 per cent of the resident population was under the age of five in 1990, and 19 per cent under 15, compared with figures for the Bahamas as a whole of 11 per cent and 33 per cent respectively.[42]

As has been true at least since 1950, probably as many Bahamian whites still live in New Providence as in the Family Islands altogether. But the Conchy Joes' love of their island homes, their determination to stay if they can and return, tends to slow the general drift away from the Family Islands towards the Bahamian metropole (and, to a certain extent, the satellite metropolis of Freeport), and may even reverse it. Island values – community, family, church and traditional lifestyles – have a magnetic attraction for Conchy Joes, and they surely have a reinforcing validity for a new generation of upwardly mobile and educated non-white Bahamians, especially given the bad features of modern life at the crowded centre.

More significant, though, are the ways that the island-based whites contribute to reversing the disastrous downward trend in the Family Islands' economy. As opportunistic as ever, they are proving adaptable as never before. Traditional boatbuilding, sadly, has become no more than a museum curiosity; but the traditional boatbuilding families of Abaco either have shifted into using powered machinery and modern materials, especially fibreglass, or have shifted laterally into the lucrative boat charter and servicing business. Others cater for tourists and foreign residents, deal in real estate and engage in housebuilding. Of more fundamental importance, Conchy Joes have led the way in modernising the Bahamian fishing industry and, with more governmental support, may yet do the same for Bahamian agriculture.[43]

The ways in which Conchy Joe culture contributes to and may meld with that of the

Bahamas as a whole may perhaps be illustrated, Simon Schama fashion, by a tentative analysis of the work of the two major Bahamian painters who happen to be of Conchy Joe provenance, Alton Lowe and Brent Malone. Both are descriptive realists, but they differ in significant ways. Alton Lowe of Green Turtle Cay, Abaco, is largely self-taught and has stayed deeply and affectionately rooted in his white Abaconian milieu. He celebrates the seas, skies, marine activities and, above all, the mariners of his native cays, their women and children. At a superficial viewing, many of his paintings seem to have no more than a charming chocolate-box verisimilitude. Yet a deeper look at the patient wrinkled old mariner, hand on the tiller, quizzical gaze over the dazzling emerald towards the dark blue of the deep, or the blond blue-eyed young women forever staring at the horizon, looking for a returning sail, suggests a more profound and complex mix of endurance, isolation and poignant longing.

If in Lowe's work there remains a deep and almost tragic nostalgia, that of Brent Malone is far more optimistic and progressive. Resident in Nassau and academically more polished than Lowe, Malone also celebrates the sea and its ways; not the elements against man as in the greatest canvases of Winslow Homer, but the accurate minutiae of sailing ships and the precise forms and physiognomies of the men who work them, blacks far more often than whites. Malone's fascination with, and sensitivity towards, Bahamian blacks, moreover, extends into a profound interaction with their Afro-Bahamian culture, especially in his obsession with the predominant Bahamian festival of Junkanoo, with its attendant bloodbeat rhythm of the goombay drums.

What this doubtless signifies is that if the minority culture is to contribute towards that of the nation it must participate at the risk of becoming almost subsumed. Bahamian whites have always had a reticent, but ineluctable, attraction towards Afro-Bahamian music and dance. Increasingly now they accept that the Junkanoo, ever changing and accepting new elements just like Trinidadian carnival, is the predominant national festival form. The once treasured 'Old Bunce' (or 'Old Skin') festival of Green Turtle Cay, with its essentially British and North American mumming and Jack-in-the-Green antecedents, is already fading in favour of Junkanoo.[44]

The same process can be observed in the Bahamian national involvement in sports. Naturally, sailing is the traditional sports activity, the first in which the Bahamas have achieved world-class honours. The first Bahamian Olympic medallists were Conchy Joe sailors from the Nassau Yacht Club. They remain national heroes, but the pre-eminent national sailing race is the Family Island Regatta held annually in April at George Town, Exuma, in which the chief races are between purported work boats, with black skippers and crews.[45] Tennis is a minor sport, but one in which Bahamians excel. Originally, the Bahamas simply participated with other territories to select a British Caribbean Davis

Cup team, but since the 1970s has produced its own team to beat all the rest. In 1993, the Bahamas was drawn to play the United States in a Davis Cup tie for a place in the elite World Group. The Bahamas team consisted of just two players; Roger Smith, a black hailing from Grand Bahama, and Mark Knowles, a white with Conchy Joe antecedents on his father's side. Although they were inevitably beaten by a five-man squad, they did their nation proud, with the memorable support of a sizeable group of fellow Bahamians, not clad in Junkanoo costume, but blowing conch shells, bugles and whistles, to the insistent beat and rhythm of cow-bell and goombay drums.[46]

Notes

1. Howard Johnson, *The Bahamas in Slavery and Freedom* (Kingston, London, 1991), p. 105.

2. For the early history of the Bahamian people and the connection with Bermuda, Michael Craton and Gail Saunders, *Islanders in the Stream: A History of the Bahamian People. From Aboriginal Times to the End of Slavery,* vol 1 (Athens, Georgia, 1992). The pre-revolutionary figures are for 1773, from Public Record Office, London, CO 23/22, 59-70, *ibid,* p. 180.

3. *Ibid.,* 179. Gail Saunders, *Bahamian Loyalists and their Slaves,* (London, 1983); Sandra Riley, *Homeward Bound: A History of the Bahama Islands to 1850, with a Definitive Study of Abaco in the American Loyalist Plantation Period* (Miami, 1983).

4. Maxwell to Sydney, 12 May 1784, CO 23/26, 103-04, quoted in Craton and Saunders, *Islanders in the Stream,* I, p. 179.

5. CO 23/48, 144; 23/59, 37, *ibid.* The salt-producing Turks Islands, more closely connected with Bermuda than Nassau, had 40 whites and 110 'reputed blacks' in 1773. In 1807 there were still only 40 whites but 1,295 slaves, as well as 75 free non-whites. In addition, there were 1,080 slaves, 20 whites and seven free non-whites in the Caicos Islands.

6. Craton and Saunders, *Islanders in the Stream,* I, pp.213-32. Most of the subsequent material in this essay is derived from the manuscript of vol. 2 of *Islanders in the Stream,* which is scheduled for publication in 1997. This material is identified here by chapter and typescript page.

7. *Islanders in the Stream,* I, pp. 358-91.

8. Louis Diston Powles, *Land of the Pink Pearl* (London, 1888), p. 112, quoted in Gail Saunders, 'The Social History of the Bahamas, 1890-1953', Ph.D. thesis, University of Waterloo, 1985, p. 76.

9. Howard Johnson, 'The Liberated Africans, 1811-1860', *Slavery and Freedom,* pp. 30-54; Craton and Saunders, 'Islanders in the Stream', vol. 2, 1:1-26. Michael Craton, 'The Ambivalencies of Independency: The Transition Out of Slavery in the Bahamas, c. 1800-1850,' in Roderick A. McDonald (ed.), *West Indies Accounts: Essays on the History of the British Caribbean and the Atlantic Economy in Honour of Richard Sheridan,* (Barbados, Jamaica, Trinidad and Tobago, 1996), pp. 274-96.

10. *Colony of the Bahamas, Blue Book, 1856* (Nassau, 1856), pp. 144-45. The simple distinction between 'Whites' and 'Coloured Population' (consonant with the polar categorisation found in United States rather than the recognition of three categories including mixed-race 'coloureds' between 'whites' and 'blacks'- more common in the West Indies) was clearly made by the enumerators rather than by those

enumerated. No subsequent attempt at racial classification was made in the Bahamas Census until 1943, for the stated reason given in 1861 by Governor Charles Bayley (interestingly, one of the most candidly racist of Bahamian governors) that it would exacerbate racial animosities. 'Islanders in the Stream', vol. 2, pp. 50-52.

11. *Ibid.*, 1:41-50; 3:30-1; 6:41-2. Howard Johnson, 'Social Control and the Colonial State: The Reorganisation of the Police Force, 1888-93', *Slavery and Freedom*, pp. 110-124.

12. Howard Johnson, 'The Share System in the Nineteenth and Early Twentieth Centuries,' 'Post-Emancipation Labour Systems', and 'The Credit and Truck Systems in the Nineteenth and Early Twentieth Centuries', *Slavery and Freedom*, pp. 55-119, especially pp, 84-105, 'Islanders in the Stream', vol. 2 pp. 56-77.

13. *Ibid.*; Johnson, *Slavery and Freedom*, pp. 96-102; Powles' *Land of the Pink Pearl*, 88-92; Michael Craton, *A History of the Bahamas*, 3rd edition (Waterloo, 1986), pp. 238-41.

14. 'Islanders in the Stream', vol. 2. 5:1-20, 7:23-28. By the time of the American Civil War, half the population of Key West was said to consist of Bahamian 'Conchs', some of them forming a kind of Bay Street commercial elite. Their predominance, and the attractions for them of Key West, faded with US slave emancipation, the migration of Cuban tobacco manufacturers and Cuban refugees from the Ten Years' War (1868-78), the migration of black Bahamians to work in the tobacco factories and sponge beds, and, finally, the building of the railroad and road along the Florida Cays by the time of the First World War. To this day, however, Key West still retains architectural traces reminiscent of the Abaco Cays, and native Key Westians are still popularly known as 'Conchs'. Howard Johnson, 'Late Nineteenth and Early Twentieth Century Labour Migration to Florida', *Slavery and Freedom*, pp. 163-180.

15. *Ibid.*, 6-11; T. Wesley Mills, 'The Study of a Small Island Community, the Bahama Islands', *The American Naturalist*, XXI (1887), pp. 875-85; George Burbank Shattuck (ed.), *The Bahama Islands* (New York, 1905), pp. 410-14.

16. Craton, *History of the Bahamas*, pp. 245-63;

Saunders, 'Social History of the Bahamas', pp. 174-240, 402-500; 'Islanders in the Stream', vol. 2. 7:36-51, 9:35-81. Though the possession of ancient Bahamian lineage was always prized among the whites, entry to the Bay Street elite was not an absolutely closed door to wealthy immigrants of the right complexion and ideas, at least in the second and third generation. Jews were always excluded (even if they contributed much to the Bahamas) and such pushy newcomers as Murphy, Collins and Oakes were never fully accepted. But in its heyday, Bay Street's political elite included two brothers called Baker whose forerunners were Christian Lebanese traders called Ouwade, as well as the descendants of white emigrés from Haiti and Cuba, and a d'Albenas, whose family hailed from Quebec. This small opening of opportunity doubtless contributed to friction between Bay Street and the genuine Conchy Joes, as well as the 'Long Island whites'.

17. *Ibid.*, 8:7; 10:37-40.

18. *Ibid.*, 8:13-14, 18-21, 54-56. The Development Board, authorised in 1914, was first constituted in 1920. The first chairman was the far from disinterested R.H. Curry, member of the Executive Council and Nassau's premier shipping agent. Harold Christie remained one of Oakes's closest associates and was allegedly fast asleep in an adjacent bedroom when Oakes was brutally murdered on the night of July 7-8, 1943. *Ibid.*, 10:48-50.

19. Originally, Christie and other Bay Street realtors, though with undoubted advantages because of their wealth, legal expertise and close access to registration records, were only able to deal in private lands. The colonial administration tended to keep a very jealous control over the prerogative of allocating Crown Lands. Governor Harry Cordeaux during the 1920s, for example, secretly wrote: 'I don't like the idea of parting [with Crown Lands], though it's difficult to refuse genuine development schemes. Americans are buying up every available inch of private land in New Providence and paying enormous prices for it and there will soon be nothing British left except the Flag!' Cordeaux to Darnley, Private, 8 August 1926, CO 23/296. Probably the most complaisant of modern governors was Lord Ranfurly (1953-7) after whom the

main intersection in Freeport is appropriately named the Ranfurly Circus. *Ibid.*, 8:19-23; 10:13-16.

20. *Ibid.*, 10:13-22. Two 'exemptions' to the law against casinos had been granted to favoured Americans to operate gaming clubs in Nassau and Cat Cay for non-Bahamians as early as 1925. As a young lawyer, Stafford Sands had attempted in vain to obtain such an exemption for a client in 1939, and between 1946 and 1956, when he was a member of the Executive Council, he made further unsuccessful applications on behalf of himself and others. Colin A. Hughes, *Race and Politics in the Bahamas* (St Lucia, 1981), pp. 98-99. 'Islanders in the Stream', vol 2 10:49-50.

21. *Ibid.*, pp. 50-52. Sands' most important traditional Bay Street enterprise was the creation of the Nassau Food Stores chain. After his fall from grace this was sold to the U.S. Winn-Dixie firm, which formed the locally registered Bahamas Supermarkets Limited for the purpose, changing the name of the chain to City Markets. Anthony Thompson, *An Economic History of the Bahamas* (Nassau, 1979), pp. 103-4.

22. In fact, the majority of the greatly increased population of Grand Bahama, predominantly non-white, lived outside the boundaries of Freeport-Lucaya. The sprawling black settlement of Eight Mile Rock alone was more populous than the Freeport-Lucaya enclave. Belonger Status was promoted by the regime as a means of distinguishing true Bahamians from mere residents, though the opposition charged that this was a fraudulent claim. 'Islanders in the Stream', vol 2, 10:42. *Report on the Census of the Bahama Islands taken 15th November 1963* (Nassau, 1963).

23. Despite the myth propounded by Etienne Dupuch that he alone had achieved the anti-discrimination legislation of 1956, it was really a case of Bay Street conceding to a culmination of pressures, with the change almost anti-climactic. Hughes, *Race and Politics*, pp. 45-46; D. Gail Saunders, 'The 1956 Resolution: Breaking Down the Barriers of Racial Discrimination in the Bahamas', paper given at 26th Conference of Caribbean Historians, San German, Puerto Rico, 1994; 'Islanders in the Stream' vol 2, 9:68-9.

24. *Ibid.*, 9:35-44; Tracey L. Thompson, 'Remembering the Contract: Insights towards a Thesis,' paper given at 25th Annual Conference of Caribbean Historians, Mona, Jamaica, 1993.

25. For a graphic personal account of the changes between 1947 and 1968, Jack Ford, *Reminiscences of an Island Teacher: Life in the Bahamas, 1948-1953*, Jack Hardy (ed.) (Decatur, 1992). Also, Ruth Rodriguez, *Out Island Portraits, 1946-1956*, (New York, 1978); Haziel L. Albury, *Man-O-War My Island Home: A History of an Outer Abaco Island* (Hockessin, Delaware, 1977); Steve Dodge, *Abaco: The History of an Out Island and its Cays* (Miami, 1983); 'Islanders in the Stream', vol 2, 10:1-12.

26. The censuses of 1943 and 1953 were the only ones after 1851 designating the Bahamian population by race. Following a more West Indian categorisation than that used in 1851 and shown in Table 1, they also relied more on self-identification than the census-takers' own assessments, especially in 1953. Though coming before the surge of black consciousness of the 1960s, the 1953 categories are particularly interesting in showing which non-white islanders (notably those from Long Island, Ragged Island, Long Cay and Acklin's) regarded themselves as 'Mixed' and those (notably in Andros, Cat Island, Mayaguana and Rum Cay) who, for whatever reason, called themselves unequivocal blacks. Note too that while Spanish Wells is separately tabulated, the almost equally white-dominated Abaco Cays are not. After 1953, racial categories were not given in the Bahamas censuses, both because of the difficulties of tabulation and of heightened racial sensitivities. After 1953, therefore, while a fair calculation of the number of expatriate whites can be given from the statistics of national origin, that of native Bahamian whites or persons of 'mixed race' cannot. *Report on the Census of the Bahama Islands, taken on the 25th. April, 1943* (Nassau, 1943); *Report on the Census of the Bahama Islands 1953* (Nassau, 1953); 'Islanders in the Stream', vol 2, 6:29-31, 12:1-12; Azellah Major et al., *Demographic Aspects of the Bahamian Population, 1901-1974* (Nassau, 1976); Norma Abdulah, *The Bahamas and its People: A Demographic Analysis* (Trinidad, 1987).

27. Hughes, *Race and Politics*, pp. 36-46;

Saunders, 'Social History of the Bahamas,' pp. 472-73; Doris L. Johnson, *The Quiet Revolution in the Bahamas* (Nassau, 1972), pp. 29-42; Henry M. Taylor, *My Political Memoirs: A Political History of the Bahamas in the 20th Century* (Nassau, 1987), pp. 122-43, 198-238; 'Islanders in the Stream', vol 2, 9:65-68.

28. Taylor was elbowed aside as PLP president in 1963, accepted posts under the UBP government, but ended his political career as the PLP's nominee as Governor General. Dupuch, after being named as one of the recipients of Freeport largesse (subsequently returned) retired from politics and went to live in Florida, though continuing to write editorials against the PLP almost up to his death in 1991. Another more complex by-product of the turmoil was the widening split between the PLP and the labour movement, which involved a personality and power clash between their respective leaders, Lynden Pindling and Randol Fawkes, as well as much subtle manoeuvring on the part of the UBP. Randol Fawkes, *The Faith that Moved the Mountain* (Nassau, 1979), pp. 127-67; Felix Bethel and Michael Stevenson, 'The State, the Crowd, and the Heroes: The Struggle for Control in the Bahamas, 1958-1968,' paper given at 24th Conference of Caribbean Historians, Nassau, 1992; 'Islanders in the Stream', vol 2, pp. 71-81.

29. Hughes, *Race and Politics*, pp. 124-64; 'Islanders in the Stream', vol 2, 10:50-60. One of the most successful FNM candidates in 1972 was Sir Roland Symonette, who was elected once more (for the splinter BDP) in 1977, but retired in 1978, two years before his death. By 1977, all constituencies were singly represented, whereas up to 1962 there were ten double and three triple constituencies (the latter all held by white UBP candidates until 1967).

30. In the almost-tied 1967 election, Grand Bahama, Abaco and Eleuthera between them elected five UBP candidates, three from the PLP, and one Independent. The UBP vote was approximately 36 per cent in Grand Bahama, 80 per cent in Abaco, and 50 per cent in Eleuthera and its cays. The Eleuthera Independent was the white Alvin Braynen, made Speaker by the PLP government and later rewarded with the High Commission in London. Both Grand Bahama

seats were won by the PLP on the strength of the non-white native-born majority outside Freeport-Lucaya.

31. Peter Barratt, *Grand Bahama* (London, 1982, originally published, 1972), pp. 106-08; 'Islanders in the Stream', vol 2, 10:67-73.

32. Dodge, *Abaco*, pp. 116-31; 'Independence and Separatism', in Dean W. Collinwood and Steve Dodge (eds), *Modern Bahamian Society* (Parkersburg, Ohio, 1989), pp. 48-64; 'Islanders in the Stream', vol 2, 10:80-82.

33. *Nassau Tribune*, 9 July 1973, quoted in Dodge, 'Independence and Separatism', p. 55. The PLP also showed tactical wisdom in not banning 'Mad Mitch' from the Bahamas. When he came he gave a speech strongly disavowing any intention of leading mercenaries in an Abaconian war of independence.

34. Dodge, Abaco, pp. 134-146; Michael Craton, 'Hopetown and Hard Bargain: The Loyalist Transformation in the Bahamas', in Ralph Bennett (ed.), *Settlements in the Americas: Cross-Cultural Perspectives* (Delaware, 1993), p. 275.

35. 'Islanders in the Stream', vol 2, 11:1-3, 40-46

36. *Ibid.*, 13:20-25.

37. *Ibid.*, 16:25-30; Barratt, *Grand Bahama*, pp. 141-160; Dodge, *Abaco*, pp. 134-164.

38. Hughes, *Race and Politics*, pp. 208-229

39. 'Islanders in the Stream', vol 2, 12:1-10; Field Research and Interviews, Spanish Wells, May 1994.

40. *Ibid.* For the drug involvement of Abner Pinder, *Report of the Commission of Inquiry Appointed to Inquire Into the Illegal Use of the Bahamas for the Transshipment of Dangerous Drugs Destined for the United States of America, November 1983-December 1984* (Nassau, 1984), p. 25. Ironically, one of the most notorious employers of Haitians was Key-Sawyer Farms on the Abaco mainland, largely owned by Edison Key, white PLP Member of Parliament. The mostly illegal immigrants' living conditions reportedly deteriorated even farther when the

enterprise was sold to American interests in the late 1980s. 'Islanders in the Stream', vol 2, 11:31, 14:12-13.

41. The victorious non-black FNM candidates were Pierre Dupuch for Shirlea in Nassau, James Knowles for Long Island, Robert Sweeting for Hope Town, Abaco, and Noel Roberts for St. John's (Northern Eleuthera), declared elected by seven votes on a recount over the PLP's white Sigillian candidate, Marvin Pinder. Brent Symonette, 37-year-old son of Sir Roland's second marriage, lawyer and businessman educated in England, was the only white in Hubert Ingraham's thirteen-person Cabinet, three of whom were women. *Nassau Tribune*, 26 August 1992, p. 7.

42. 'Islanders in the Stream', vol 2, 12:1-10; *Bahamas Census 1990: Preliminary Results*, (Nassau, 1993); preliminary tables, 19:1. Spanish Wells: *Population by Sex and by Age in Years Last Birthday*, personal communication, 1994.

43. Dodge, *Abaco*, pp. 34-61, 134-64.

44. Michael Craton, 'Decoding Pitchy-Patchy: The Roots, Branches and Essence of Junkanoo,' *Slavery and Abolition*, 16:1 (1995), pp. 14-44.

45. Durward Knowles, Sloan Farrington, and Cecil Cook were World and Olympic champions 1952-56. Douglas Hanks Jr, *Driven by the Stars: The Story of Durward Knowles* (Nassau, 1992). The George Town Regatta, begun by Linton Rigg and R. H. Symonette (son of Sir Roland, and then the local parliamentary representative) in 1954 as an entertainment for white foreigners and the Bahamian elite, was democratised and virtually nationalised by the PLP in the later 1960s. From then, and particularly after the cessation of local horse-racing, informal betting on sail races became one of the most active forms of Bahamian gambling. Long Island Whites raced with Androsians, Exumians and other black sailors from the beginning; white Abaconians tentatively joined in around 1975; Spanish Wells sailors had not participated up to 1983. Interview with Howland Bottomley, Regatta Point, George Town, Exuma, 26 June 1983.

46. *Tennis Magazine*, (December 1993), pp. 84-88; Craton, 'Decoding Pitchy-Patchy,' p. 15.

5

The Culture of the Colonial Elites of Nineteenth-Century Guyana[1]

BRIAN L. MOORE

The abolition of slavery in the British Caribbean (1834–38) ushered in a prolonged period of uncertainty and instability to the colonies as the established societal order characterised by white dominance and privilege came under direct attack from the emancipated ex-slaves and their descendants. Despite white fears of a 'reversion to barbarism' associated with things black and African, for the most part this was a non- violent challenge to the white power structure. The ex-slaves sought social and economic mobility and the means to achieve it. They wanted land, higher wages, educational facilities, better jobs and the franchise. These aspirations, however, were considered inimical to the interests of the white elites: they were translated to mean 'black power', tantamount to barbarism, of which Haiti supposedly served as a good example. For the white minority the continued prosperity of the colonies, and of 'civilisation' itself therein, necessitated continued white dominance. This meant that the ex-slaves had by all means to be kept 'in their place', at least until they showed a readiness to enter the society of 'civilised' beings, and it was generally taken for granted that that would be long in coming.

But emancipation posed practical problems of keeping the ex-slaves down. In a theoretical 'free society', all 'men' were considered equal before the law; and under the watchful eye of the humanitarian movement in Britain the overt use of 'race' to preclude black-coloured advancement was not likely to be tolerated by the Colonial Office, even though imperial officials shared the view that the established social order should be preserved for as long as possible. No institutionalised system of apartheid, therefore, would be permitted to develop in the Caribbean colonies. But then how were the ex-slave majority to be kept subordinate to the will of their erstwhile masters? How long could a tiny white minority continue to preserve their dominance at the expense of a potentially hostile and overwhelming black majority? These were the issues which preoccupied the white elites in colonial society after emancipation.

It is this social context that helped to shape the cultural attitudes of these elites in the post-emancipation British Caribbean. They felt more vulnerable than ever before and were consequently increasingly dependent on the metropolis. But British policies and changing circumstances in the colonies deepened their sense of insecurity. In an era of international peace after 1815, Britain was less committed to maintaining large garrisons in the Caribbean. The drift towards free trade after 1820 gradually knocked the bottom out of the West Indian sugar monopoly in the British market. By the mid-1840s several of the colonies were in the throes of depression. The decline in personal fortunes and new laws and regulations opening up the political system on the basis of 'equal' footing (without regard to 'race') threatened to undermine the monopoly of the planters and merchants in this area of colonial life. Some chose to leave, either to return home or to seek greener pastures in North America. Those who remained became more psychologically and physically dependent on the motherland. If in bygone times they had been tempted to claim autonomy in relation to Britain, now they became wholly dependent on her for their well-being, even their very survival.

There was thus a greater perceived need among the white elites after emancipation to align themselves closer to their British roots. If their British kith and kin were to sympathise with their dilemma, they needed to demonstrate that despite generations in the tropics away from the 'civilising' influences of the metropolitan society and institutions, they had not degenerated and were still British at the core. Moreover, British institutions, ideas, values and customs were all the more important in the changing circumstances in the colonies if the ex-slaves were to be 'civilised' and conditioned to accept the *status quo*. Force was still very necessary to maintain law, order and social stability, but culture was an essential softer side of imperialism aimed at achieving consensus while preserving existing social inequalities.

For most of the post-emancipation nineteenth century, the colonial elites of Guyana were composed essentially of British whites and their descendants.[2] These were mainly Scottish, English and Irish immigrants serving in different capacities, from lowly overseers and book-keepers on the sugar estates to planters, merchants, and colonial officials. In between there were professionals such as lawyers, doctors and priests, army and police officers, bank and store clerks. With few exceptions, most of these had middle- and lower-class origins in the British Isles and were intent on making their fortune in the colony before returning home to enjoy an upper-middle-class life of luxury and leisure. There were in addition a few Dutch and North American residents and a hand-ful of Jewish families. Finally there was a body of local-born whites who formed 42–45 per cent of the total white population.

Altogether this dominant white section increased from 2,776 (2.8 per cent) in 1841 to 4,551 (1.6 per cent) in 1891. Very importantly, most of them were single males; indeed as late as 1891 there were just 67 females per 100 men among the European pop-ulation. Throughout the post-emancipation nineteenth century over 60 per cent of the white population were urban, concentrated mainly in the capital, Georgetown, and to a lesser extent in New Amsterdam in Berbice.[3]

Despite the uncertainties ushered in by emancipation, this elite class of whites was able to maintain almost absolute dominance over both the colonial polity and economy almost until the end of the nineteenth century. The economy was of course based large-ly on sugar plantations which were owned both by private individuals and increasingly by British companies such as the Colonial Company, Thomas Daniel and Sons, James Ewing & Company, and Booker Brothers & J. McConnell. Until the late 1880s the plan-tation sector accounted for over 90 per cent of the total export trade.[4]

Notwithstanding the opening up of the franchise after emancipation to all colonial subjects regardless of race or colour, the polity was likewise controlled by the planting interests who shared power only with colonial officials representing the imperial gov-ernment. Under the old Dutch-style colonial constitution which remained in force until 1891, only persons with 80 or more acres of land (that is, the planting interests) were eligible for election to the Court of Policy (the legislature), where they enjoyed equal representation with the appointed imperial officials. The annual budget, however, had to be approved by the Combined Court composed of all the members of the legislature adjoined to another body of elected members (the Financial College). This gave the wealthy planting and commercial classes an absolute majority over the colonial officials in financial affairs.

Under those circumstances, colonial revenues and expenditure, and the process of law-making were largely influenced by and reflected the economic and social interests of the colonial elites for almost the entire nineteenth century. In addition, and naturally because of such political and economic dominance, this class controlled all the statuto-ry boards responsible for sea defence, drainage, the vestries, village administration, health, and so on as well as the local armed forces (police, militia and volunteer forces) and the judiciary. It also controlled the three major newspapers in the colony, the *Royal Gazette,* the *Berbice Gazette* and the *Colonist.*5

This economic and political power was not enjoyed by the entire white population. It was largely the preserve of a small number of wealthy planters and merchants. Beneath them were a few persons engaged in various occupations and professions who, while aspiring to such elevated status, were largely dependent on the patronage and favour of this extremely powerful elite minority for their livelihood. Class differences were very discernible among the white population, and very serious attention was paid to social ranking. This was not only reflected in the jobs and incomes of individuals and families, but also in their residences, material possessions, means of transportation, leisure activities and membership of social clubs.

Great pains were taken by those at the apex of colonial society to preserve the exclusivity of their social circles, whilst at the same time every effort was made by those lower down to gain admission into the highest social ranks. In this situation snobbery and blackballing, fawning and cringing were rife. Yet these were very much integral aspects of middle-class Victorian culture which the colonists had taken to Guyana and other British colonies. Overseas, however, class consciousness was perhaps accentuated by the fact that the acquisition of wealth cut through the restrictive barrier of heredity that obtained at home and offered a short cut to social elevation, thereby presenting a greater threat of dilution of what was considered pedigree: hence there was a need to guard zealously against that. Furthermore, as Brereton has observed in Trinidad, the small size of the white community meant that everyone knew everyone else.6 Thus to be seen in the 'wrong' company was a very serious matter. For the social aspirant, association with his or her social 'superiors' was vital for admission into the highest social ranks.

For the generality of the dominant British section of the white population, however, whatever their status, middle-class British (Victorian) culture served as the model to be emulated. In this respect they were no different from fellow British migrants overseas. But what made those in Guyana (and other tropical colonies) different from those who went to settler colonies like Australia, New Zealand, Canada or South Africa was their perception of their sojourn as temporary. No matter how long they remained in the colony, they always harboured the notion that they would retire to the metropolis to a life of leisure and luxury befitting the upper-middle class status to which they aspired.

It was perhaps only in architecture that these elites were forced to make significant adjustments to local conditions and forego seeking to replicate the British model. Houses and public buildings had to be designed and constructed with the tropical climate in mind and with proper ventilation. Buildings were generally constructed of wood, because of the abundant and cheap supplies of local hardwoods. Even so, some wealthier residents preferred to import pine and oak from the United States which carried prestige. Roofs were generally made of shingles which further helped to keep room temperatures down.

Because the coastal areas were prone to flooding, practically all elite buildings were constructed on stilts with external stairways providing access. Most houses of the wealthy were two-storied, with large airy galleries, drawing and dining rooms downstairs, and commodious sleeping quarters upstairs. The less well off (if families), however, had to settle for smaller houses or (if single) mere rooms in hotels or guest houses.

The difference in wealth and status was vividly demonstrated on the sugar estates in the accommodation provided for owners or managers on one hand and for bookkeepers and overseers on the other. The manager's mansion stood huge and splendid in stark contrast to the overseers' quarters which were no more than dingy single rooms in single-storied buildings, normally quite wretched in appearance and condition. The wealthier whites both on the plantations and in the towns also made ample use of the wide variety of exotic tropical flowering trees and plants to beautify their premises and residential areas. This of course added to the spectacle of elegance associated with high status that was so very important to these colonists.[7]

If largely for practical reasons the white elites displayed a willingness to be creative in house construction, they were less accommodating in their furnishings. These were either imported or, if made locally, patterned after an imported model. Typical drawing room furniture, for instance, included suites, couches, rocking chairs, whatnots, flower stands, pianos and several types of tables — loo, gipsy, *papier maché*, centre, sofa and card tables. In the dining room, there would be 'a splendidly roomy dining table and chairs. Plenty abounds everywhere, and the snowiness of the cloth and napkins, the beauty of the flowers and ferns that adorn it, all tend to enhance the pleasures of the table'. Other furnishings included waggonettes or dinner waggons, sideboards, chiffonniers; by the 1880s the very wealthy might have a refrigerator or water cooler. Bedroom furniture included four-poster beds, dressing tables, chests of drawers, wardrobes, bedroom chairs, commodes, clothes and towel horses. Despite obvious differences in the architecture of their houses, these imported household furnishings reflected the strong desire of the white elites to recreate some of the domestic comforts of their middle-class peers back home as symbols both of high status and of their Britishness.[8]

These were even more vividly seen in their dress styles which conformed as closely as possibly to metropolitan forms and fashions. The newspapers of the period were replete with advertisements which give a clear idea of the items and materials used for clothing. These included for the men, tweed suits, morning coats, trousers, white and regatta shirts, merino and cotton vests, broadcloths, doeskins, linen and cotton drills, serge and flannel. In 1897 a visitor, Arthur Sawtell, was struck by 'the extremely English appearance of the business and professional classes'. 'Except for the head-gear . . . there is little to distinguish nine out of ten of the whites of the colony from their brethren oversea. Here and there you occasionally see a man in a drill suit.... But on the whole cloth, frequently dark and heavy-looking, prevails'.[9] For the ladies, black lace and lama shawls were popular, as were coloured cashmere, coloured and black cloaks, white quilted petticoats, white and coloured muslin robes, hair nets, gloves, hats, chêne Mohair, checked satin cloth, checked Mozambique, checked Leno cloth, sky, scarlet, green and French de Laines, coloured French *barège*, black Norwich *barège*, plain circassian, silk and cotton check dresses.

Several of these dress materials were clearly inappropriate to a tropical environment. But for the white elites good taste in dress was equated only with what was fashionable in the metropolis; and since one's appearance was considered important if one hoped to be considered a part of the upper echelons of colonial society, considerable attention had to be paid to wearing the latest European fashions. Therefore no expense was spared to appear elegantly clad in public no matter how incongruous that may have been in relation to the climate. As one writer put it, 'When light and flowing garments might be worn with comfort, both sexes try to imitate the London fashions, with this difference that their clothes seldom fit them, and they are generally twelve months behind the *mode*'.[10]

Just as 'high society' entertainments were integral features of the cultural life of the Victorian bourgeoisie in England, so too were these cultural institutions imported into the colonies. Status seekers focused most of their energies and attention on two primary objectives in their quest for social acceptance: invitations to public high-society events and membership of the elite social clubs. Balls were among the most popular pastimes of Guyanese elite cultural life. One had merely to whisper an intention of planning a ball or reunion of some sort to be inundated for weeks before the event with requests for invitations 'by callers of both sexes, many of them strangers'; and no rebuke would discourage those persons who would persist until granted their wish.[11]

It is not surprising that these status-seeking white residents, mainly male, should have taken the elite social club, patterned on the grand men's institutions of Pall Mall and St James in London, to the colonies. It satisfied their twin principal desires: reaffirming their Britishness and their quest for high social status. Membership of one of the leading social clubs was vitally important in signalling one's arrival at the apex of the social hierarchy, and consequently was avidly sought by all white males. The Georgetown Club, founded in 1858, was by far the most prestigious of its kind and earned its highest accolade when Governor Kortright became the first chief executive to apply for membership in 1878. The leading planters, merchants and government officials belonged to this club, but women were explicitly excluded from membership.[12] Of lesser pedigree were the British Guiana Club, formed in 1871, and the Demerara Club founded in 1880.[13]

As in England, elite men spent most of their spare time at these clubs which offered many facilities for relaxation: indoor games such as cards, chess and billiards, good bars, reading rooms, and excellent dining and sleeping facilities.[14] Strict procedures for membership (accompanied by snobbery and blackballing) limited it to a very exclusive circle indeed and kept out those who were not considered socially acceptable.[15] In the colonial context, these clubs served as important institutions for enforcing conformity to the social norms and values of a prejudiced narrow class-conscious white male elite.[16]

In the colonial environment, it was not enough to be wealthy, one had to flaunt it. Even persons who could ill afford it indulged in lavish entertainment to impress their guests. Formal dinner parties, by far the most common form of social intercourse among white families, were marked by undue extravagance. They had to be 'elaborate and according to the most approved style and fashion of what is considered *ton*.'[17] Generally they consisted of several courses with a variety of meats and wines on offer.[18] Mr Pepps, an usually cynical contemporary, mused on one occasion that had he not known his host well he would have thought that he had been at the table of one of vast wealth. His wife, however, was adamant that if she could not match such lavish entertainment, she would rather not do it at all.[19] To do otherwise would have been to lose status and esteem among one's social peers and risk being blackballed.

Although the elites made effort to preserve a strong sense of Britishness by holding fast to Victorian culture, social conditions in the colony promoted significant deviations from the metropolitan model. This has already been noted with reference to architecture. Beyond that, however, not only were the white elites a very small minority amidst a heterogeneous mass of non-white ethnic groups, but even among themselves men far outnumbered women. These social circumstances significantly affected their cultural attitudes and behaviour, particularly as they related to sex, marriage, artistic and intellectual life.

The reality of almost absolute social and political power in a frontier environment, combined with a shortage of white women and a strong desire for the pleasures of the flesh, found full expression in the sexual proclivities of elite males. During the slavery period marriage of white estate personnel was discouraged on the grounds that they would require more domestic servants.[20] This was fairly typical of most plantation colonies because of the low salaries and poor living conditions.[21] Therefore, instead of a monogamous Christian marital relationship, it was customary for estate managers and overseers, merchants and even government officials to have a domestic 'establishment' presided over by a black or coloured woman who looked after the servants and provided all 'comforts' for her master.[22]

Such deviant mating relationships remained prevalent in the post-emancipation period,[23] as managers and overseers on estates continued to cohabit with or sexually harass and abuse female workers, with Indian immigrant women replacing Creoles.[24] Even white missionaries from time to time yielded to temptation and succumbed to the pleasures of female flesh in 'illicit' relationships.[25] But during the second half of the century as the need to reaffirm their Britishness (by adhering to Victorian middle-class morality) intensified, Christian monogamous marriage gradually became the standard of respectability particularly among the upper classes.[26] This tendency was encouraged both by religion, as more priests and missionaries were stationed in the colony, and by technology, as steamships cheapened and shortened the travel time between colony and metropolis and made the voyage less difficult. Thus, more white men returned to England to marry women of their own kind; and as the latter began to accompany their husbands to the colony and a more stable white community developed, the old 'establishments' became regarded with disfavour and gradually diminished in number among upper-class urban whites,[27] although they remained prevalent on the estates.

The presence of women also influenced the behaviour of their male counterparts. Stoler observes that white women became the 'custodians of morality' in colonial society, and argues that wherever they were introduced in significant numbers they seemed to exert 'a civilizing, cultured, and restraining check on the rowdy, crude, and hard-drinking life style' of the rural plantocracy.[28] This was certainly the case in Guyana as well as the wider Caribbean, and wherever wives were present there was a fairly high degree of order and decorum.[29] The increased female presence also put religion into a more central position in the lives of the white elites. There was greater attendance at church on Sundays, and the women themselves became very involved in the social activities of the churches largely for want of anything else to do with their time.[30]

If the increased presence of white women and priests caused an upliftment in the morality of the colonial elites by discouraging concubinage (or cohabitation outside formal marriage) particularly in the urban centres, it did not materially curb male sexual appetites because there was always a substantial number of young men who did not consider themselves sufficiently well off financially to get married and enjoy a lifestyle befitting that status in Creole society: 'salaries are small and, until they are in a position, the boys are shy; to occupy a small house and to work honestly together to endeavour to make provision for the future never seems to suggest itself to the *jeunesse dorée* of the colony.'[31]

The craving for high status reinforced a prejudice among middle-class British men against early marriage. According to Hyam, in the mid-nineteenth century the average age of marriage for British men was 29, and about 10 per cent never married at all. This pattern was maintained in the colonies for more or less the same reason: the desire to become economically and socially established before getting married. Thus both at home and abroad it was customary for young men simply to play the field (with both single and married women, including prostitutes)[32] until their middle years when they would decide to marry much younger women of suitable status. Young elite women on the other hand, while being courted by men young and old, were generally only likely to receive an offer of marriage from a much older man. In Guyana age did not seem to matter: men as old as 70 reputedly regarded themselves as likely suitors for teenage girls.[33]

Sexual promiscuity, therefore, was rampant among the colonial elites beyond the end of the century. Contrary to Stipendiary Magistrate Hancock's impression in 1845 that the phenomenon of the roving single white male with a series of female connections had decreased,[34] the white stud or 'lady-killer' remained very much alive beyond the end of the century. As the *Royal Gazette* put it, instead of early marriage, 'the young men here indulge in dissipation': 'Libertinism seems to be accepted here as a thing of course; in fact a young man without a touch of Don Juan in composition is said to be a "duffer" or an "impostor". To lead a regular and virtuous life exposes a man to the ridicule of society in general.'[35]

No less interesting is the strong suggestion that sexual promiscuity was not limited to heterosexual activity: the *Royal Gazette* actually labelled Georgetown the Sodom of the nineteenth century![36] Homosexual activity would not have been abnormal for, as Hyam notes, many colonial officials and male colonists were sexually initiated in British public schools where they frequently shared beds; and even though middle-class Victorian Britain developed a pathological abhorrence of homosexuality, driving homosexual people underground, the colonies offered ample opportunities for, and fewer sanctions against, such 'deviant' sexual behaviour.[37]

The high incidence of sexual promiscuity and the unwillingness or inability of men to get married at an early age, naturally affected elite women who, like their middle-class peers in Britain and in other colonies, were socialised to consider marriage and child-rearing as their natural destiny. Indeed the Victorian middle-class convention that women should be confined to the home was reinforced in colonies like Guyana where there was an added security fear. Most colonial elite women seemed to accept this prescribed position in exchange for the high social status and material benefits that marriage to an older well-established man offered. They thus expected a large house with its full complement of expensive furnishings, horse and carriage, and the means to entertain lavishly. Complementary with this was a large army of house and yard servants;[38] for in the colonies, no upper class woman worthy of the status was prepared or expected to do household chores. The notion of the genteel elite woman of leisure received its fullest expression in the plantation society of Guyana: 'The ladies of the higher classes usually spend their time in reading, and now and again, though only to break the tiresome monotony, in light feminine tasks. The kitchen only knows the lady of the house and her daughters by name, and the remaining cares of a housewife are just as much unknown to the former as to the latter'.[39]

Although the white colonial woman was not expected to go out to work and had a considerable amount of spare time while at home, she was not encouraged to pursue artistic and intellectual activities especially if that meant going out of the home on her own. Even in nineteenth-century Britain it was held that if women indulged in too much intellectual activity it would adversely affect their primary childbearing functions.[40] Thus in the colonies women who certainly had the spare time were denied the opportunity to engage in serious intellectual or artistic activities. The men, on the other hand, were either too busy seeking their fortunes or simply lacked the interest.[41]

The result was that there was precious little activity in those spheres although ironically they enjoyed a high status appeal among the elites. To show that one had arrived socially one had to feign an interest in the fine arts and intellectual activity. Thus every upper class house had to have a few books on display whether they were read or not. Similarly if there was an artistic show on in town, anyone with pretensions to 'high culture' was expected to attend. But even in artistic and intellectual activity, the emphasis was on import and consumption rather than creation. There were precious few persons who had a genuine interest in activities beyond day-to-day politics, economics and fawning for social advancement. Those few did try to build cultural institutions, but since their primary objective was to assert their Britishness, the accent was on importing, not creating new indigenous art forms.

During the 1840s and 1850s a few institutions were established in Guyana to stimulate intellectual and artistic life. These were a small public library, a grammar school (Queen's College), the Agricultural and Commercial Society and the Athenaeum Society in Georgetown, and the Berbice Reading Society. The Astronomical and Meteorological Society and the Society for Natural History and Geology were also established, but do not appear to have survived very long. Membership of all these institutions, however, was always very small.[42] Some short-lived organisations were formed from time to time, such as a Literary and Debating Club, the Georgetown Philharmonic Club, the Demerara Musical Institute, the Amateur Orchestral Club and a few dramatic and musical clubs.[43] But these represented no more than sporadic and generally unsuccessful efforts to generate a genuine interest among the elites in the fine arts. It was easier to import European artistes than to stage local theatrical productions, which in any event were invariably British. No drama focusing on aspects of local life and culture was put on by the white elites in nineteenth-century Guyana. Elite cultural activity was thus renowned for its sterility. A key reason for this cultural desert was a singular unwillingness to incorporate aspects of the other cultures present in the society because they were not British or European and were thus deemed inferior.

While the desire to emulate the Victorian cultural model by the white colonists was designed to assert their Britishness in a far-off colonial frontier, it was also intended to promote the development of a consensus of values throughout the society with a view to maintaining the British imperial order and the divisive social *status quo* which it spawned. One of the striking characteristics of British migrants overseas, particularly in colonies with a large non-British or non-white majority, was their fierce loyalty to the British Crown and things British. As one contemporary put it, 'England is far dearer to exiled affections than to the cold contents of home'.[44] The colonial press played a major role in this regard, printing news and features about life in the metropolis. In addition, metropolitan newspapers were also readily available at the elite social clubs and hotels.

British colonials harboured a strong sense of the imperial idea and identification with the British monarchy[45] even when mid-Victorians at home were reputedly anti-imperialist. Cannadine has shown how uninterested, indeed even hostile, the mid-Victorian Britons were towards their monarchy until the 1870s. Hence there were few public ceremonies centred on royalty and very little public pageantry. It was only during the last quarter of the century, particularly following the proclamation of Queen Victoria as 'Empress of India' and the acquisition of new colonies, that the monarchy was transformed into a grand national and imperial institution, and every royal occasion became an imperial one, a development that reached its climax in Victoria's jubilees and the coronation of Edward VII.[46]

In the colonies, however, the monarchy assumed tremendous significance much earlier. More than anything else, loyalty to the Crown signified how British the white colonists were despite their distance from home. In the Caribbean, Africa and South Asia the monarchy also symbolised the might and glory of the imperial power, which was important to extol particularly where white residents were vastly outnumbered by people whom they considered uncivilised and potentially hostile. But it did not merely symbolise imperial military and political domination. It was also a symbol around which a consensus of ideological values could be cultivated to unite both rulers and ruled based, however, on the latter's 'voluntary' subordination to the crown and constituted authority (and to whites in general). Traditions associated with the monarchy were thus invented[47] even when they did not exist in the metropolis, and the skilful manipulation of these placed in the hands of the colonial elite group the means to promote social consensus and stability. Thus whereas in England for a long time the birthday of Victoria passed almost unnoticed, in Guyana (and elsewhere in the British Caribbean) it was always celebrated annually in May or June as a public holiday with colourful military parades and gunfire salutes, levees at Government House (the governors' residence) and grand balls. Ships in the port hoisted bunting in celebration.[48]

By the late nineteenth century when the monarchy had become a national symbol in Britain itself, the two jubilees of Victoria's reign were celebrated there and throughout the British empire with great festivity. On both occasions – the golden (September 1887) and the diamond (June 1897) – public holidays were declared and the colonial elites organised events not only for their own gratification, but also to impress upon the subordinate social groups the might, splendour and benefits of the British empire and its empress queen. After many years of witnessing repeated rituals in association with the invented traditions of the monarchy, these became fully inculcated by the black and coloured population. In the words of the coloured newspaper, the *Echo,* 'It has been providentially given her to see the growth of her Empire into these imperially magnificent proportions that now astonish the world and honour all who bear the name of Englishman'.[49]

Thus with the adulation of the black and coloured colonial 'Englishmen', public buildings and streets were gaudily decorated and illuminated; churches held special thanksgiving services; there were parades of military and civilian organisations, including schoolchildren; fireworks displays, dinners for the poor at several churches, entertainment for the Indian immigrants at the Immigration Depot; balls and concerts; special horse-racing meetings and athletic sports meetings. As further tributes to the queen, in 1887 the Court of Policy approved the erection of her statue as a memorial of the jubilee; and in 1897 they approved the construction of a bandstand in her honour at the Sea Wall (the main promenade in Georgetown where the social elites congregated each afternoon to socialise and relax).[50]

Sports which became increasingly popular in the later nineteenth century also played a very significant role in the transmission of Victorian socio-cultural values. They formed a major part of the leisure activities of the white elites (mainly the males) and, as in other areas of their lives, duplicated those in England. In the metropolis itself there was literally a sports revolution from the 1860s onwards as both the middle and lower classes began to enjoy more leisure time. Organised sport was one means of putting this spare time to constructive use, and this was undertaken largely under middle-class leadership and sponsorship, and promoted mainly by the churches, public schools and elite universities. Games were standardised by rules and regulations governing not only how they were played, but the conduct and dress of the players; and supreme governing bodies like the Marylebone Cricket Club and the Football Association were set up in all major sports (tennis, hockey, netball, golf, racing, athletics, etc).[51]

In the late nineteenth century the doctrine of 'muscular Christianity' held sway. According to Sandiford, this revolved 'around the basic notion that there [was] something innately good and godly about brute strength and power. Physical weakness [was] unnatural since it [was] only a manifestation of moral and spiritual inadequacy. It could be overcome by prayer, upright living, discipline, and exercise'. Sport, especially team sport, was thus good for the body as well as the soul. It was considered a civilising agent, one that instilled such middle-class values as teamwork, self-discipline, respect for the rules, obedience to authority, courage in the face of adversity, and so on. In short, sport was the training ground for life's challenges.[52]

Given the importance which sports assumed in late Victorian British social life, it is not surprising that they should have been taken to the colonies. Holt observes that they were vital both for the colonial official and colonist. For the former, they 'helped both to relieve the tedium of a distant posting and to integrate new arrivals into the small world of colonial society'. For the latter, they 'served overwhelmingly to express and enhance the solidarity of colonial society. Providing amusement for those far from home isolated amidst an alien and sometimes hostile population, sport was not so much a luxury as a necessity, a means of maintaining morale and a sense of shared roots, of Britishness, of lawns and tea and things familiar. For the more humble middle-class emigrant sports also underlined that transition from a suburban to an essentially landed style, which added to the appeal of the Empire'.[53]

But sport was taken to the colonies with all of the class and gender prejudices with which it was engulfed in Britain. The British working classes were systematically excluded from middle-class sports clubs and associations, and there was a rigid differentiation between amateur and professional players.[54] This class bias, when transferred to colonies in the Caribbean, Africa, India and the Pacific was reinforced by racial prejudice; and, as Holt notes for the Caribbean, 'racial segregation was built into colonial sport. Many whites simply refused to play in or against teams with black players'.[55]

While maintaining a *social* distance between white and non-white in the colonial context, sport was at the same time intended to serve as an assimilative *cultural* mechanism in order to promote a consensus of shared values, beliefs and attitudes between rulers and ruled. Stoddart points out that dominant British beliefs about social behaviour, standards, relations and conformity were transferred through sport. But it is important to note that British sport, indeed British culture generally, was not imposed formally by the state as the French did in their colonies. Sport was acquired by the subordinate population on a voluntary, subconscious basis. In this way, resistance to the values that were part and parcel of the baggage of sport was lessened. This method of transfering sporting traditions and values gave the elite tremendous power in the colonial situation.[56]

British sport was also enveloped by gender bias against female participation. With the strict separation of sex roles in British society and the philosophy of muscular Christianity with which sport was imbued, there was little place for women who were characterised as 'the weaker sex'. According to McCrone, the stylised image of the genteel middle-class woman held her as a person 'imbued . . . with qualities of mind and body that destined her for specific tasks, such as being man's helpmate, nurturing his children, and protecting the sanctity of his home. [This] ideal woman was antithetical to sport. Passive, gentle, emotional, and delicate, she had neither the strength nor inclination to undertake strenuous exercise and competitive games.'[57]

Although noble women had hunted, hawked and ridden horses ever since the Middle Ages, there was a popular perception that sport was a male sphere of activity and 'scientific evidence' was employed to 'prove' that strenuous exercise was harmful to women. It was not until the late Victorian period that women gradually, quietly, almost clandestinely, began to participate actively in sports, a process facilitated by the new girls' public schools and womens' colleges of the elite metropolitian universities.[58] One consequence of this was that, with few exceptions, female sports developed in a totally separate sphere from that of males, thus mirroring the gender separation in public and private life.[59] The ideal of the genteel woman attained its highest expression in the colonies where there was an even greater perceived necessity to protect their 'vulnerable' physical beings and honour from the 'lusting natives'. In the colonies the lady of high status had to conform to strict social codes governing her deportment and physical activity which consequently ruled out participation in those sports that required 'unlady-like' exertion.

Because of Guyana's large forest and wildlife resources, the British aristocratic sport of hunting could be engaged in. In Britain working-class 'blood' sports such as cock and dog fighting were driven underground by the dominant middle class,[60] but the aristocracy were able to preserve their own hunt for recreation. Holt asserts, however, that in the colonies hunting was not just a form of amusement: 'It was often vital for a man to ride in order to be able to fulfil official functions and the ability to shoot was a useful reminder to subject races of the underlying reality of imperial rule'.[61] The demonstration effect of hunting therefore added to the power of the elites. In Guyana, hunting excursions deep in the interior of the country were prestigious but expensive pastimes. Only the very rich could afford them. Even a short trip of three or four days would cost a party of four $25 per head.[62] Hunting was often combined with picnicking behind the canefields of the plantations. This, however, perpetuated the separation of gender roles as the men went hunting in the bush while the women remained safely behind with the children.[63]

Both Demerara and Berbice had rifle clubs. The former was established in 1867 and later was placed under the governor's patronage. It lasted beyond the turn of the century. The Berbice club was founded earlier, but does not seem to have survived for very long. These clubs were composed of the leading planters and merchants, and members of all branches of the militia service. Practice shoots were held weekly. Prize meetings were organised at which money, cup prizes and medals were awarded; and from time to time teams from similar rifle clubs in neighbouring colonies, as well as visiting warships, competed against the local teams. Very significantly, women were allowed to compete for a special ladies' purse.[64] This may seem to be a departure from the stylised image of the delicate, defenceless, genteel being; but perhaps it was felt that living amidst lusting black and brown 'savages', the white colonial woman needed to be capable of protecting herself in an emergency. Rifle shooting, like hunting, enhanced the power of the elites through its demonstration effect.

As in Trinidad and Jamaica, horse-racing was very popular among the white elites,[65] but it also attracted large numbers of blacks, Indians, Chinese and Portuguese. This represented a good example of the subordinate ethnic groups voluntarily adopting a cultural pastime of the dominant white minority, although gambling, frowned upon both in Britain and the colonies by the churches, did not fit in with the sort of values which imperial officialdom wished to impart.[66] The principal venue for horse-racing was the D'Urban Race Course, built in 1829 on the outskirts of Georgetown, where two major meetings were held each year. Horse-racing was also held twice a year at Belfield on the east coast of Demerara, and occasionally at Capoey Lake in Essequibo. Horse-racing was particularly fashionable among the elites because, apart from the thrills of competition, it provided yet another opportunity to flaunt wealth and status.[67]

Other sporting activities engaged in by the white elites with varying enthusiasm were archery, golf, cycling, rowing, football, rugby, athletics and such indoor games as chess, checkers, card games, darts, fencing and billiards. Lawn tennis became increasingly popular largely because it was considered a social game in which women were allowed to play with men. This broke down the strict separation between sexes so rigidly upheld both in Britain and its colonies. Indeed in Guyana the tennis clubs admitted women as 'lady members'.

Of all the sports introduced by the British into their colonies, cricket became the most popular not only among the British elites, but also among the subordinate populations. According to Sandiford, the Victorians glorified cricket 'as a perfect system of ethics and morals which embodied all that was most noble in the Anglo-Saxon character'. Originating with the aristocracy, it was adopted with great enthusiasm by the middle classes who regarded it as an excellent training ground for military and other purposes: 'It taught discipline, self-sacrifice, and loyalty to team and country'. All classes were encouraged to play cricket primarily because it was seen as a useful instrument of socialisation, although it perpetuated the gap between the classes in British society. In the wider empire it became a vital part of the white man's burden because it helped to facilitate the process of imperial cultural assimilation.[68] Stoddart thus asserts that 'cricket was considered the main vehicle for transferring the appropriate British moral code from the messengers of empire to the local populations'.[69]

Although it is known that cricket was played in Barbados from the early nineteenth century, the earliest documentary reference to it found so far for Guyana was a report that when the militia went to drill at the Parade Ground on 21 October 1858 it was already being used by a group of cricketers;[70] and indeed until 1885 that ground remained the principal venue for organised cricket matches in the colony. The Georgetown Cricket Club (GCC) was directly linked with the sport from the moment organised cricket took root, and for a long time its playing members were the only ones who composed teams to represent Guyana in intercolonial matches. The first of those may have been against a Bermudan team in March 1859.[71] The main rival of the GCC in the colony was the Garrison Club composed of soldiers who were probably responsible for introducing the game in the first place.[72] The year 1865 witnessed the first overseas tour by a Guyanese team when in February the GCC visited Barbados. That visit was returned by the Barbadians in September.[73] In 1868 the GCC hosted the first visit by a Trinidadian team, the Sovereign CC, and returned the visit the following year.[74] In the following years matches were organised among these three territories on an *ad hoc* basis, but from 1893 a regular tournament was played by them for a Challenge Cup.[75] Matches were also played against teams composed of officers of visiting warships. The high point was the visit of Lord Hawke's English team in 1897.[76]

For the entire post-emancipation nineteenth century, the main focus of cultural life of the white, mainly British, elites was on adhering as faithfully as possible to the Victorian middle-class model of industrial Britain. This was not merely because it was equated with what was considered best in British civilisation and consequently perceived as superior to any other culture extant in the colony, but also because the principal bearers as a white minority in a 'sea of blackness' felt physically and culturally vulnerable, and thus harboured a psychological need to to reassure themselves and their kith and kin at home that they were still British in every way. Besides, since they had a short term view of their sojourn in the colony and intended to retire to Britain to enjoy an upper-middle class life with their accumulated wealth, they had no incentive to change their cultural orientation or values; and they certainly made no conscious effort to borrow from the 'inferior' cultures in their midst. Instead they felt the need to cling steadfastly to British middle-class values in the hope of attaining the desired social status that was attributed to their possession. This helps to account for the high level of snobbery within the white community. It also helps to explain why they contributed so very little to the development of indigenous art forms, for their emphasis lay on cultural imports from the metropolis.

But the physical and social environments of plantation Guyana were not similar to those of industrial Britain, and in some spheres of cultural life they were obliged to make significant adjustments to the borrowed metropolitan model. This was most noticeable in their mating patterns, largely on account of the shortage of white females. Sexual promiscuity was common and concubinage, if on the decline after emancipation, was still very much present particularly on the plantations. The flaunting of their new money and love of extravagance (the exhibitionist mentality) was also a marked departure from the more frugal ways of the Victorian middle-class model which they tried so hard to emulate. Even in their intense loyalty the monarchy in the middle decades of the century they seemed to depart from the sentiments of their peers at home. Circumstances of life in the colony therefore wrought cultural changes within the white elite community despite its tremendous efforts to cling to metropolitan patterns and forms.

Despite their primary motivation to make a fortune and then leave the colony, the white colonists were also imbued with a civilising mission which translated itself in a desire to transmit their 'superior' culture to the subordinate non-white majority. Most of them never actively undertook this task, but certainly supported any efforts that were made by state, church, press and other institutions and individuals. There was a strong body of elite opinion which felt that social stability could be enhanced if British cultural values were shared by all segments of the society. The colonial state itself did not set out any formal plans to promote the assimilation of British culture, but by the subtle use of invented traditions through symbols and rituals it succeeded in fostering a sense of cultural unity around a common allegiance to a benevolent monarch. Sport also played a very important part in transmitting British cultural values to the subordinate population. In these ways, the culture of the white elites assumed the important function of social stabiliser aimed at preserving the imperial idea and the social order with all the inherent inequalities which it spawned.

Notes

Abbreviations

BG	*Berbice Gazette*
CO	British Colonial Office Papers
CSSH	*Compararive Studies in Society and History*
(D)DC	*(*Demerara*) Daily Chronicle*
IJHS	*International Journal of the History of Sport*
JBS	*Journal of British Studies*
JICH	*Journal of Imperial and Commonwealth History*
JSH	*Journal of Social History*
MMS	Papers of the Weslyan Methodist Missionary Society
B.P.P.	British Parliamentary Papers
RG	*Royal Gazette*
SPG	Papers of the Society for the Propagation of the Gospel in Foreign Parts
VS	*Victorian Studies*

1. This paper was first written in 1993 as part of a larger research project which culminated in the publication of a book by the author entitled *Cultural Power, Resistance and Pluralism: Guyana 1838-1900* (Kingston, Montreal, 1995). Fuller details of the data treated here can be found in that publication.

2. In post-emancipation Guyana, a distinction needs to be made between the British whites and the newer Portuguese immigrants from Madeira. Although white, the latter were ethnically and socially different and were treated as such. During the nineteenth century there was very little mixing between the two groups. This paper focuses on the British whites.

3. See decennial censuses, 1851-91. In 1840 there were only 71 Dutch residents still remaining in the colony (Light to Russell, No. 160, 24 December 1840, CO 111/173; see also Brian L. Moore, *Race, Power and Social Segmentation in Colonial Society* (New York 1987), pp. 51-53.

4. Adamson shows that as the century wore on, more individual owners were obliged to seek

partnerships with large absentee capitalist companies which led to a greater concentration of sugar plantations in the hands of the latter. In addition to those listed in the text, other leading companies were Charles McGarel, Quintin Hogg & Bosanquet, Curtis & Co, Sandbach, Parker & Co, and George Little & Co Sugar and its major by-products, rum and molasses, accounted for over 90 per cent of the colonial export trade until the late 1880s, when gold production began to rise. Even so, at the turn of the century, they still accounted for over two-thirds of the export trade. See Alan Adamson, *Sugar without Slaves* (New Haven, 1972), pp. 199-216.

5. Moore, *op. cit.,* pp. 51-61.

6. Bridget Brereton, *Race Relations in Colonial Trinidad, 1870-1900* (Cambridge,1979), pp. 61-62.

7. E. Jenkins, *The Coolie: His Rights and Wrongs* (London, 1871), p. 45; B. Premium, *Eight Years in British Guiana* (London, 1850), pp. 12-13; J. W. Boddam-Whetham, *Roraima and British Guiana* (London, 1879), pp. 121-27; L. Crookall, *British Guiana* (London, 1898), pp. 85-95; 'A Demerara planter's hospitality', in *RG,* 4 October 1888; R. Schomburgk, *Travels in British Guiana, 1840-44,* vol. 1 (Georgetown, 1922), p. 41; enclosed in Scott to Boyce, No. 481, 1 May 1875, *MMS*/W.v/2; *RG,* 10 June 1879, 'A glimpse of overseering in Demerara'; and *RG,* 21 June 1879, 'Overseering in Demerara'.

8. *Ibid.*

9. W. Arthur Sawtell, 'First Impressions of the Colony', in *Echo,* 4, 1897 (extracted from his paper published in the June 1897 issue of *Timehri*).

10. *RG,* 29 January 1881, letter by a visitor.

11. *RG,* 23 October 1880, 'Local Sketches'.

12. H. Kirke, *Twenty-Five Years in British Guiana* (London, 1898), pp. 24-25; *RG,* 18 March 1875; *RG,* 12 January 1878, 'Argus' column.

13. *Colonist,* 11 March 1871; *RG,* 18 March 1875, 14 December 1880.

14. *RG,* 13 March 1875.

15. *RG*, 7 August 1880 'Local Sketches'.

16. See also Patrick Bryan, *The Jamaican People, 1880-1902* (London, 1992), p. 72.

17. *RG*, 1 December 1874, letter by 'Paterfamilias'.

18. *RG*, 1 December 1874, letter by 'Paterfamilias'; see also *RG*, 29 January 1881, letter by a visitor; and Kirke, *op. cit.*, p. 11.

19. *RG*, 14 April 1877, 'Mr. Pepps' Diary in Georgetown'.

20. Comment of M. Macpherson, enclosed in Light, No. 83, *loc. cit.*

21. In Indonesia, estates neither hired married applicants nor allowed employees to marry while in service because marriages took up too much of the their time and salary. As in the Caribbean during slavery, concubinage was actively encouraged. This marriage restriction lasted until this century in Sumatra. See Ann Laura Stoler, 'Rethinking colonial categories: European communities and the boundaries of rule', *CSSH*, 31, (1989), p. 143.

22. Kirke, *op. cit.*, p. 34; Schomburgk, *op. cit.*, p. 46.

23. Letter by 'A Country Curate', in *Colonist*, 30 May 1866; Schomburgk, *op. cit.*, p. 46; H.V.P. Bronkhurst, *Among the Hindus and Creoles of British Guiana* (London, 1888), p. 200.

24. *Colonist*, 30 May 1866, letter by 'A Country Curate'; D. Wood, *Trinidad in Transition* (Oxford, 1968), p. 83; see also Brereton, *op. cit.*, p. 60.

25. Greathead to Boyce, No. 891, 7 September 1871, and Silcox to Boyce, No. 962, 21 September 1871, *MMS*/W.v/2. Three Wesleyan Methodist missionaries, Reverends Irvine, Dickson, and Bronkhurst, were accused of having affairs with unmarried women. It is not clear if they were married, although reference to the fashion of having two wives would suggest so.

26. Comments of F. Fothergill and R. Hancock, enclosed in Light, No. 83, *loc. cit.*

27. Kirke, *op. cit.*, pp. 34-35.

28. *Ibid.*, p. 144.

29. *RG*, 4 October 1888, 'A Demerara Planters Hospitality'.

30. Light to Stanley, 23 November 1843, CO 111/203; see also comments of J. Edgehill and R. Hancock in Light to Stanley, No. 83, 18 April 1845, CO 111/227. It was natural that in a British colony the Church of England should be the established church (meaning that it was supported out of public revenues); but there was such a substantial Scottish community that the Church of Scotland was also on the colonial payroll. There were two state churches in nineteenth-century Guyana, each with a major centre in Georgetown (Demerara) and New Amsterdam (Berbice), and the parishes were equally divided between them. The Roman Catholic church had a smaller presence until the arrival of the Portuguese immigrants, while the Dutch Reformed church rapidly faded out of existence because of the disappearance of Dutch residents after emancipation. Generally speaking, however, the expansion of the established churches and the increased number of priests helped to improve the moral and religious tone of the white community.

31. *RG*, 11 January 1881.

32. Ronald Hyam, 'Empire and Sexual Opportunity', *JICH*, 14, (1986), pp. 41-42.

33. *RG*, 22 February 1877, letter by 'Clarinda'; *RG*, 17 March 1877, letter by 'Jessie'.

34. R. Hancock's comment in Light, No. 83, *loc. cit.*

35. *RG*, 11 January 1881.

36. *RG*, 11 January 1881.

37. Hyam, *op. cit.*, pp. 54-63.

38. 'Jessie', *loc.cit.*

39. Schomburgk, *op. cit.*, p. 43.

40. Kathleen E. McCrone, 'Play up! Play up! And Play the Game! Sport at the Late Victorian Girls' Public School', *JBS* 23, (1984), pp. 113-15.

41. Answers to the Anti-Slavery Societys Queries enclosed in Light to Stanley, No. 255, 12 December 1844, CO 111/215.

42. Reports of Stipendiary Magistrates Fothergill and Macpherson, enclosed in Light to Stanley, 18 April 1845, No. 83, CO 111/227; Light to Stanley, No. 96, 3 May 1844, CO 111/210; No. 166, 31 July 1844, CO 111/212; also No. 264, 29 December 1844, CO 111/215. In September 1844, the Secretary of State informed the governor of the queen's accession to patronage of the society (Stanley to Light, No. 451, 27 September 1844, CO 111/212); *Blue Books of Statistics for 1869-1900* (CO 116); Barkly to Pakington, No.159, 9 October 1852, CO 111/291; *RG*, 4 March 1854; 18 August 1859; 24 November 1866; *Colonist*, 5 December 1866.

43. These included the Demerara Musical Society, the Berbice Amateur Dramatic and Musical Club, the Georgetown Histrionic Club and the Demerara Dramatic Club. In 1873 a Philharmonic Hall was erected in Georgetown. See *Colonist*, 10 February 1864, 4 November 1865, 20 January 1866, 15 December 1866, 18 September 1869, 20 March 1875; *BG*, 19 August 1882; 2 and 16 October 1889, 3 May and 2 August 1890; *RG*, 18 & 27 January 1866, 8 May 1873, 11 April 1874, 12 April 1883; 13 November 1883 *DDC*, 14 November 1883; *Argosy*, 3 May, 15 November 1890; *DC*, 27 January 1885; 1, 13, 14, 23 September, 26 October 1898.

44. Jenkins, *op. cit.*, p. 33.

45. Bradlow notes that imperialism and its corollary, loyalty to the royal family, were widespread among British settlers in the Cape Colony. See Edna Bradlow, 'The Culture of a Colonial Elite: The Cape of Good Hope in the 1850s', *VS*, 29,(1986), pp. 391-92.

46. Cannadine states that royal ceremony was not for the delight of the masses, but a group rite for the elite sections: the royal family, the aristocracy and the church. The monarchy was thus not a symbol of national unity, but the head of the elite corporate groups. In fact the celebrations focusing on national heroes such as Nelson and Wellington were far more popular than even coronations. The growth of the monarchy as a symbol of national and imperial unity was aided by Victoria's longevity, the growth of a new empire, national press which made use of new photographic techniques, and new modes of transport (bicycles, tramcars, buses and cars). See David Cannadine, 'The context, performance and meaning of ritual: the British monarchy and the Invention of Tradition, c. 1820-1977', in *The Invention of Tradition*, E. Hobsbawm and T. Ranger (eds), (Cambridge, 1983), pp. 101-64.

47. The term 'invented tradition' is used here in Hobsbawm's sense: 'a set of practices, normally governed by overtly or tacitly accepted rules and of a ritual or symbolic nature, which seek to inculcate certain values and norms of behaviour by repetition, which automatically implies continuity with the past' (see Eric Hobsbawm, 'Introduction: Inventing Traditions', in Eric Hobsbawm and Terence Ranger (eds), p. 1.

48. See for instance *RG*, 25 May 1844, 28 May 1859; *Creole*, 25 May 1861; *Colonist*, 15 June 1865; *Argosy*, 31 May 1890; *BG*, 11 May 1892.

49. *Echo*, 18 June 1887. The Barbadians had a reputation for being fiercely loyal to the imperial monarch. According to the *Argosy*, they had 'unbounded loyalty to ... the Queen', called their country 'little England', and boasted that they would always defend the Crown against all comers: 'As long as Her Majesty has Barbados and the Barbadians on her side no harm can come to Her' (*Argosy*, 29 March 1884).

50. *RG*, 19 June, 20 and 21 September 1887; *Echo*, 24 September 1887; Irving to Holland, No. 146, 14 April 1887, CO 111/438; Bruce to Holland, No. 370, 1 October 1887, CO 111/440; *DC*, 20 and 22 June 1897, 28 October 1898.

51. Peter Bailey, *Leisure and Class in Victorian England* (London, 1987), pp. 69-153; Keith A.P. Sandiford, 'The Victorians at Play: Problems in Historiographical Methodology', *JSH*, 15 (1981), pp. 271-78; Timothy J. L. Chandler, 'Games at Oxbridge and the Public Schools, 1830-80: The Diffusion of an Innovation', *IJHS*, 8 (1991), pp. 171-201. There is a fast growing body of literature on sports in Victorian Britain and the empire. See, for instance, Richard Holt, *Sport and the British: A Modern History* (London, 1989); J. A. Mangan, *The Games Ethic and Imperialism* (London, 1986), and *Pleasure, Profit and Proselytism: British Culture and Sport at Home and Abroad, 1700-1914* (London,

1988); and Brian Stoddart, 'Sport, Cultural Imperialism, and Colonial Response in the British Empire', *CSSH*, 30, (1988).

52. Sandiford, *loc. cit.;* also his 'Cricket and the Victorian Society', *JSH*, 17 (1983), p. 305; Stoddart, p. 653.

53. Holt,*op. cit.*, pp. 207-08.

54. Bailey, *loc. cit.*; Sandiford, 'The Victorians', pp. 279-80.

55. Holt, *op. cit.*, p. 221.

56. Stoddart, *op. cit.*, pp. 650-56; Holt, *op. cit.*, pp. 212-23.

57. McCrone, *op. cit.*, pp. 107-08. See also, Sandiford, 'The Victorians', pp. 281-82; and J. A. Mangan, 'The Social Construction of Victorian Femininity: Emancipation, Education and Exercise', *IJHS*, pp. 1-4.

58. McCrone, *op. cit.*, pp. 108-34; Mangan, 'The Social Construction', pp. 4-7.

59. Jihang Park, 'Sport, Dress Reform and the Emancipation of Women in Victorian England: A Reappraisal', *IJHS*, 6 (1989), p. 11.

60. Bailey, *op. cit.*, p. 98.

61. Holt, *op. cit.*, p. 208.

62. Kirke, *op. cit.*, p. 19.

63. *Ibid.*, pp. 97-98.

64. *RG*, 27 August 1864, 11 February 1865, 6 August 1884, 25 August 1888, 18 September 1889, 22 February 1893; *Colonist*, 3 and 25 June 1867; Hincks to Buckingham and Chandos, No. 52, 18 April 1868, CO 111/367; *RG*, 27 July 1869, 18 September 1880 'Local Sketches'; *DC*, 24 March 1885, 6 March 1891, 7 September 1898.

65. Brereton, *op. cit.*, p. 6; Bryan, *op. cit.*, pp. 194-95.

66. Stoddart, *op. cit.*, pp. 656-57.

67. *RG*, 9 February 1878.

68. Sandiford, 'Cricket and the Victorian Society', pp. 307-11.

69. Stoddart, *op. cit.*, p. 658.

70. *RG*, 23 October 1858.

71. *RG*, 17 March 1859.

72. *RG*, 31 December 1863, 6 January and 26 February 1864; *Colonist*, 4 January and 26 February 1864.

73. *Colonist*, 23 February 1865 and 12 September 1865.

74. *RG*, 28 January 1869.

75. Kirke, *op. cit.*, pp. 63-64.

76. *RG*, 26 August 1869. Hawke's team played two games against supposedly representative Guyanese teams, but which were composed entirely of members of the GCC (see *Echo*, 27 February, 3, 10 and 24 April 1897).

6

The White Minority in Jamaica at the end of the Nineteenth Century

PATRICK BRYAN

At the end of the nineteenth century the whites in the island of Jamaica constituted a dominant minority. This fact is not particularly surprising since from the foundation of the British regime in the second half of the seventeenth century whites had enjoyed control of land, labour and capital. They also enjoyed nearly undisputed control of the political system by enforcing a limited suffrage that effectively eliminated access to political decision-making by all except a powerful white minority. Control of the means of production and of the political system conferred on them considerable social authority. The white oligarchy curbed the threat of upwardly mobile mixed bloods from the end of the eighteenth century, and Jews were subject to levies on their income. Both Jews and mixed bloods were deprived of civil rights. Since slaves were property, they could not, by definition, be citizens.

The sole restraint on white power up to the nineteenth century was the Parliament in Britain itself, but rule from the metropolis was often challenged by aggressive planters who insisted on their rights as Englishmen. They vigorously defended (not always successfully) the colonial interest when that interest was adversely affected by metropolitan interest.

There was a struggle to the bitter end over abolition, a battle that the oligarchs lost. They won, however, the major concession of £20 million in compensation for the loss of their slaves. More important, the principle was accepted that abolition would give legal freedom to the slaves and nothing more. Post-emancipation society was to be more of the same thing: white oligarchical hegemony buttressed by new legal sanctions, continued domination of the resources of the colony and the conversion of the slave force into a proletariat tied to the sugar estates.

The white population of Jamaica continued to be a dominant minority, its power being in inverse proportion to its numbers. In 1871 there were 13,101 whites, 100,346 coloured, and 392,767 blacks. In 1911 there were 15,605 whites. But they had declined as a percentage of total population, from 2.29 per cent in 1891 to 1.88 per cent in 1911. On the other hand, the coloured (brown) population had increased by 33.8 per cent and the black population by 28.9 per cent between 1891 and 1911. By 1900 the majority of whites lived in Kingston and St. Andrew and were therefore largely an urban population.[1] Others had left Jamaica entirely. The number of doctors in 1833 (some 200)[2] exceeded the number of doctors (100) in the island in 1900. An analyst in the *Daily Gleaner* in 1903 described the situation in the following way: 'A hundred years ago towns like Savanna-la-mar, Montego Bay, Falmouth, had a considerable white population. Their descendants today form a mere handful of white and coloured families who have inherited the prejudices but not the wealth of their ancestors.'[3] A few hundred whites from Palestine, Lebanon and Syria at the end of the nineteenth and early twentieth centuries did not alter the demographic profile. The Middle-Easterners who entered the island mainly as dry goods merchants proved upwardly mobile and found for themselves a secure niche as a closed ethnic group.

Despite the decline of sugar, white economic power relative to the rest of the population did not diminish. In any case, sugar held its own in the parishes of St James, Hanover, Trelawny, parts of Clarendon and St Elizabeth. Just as important, however, is that a new market for bananas had emerged in the United States, and parishes such as Portland and St Mary that had gone out of sugar production launched themselves into competitive banana production. By the start of the new century banana was challenging sugar as the major export crop. The United States market also offered favourable tariffs for citrus, cocoa and coconuts. Economic growth at the end of the nineteenth century, linked to the United States market, brought back idle land into cultivation, and tenant farmers and squatters were ruthlessly pushed off their precarious holdings.

The great banana entrepreneurs had originated in the mercantile sector and the professional areas of Jamaican life. J. E. Kerr, for example, who started a business in Montego Bay in the 1870s, shipped logwood to Boston and imported flour from New York. In the 1880s he went into the export of bananas and oranges in his own ships, and in 1887 produced bananas on 350 acres at Llanrumny.[4] Other significant banana producers were Dr (later Sir John) Pringle, who produced bananas on several estates in St James and St Mary, some of the properties having been secured from his father-in-law at a very favourable price.[5] There were, too, A. L. DaCosta, Robert Butler Braham and Francis Bather. Alfred Pawsey, a prominent merchant of Kingston, was also the proprietor of Gibbons estate in Clarendon and of Bog Estate. William Malabre was a prominent merchant and substantial planter. Malabre was a descendant of a French family that had fled St Domingue early in the nineteenth century to escape the ravages of the slave rebellion there. Sugar plantations owned by another French *emigré* descendant, James Celeste Lecesne, at Harker's Hall and Grey's Hill were converted to banana production by a syndicate that established the Jamaica Fruit Company.[6] Charles E. De Mercado, a Jewish merchant of Kingston, shareholder of the *Daily Gleaner* and a partner of Lascelles of New York, was also in partnership with David Gideon of D. S. Gideon and Nephew, general importers and commission merchants of Port Antonio. The partnership grew into the larger one of De Mercado, Gideon, DiGiorgio, Johnston and the Atlantic Fruit Company.[7] $+$

Political power continued to march in tandem with economic power. Crown Colony government, imposed in 1866, deprived the oligarchy not so much of representation but of elected representation. The governor's veto powers were never mobilised to affect adversely the interests of the oligarchs, who were able to persuade the Crown Colony governors to underwrite a system of East indian immigration in order to depress wages in the sugar industry. When the governor, Sir Anthony Musgrave, made statements that showed some sympathy for small farmers, he was promptly dubbed a planterphobe. By 1884 the electoral principle was restored with a franchise which ensured that 1,001 whites out of 15,000 could vote, 3,766 blacks out of 444,186 and 2,578 coloureds out of 109,946.[8] The franchise was narrowed even further in 1893 by removing the facilities for illiterates to vote. In August 1887 there were 42,266 voters, in 1900-01 only 16,256 could vote.[9] Despite Dr Robert Love's efforts in the *Jamaica Advocate* to broaden political representation, political leadership before 1900 was dominated by the landed and business interests of the island. These interests had an able collaborator in the person of the governor, Henry Blake, who succeeded Governor Henry Norman in 1889. Among the men who served in the nominated and elected houses were Pringle, George Stiebel, Malabre and Gideon. Stiebel, it is true, was coloured, but his enormous wealth, earned in Spanish America, made him a natural ally of the white oligarchy.

A sense of community is often given visibility by the formation of associations. This was true of Jamaica's white oligarchy. Among the business associations established was the Jamaica Society of Agriculture in 1885.[10] This association addressed the sugar issue very vociferously. In recognition of the common interests of the planters and merchants the society added Merchants' Exchange to the existing name of the organisation in the following year, receiving a small subsidy from the government and the patronage of

Governor Norman. In 1895 the organisation became the Royal Jamaica Society of Agriculture and Commerce and Merchants' Exchange.[11] Prominent members of the society included Malabre, Colonel James Ward, James Verley, P. E. Auvray, J. E. Kerr, J. M. Farquharson, F. B. Lyons and J. L. Ashenheim, all merchants, planters or a combination of both. Ten members were added between 1894 and 1900, including Lorenzo Dowe Baker, the pioneer of large-scale banana production for export, F. L. Myers, Thomas Aguilar and Isaac Brandon. Another club was the Jamaica Club, which was not a business association although most of its members were prominent businessmen. The entrance fee was five guineas; the annual subscription was three guineas. Membership included the inevitable Colonel James Ward, Hon. Jonathan Pringle and Alfred Pawsey.[12] Another exclusive club was the Royal Yacht Club, whose headquarters boasted a billiard room, whist tables, and a cool and airy reading room. In fact, the *Daily Gleaner*, in 1894, concluded rather scathingly that yachting was a farce and that the Jamaica Yacht Club had practically no connection with yachting, apart from one or two enthusiasts. 'Yachtsmen', continued the *Gleaner*, 'among the several hundred members cannot justify the institution using the indicative prefix before "club". We suggest that the word "yacht" be omitted. The "Royal" would distinguish it from the other social club [presumably the Jamaica Club] on Hanover Street.'[13] In sport there was the same tendency. The Kingston Cricket Club, Manchester and St. Elizabeth Cricket Clubs, Lucas and Kensington, and the St Andrew Lawn Tennis Association were white elite organisations. In May 1894, H. S. Braham, a businessman, founded a gentleman's social club in Porus.

It is difficult to escape the conclusion that white society conducted itself as something of a caste. This can be explained by their existence in a predominantly coloured society and the consequent need for 'mutual protection' against 'combustible' coloured people. This conduct was justified in the following way by Frank Cundall, a resident Englishman, who was the Librarian of the Institute of Jamaica:

> With the exception of the planters, government servants and professional men are almost the only cultured members of any community for there are so few residents of leisure that they may be disregarded entirely. The only residents in any district are there by necessity, engaged in agriculture or trade, the affairs of the Church, education, medicine, law or the collection of taxes, with the occasional retired naval or military officer, who from doing duty in the West Indies, has come to adopt it as his residence.[14]

Cundall's view was shared by the rest of the white community, who thought that culture was an attribute enjoyed only by the white minority group, and that social intercourse between whites and coloured was not possible.

The caste-like conduct of the white community was partly a consequence of a conviction about their cultural superiority and cultural difference from the rest of the population. The realities of race in Jamaica facilitated a 'sham criteria of eminence' partly because the social power of the elite rested on the belief that, as whites, they were the island's repositories of culture. The inequalities of Jamaican society made possible the existence at the top of the society of a minority who thought that their way of life added tone to the society. The relationship between elite status, inequality and culture is described by R. H. Tawney: 'Like an oasis which few can inhabit, but the very thought of which brings refreshment and hope to the sand-weary traveller, inequality it is argued, protects the graces of life from being submerged beneath the dust of its daily necessities. It perpetuates a tradition of culture, by assuring the survival of a class which is its visible embodiment, and which maintains that tradition in maintaining itself.'[15] Whatever the imperfections of the white minority elite, they viewed themselves and were viewed as the natural 'centre of light and authority'.[16] The elite concept of social distance, founded on racial and economic considerations, was buttressed in practical terms by aesthetic distance. The landed class, the ruling class, the social elite, the white minority, were very much the same people.

Whites were also constrained into caste-like conduct because of a fear of social ostracism, which, as a British observer commented, ensured the whites' reluctance to look at blacks and coloured sympathetically: 'For a white man to champion the cause of his black fellow citizens is to risk social ostracism and where culture and intelligence and everything that makes life of a refined and educated man worth living is confined to a limited circle, such a penalty is too great.'[17] There was considerable interaction in the white community at home gatherings. The British novelist, Alice Spinner, noted the tremendous number of call cards used by whites in calling on each other.[18] Ostracism would make such house-calls impossible or unpleasant, as Justice Gibbons, a British magistrate, was to find. Gibbons had personally intervened in the credit relationship between shopkeepers and rural farmers, and had exposed the relationship between logwood theft, big business and the magistracy. He had also exposed practices related to dishonest conveyancing of land, leading to the loss of land and financial deposits made by small farmers. Originally posted in St Ann, Gibbons was transferred to Mandeville, where he was involved in a fight with a local lawyer. Gibbons takes up the story: 'I had no acquaintances in Mandeville, and with very few exceptions, no one called on me. W. Coke called and I returned his call, but finding his wife would not call on my daughter because, I have since been informed, my sister, who was in the island some years ago, had not called on her, the acquaintance dropped and Mr Coke assumed an attitude of hostility towards me.'[19] Gibbons would have been blackballed had he sought membership in the Manchester Club. Eventually he was hounded out of the island.

This sort of conduct was also related to insecurity. Morant Bay and Haiti were always at the forefront of the white mind, which routinely described black people as combustible. A contributor to the *Daily Gleaner* recommended that a statue be erected to honour the memory of Governor Eyre, whose massacre of blacks at Morant Bay in 1865 was, for besieged whites, an act of heroism.[20] Whites did not ever rule out a re-enactment of the Morant Bay Rebellion, with blacks slaughtering whites indiscriminately. In her novel *Lucilla*, Alice Spinner describes the position of Mr Baxter, the education officer, who is a white Creole:

> [His] horror of any row or disturbance was only equalled by his conviction that the only chance of improving the coloured population was to preserve strictly one's own authority .... Like most creoles of pure British extraction he had a far more invincible prejudice and dislike to the coloured population than any Englishman could possibly possess; but he kept this in the background, as far as popular education went, swam with the current of modern opinion in the island.[21]

Whites also did not rule out the possibility of a coloured-black alliance against them. It is clear that some whites considered the wealthy brown segment as more dangerous than blacks. This issue arose in the 1880s when efforts were being made to re-establish a militia. There were fears among some of the white minority that coloured men officering blacks would be receiving armaments which could be used against whites. Bancroft Espeut, a planter, went directly to the Colonial Office to address the matter. His remarks were recorded by a Colonial Office official:

> He [Espeut] wanted to know whether HM's government were really committed to such a policy as that of raising local militias and whether they knew what such a policy meant. He pointed out that annually some 100 men retired from the police and others from the West India regiments – that these formed a nucleus of a force which we were now teaching the coloured man to organise and lead .... It was better that these black men should go to their plots of land and forget as soon as possible all the training they ever knew. In themselves they are not dangerous, but once teach the 'coloured' men to lead them and the community would never be safe. This was just what the militia was doing and it was giving instruction to *the deadly enemies of the whites,* and this would be used one day against them. There was clearly hatred between 'coloured' people and the whites and it would never be removed. Herein was the real meaning of opposition of the Legislative Council to the Militia Bill, and they intended to oppose it is every legitimate way. At the same time, they would not for a moment venture to let the coloured question come up or even be suspected, it was too dangerous.[22]

There was, then, a strong, material basis for white economic power which was reinforced by formal and informal associations between them. Since, in Jamaica, as in the rest of the Caribbean, being white means 'above all, *not* being black', and the ideas and values that developed in the white 'culture section' were 'permeated by the necessity of defining itself against its despised and feared opposite',[23] whites endeavoured to intermarry, and thereby keep the race pure. The social, political, bureaucratic and cultural authority of the white segment was partly assured by the fact that 'a society may perpetuate social inequalities far more effectively when the maldistribution of income is buttressed by phenotype'.[24]

Whites maintained social exclusiveness through their marriage patterns and mating patterns. Caste-like courtship and marriage patterns among the white minority effectively defended 'aristocratic status'. In 'white society' courtship was formal and chaperoned, although no doubt chaperoned barriers were sometimes broken by elopement, for example. In theory, and to a large extent, in practice, young women were anxiously watched by their matronly chaperones who had to be present at balls or dances, where etiquette was strictly observed. Legitimacy of birth was the norm to which white people aspired, and usually achieved. It was also the norm which they encouraged among the rest of the population. Illegitimacy was considered the source of all other social evils. Colonial statistics even linked legitimacy and health.

As in so many other things, however, there was a contradiction between theory and practice. White males were themselves responsible for some of the illegitimacy and 'immorality' in Jamaican society. White males permitted themselves the luxury of coloured or black mistresses. Sexual relations between the races was permissible, but not marriage. In this way white males enjoyed the best of both worlds. The historian, W. J. Gardner, whose work was published in 1870, outlined the nature of concubinage between white and coloured. Only rarely, according to him, was an offer of marriage received from someone who did not maintain at least one coloured or black housekeeper, 'for so in the colony it was customary to designate a concubine'. Gardner noted that both white bride and coloured concubine were resigned to the situation: 'If a good natured person, as was usually the case, she [the concubine] would prepare the home she was quitting for the expected bride, while that lady would often take an interest in the future welfare of herself and children, astonishing to any woman trained amidst other associations. It was well for her domestic peace if she had not to submit to the existence of one or more establishments other than that of which she was head.'[25] White/coloured concubinage thus allowed for the continuation of marriage among whites, while permitting semi-permanent liaisons with coloured women.

The Jamaican press, at least the *Daily Gleaner*, often remarked on the sexual excesses of many white heads of households. Gentlemen were accused of keeping mistresses during Legislative Council sessions in Spanish Town; other 'gentlemen' were accused of living lives of open shame or of siring numerous illegitimate progeny. A public official, who died in 1889, left substantial property for his seven 'natural' children as well as for his two legitimate ones. Yet another 'gentleman' left his property to his two natural daughters in 1882. Others left property for their 'reputed' children'.[26] In her novels, Alice Spinner included sub-plots in which coloured women opted for concubinage with white men in preference to marriage with people of their own race.[27]

Patterns of leisure contributed to making white society caste-like in its activities. It is true, however, that leisure pursuits were linked to their greater wealth and to perhaps greater cultural preparation. The races, gambling, golf, state balls, tennis, elaborate home entertainments, impromptu concerts (which were not necessarily impromptu), bicycle riding (the bicycle was a luxury in Jamaica), freemasonry, literary and debating societies, outings to Rockfort and Port Henderson, horticultural and dog shows were among the pursuits of the elite. Nor was it unusual to patronise the theatre, which not only enjoyed local productions (pantomimes for example), but also imported choral groups which performed at the Theatre Royal before it was destroyed by the earthquake of 1907. Gambling cut across caste or class barriers; the urban working class was more involved with Chinese-style gambling which members of the elite tried to stamp out on moral grounds, while they themselves drove their families sometimes into bankruptcy with card games. All classes participated in gambling at the races. Cockfighting, though illegal, also attracted an enthusiastic elite following.[28]

White society was not monolithic. The cohesiveness of white society had to do with the formation of a common position as whites in an island of dark men. There was not a generalised position about how blacks should be treated, although there was a general view that they were inferior in terms of either race or culture. The first position coincided with that of the Spaniard Gines de Sepulveda in the sixteenth century that Indians and coloureds were an inferior species of human being, and that their enslavement or other forms of servitude was justified. In the late nineteenth century this view was expressed in the form of a belief that blacks should constitute a permanent proletariat, in existence only to serve whites. It was really the old Aristotelian view that divided human kind into those with and those without intelligence, the latter destined to serve the former. Curiously enough Las Casas' interpretation that Indians and coloureds would be perfect 'if only they worshipped the true God' was echoed in Archbishop Enos Nuttall's dedication to altering the superstitious tendencies in 'native religion', and removing the mental construction of people of African ancestry to make them more amenable to Anglo-Saxon civilisation's norms. The pro-slavery ideology so amply discussed by Gordon Lewis continued, albeit in modified form.[29]

The white planter class believed that blacks should be kept tied to the plantation in order to ensure their access to 'civilisation' after emancipation. Without that tie, it was assumed, blacks would revert to barbarism. The outcome of this kind of thinking was the importation of white farmers to occupy the hillsides to make it difficult for blacks to find land for their own cultivation. Other whites thought that the black and white races should be allowed to develop separately. In this view the white and black races were like two banks of a river, perhaps equal but very different.[30]

The late nineteenth century was the period of pseudo-scientific racism linked to Spencer's Social Darwinism and to Positivism. The latter was definitely a *status quo* ideology that favoured progress within order, moral reform, hierarchy and 'obligation'. In the minds of some positivists, particularly those with a religious bent, history functioned according to divine law. Hence, slavery, as undesirable as it was, proved to be the first step to expose the 'African savage' to 'free' conditions. Crudely interpreted Social Darwinism condemned coloured people to extinction because of a supposed inherent inability to compete with their racial superiors. In Jamaica, however, Archbishop Nuttall's Darwinism became linked to Christian humanism. The importance of Nuttall cannot be overestimated in terms of his contribution to the expansion of both secular and religious education at the end of the nineteenth century. In his view, because of their demographic history, blacks would not die out as a racial category. Second, the outlook of blacks was shaped not so much by race as by culture (especially religious culture). Consequently, a reshaping of black culture according to Anglo-Saxon norms (and Nuttall believed that Anglo-Saxon civilisation was superior) was all that was required to make blacks the equals of the white race. There was only one problem, however, the re-education or reshaping of the black mind would take centuries. Third, the British Empire, in its paternalist rule over the 'subject people' of the empire, served the function of 'uplifting' the subject people. Fourth, Jamaican blacks brought to religion certain forms – a sense of community, and an attachment to music which could stimulate 'vital religion'. Nuttall's main importance, however, lies in his expansion, through the Anglican Church, of elementary education. He considered that the Church had an obligation to oversee the spiritual and the temporal needs of its collective congregation.[31]

Nuttall was joined by other whites in the belief that it was better to spend money on education rather than on the police. Although this liberal segment formed only a small group within the white minority, their views helped to strengthen the credibility of the white ruling elite among the black population. A logical extension of this orientation was a programme of action to encourage basic numeracy and literacy and philanthropic action, which concerned itself with women, children, prison reform, mutual aid and moral reform. A branch of the Young Men's Christian Association was established in the colony and the Women's Self-Help Society was founded by Lady Musgrave, wife of the

Governor, Sir Anthony Musgrave.[32] The Kingston Charity Organisation Society, patterned on the Charity Organisation Society (COS) in England, was introduced to see to the needs of the deserving poor.[33] The Upward and Onward Society, established by the Moravians, joined the Women's Self-Help Society in teaching marketable skills to poor women or to genteel women who had fallen on hard times; it was especially concerned with moral education, home-making and healthy leisure pursuits. There were also individual acts of charity. In 1902, for example, Eliza James Verley, widow of the planter Louis Verley, granted £5,000 for a home for respectable gentlewomen who were widows or spinsters in indigent circumstances.[34]

Mutual aid societies emerged before the mid-nineteenth century, and although some of them had a precarious existence, the more promising ones were from time to time revitalised. Rev. T. B. Turner, for example, founded the St George's Church Mutual Relief Society in November 1828 to assist members during illness and with funeral expenses. It went into abeyance but was reorganised in 1864. In 1866 Enos Nuttall became its president. In 1871 the Trinity Catholic Church Benevolent Society was established with Rev. Joseph Dumont as president, treasurer and secretary. In 1883, Rev. William Spillman, SJ, founded the Catholic Burial Association whose object was to 'procure Christian burial for the deserving of the Catholic Faith'.[35] The Salvation Army, established in Jamaica in the 1880s, quickly became associated with social and charitable work. White leadership in many Christian churches, therefore, provided increased credibility for white minority rule.

There were other areas in which the white minority was not monolithic. A clearly defined ethnic group within the white minority were the Jews, who had had a long residence in Jamaica. Up to 1830 the Jewish population, wealthy through trade and tolerated, in terms of freedom of conscience, were discriminated against. They did not until then enjoy the civil liberties of the rest of the white population, and even with the grant of civil liberties in 1830 they were not free from various psychological and social barriers. By the end of the nineteenth century, however, it is clear that Jews were members of the same organisations as whites, for example, the Jamaica Society of Agriculture and Merchant Exchange. The fact is that the 'Jews who constituted an increasingly affluent and influential urban-based merchant class could . . . no longer be ignored'.[36] By the end of the nineteenth century the Jews were being co-opted into politics, with elected Jews increasing their representation in the Legislature from eight in 1849 to 13 out of 47 in 1866.[37] Whatever their links with planters at the political and economic level, however, the Jewish population 'fostered a socio-cultural environment that promoted their self-preservation along religious and cultural lines'.[38] Only Jews, for example, could be buried in Jewish cemeteries. The Jews continued to maintain their own institutions and voluntary associations which provided a 'cultural boundary that sets Jews apart from non-Jews'.[39] Jewish flexibility, partly a consequence of declining numbers since the end of the nineteenth century, has ensured that they are fully integrated into the marketplace, while maintaining a distinct identity within the white minority group. In the nineteenth century, however, the Jewish population was not uniformly wealthy. Richer Jews were major agents in the trade with Spanish America, owners of urban real estate, gradually gained control of some plantations through defaults in debt payment and were big wholesale merchants. Other Jews' economic existence was associated with the retail trade, and, to some extent, petty trade. The cholera epidemic of the 1850s appears to have exposed far more poverty among the Jews than expected. The solution was the formation of the Hebrew Benevolent Society. The Jewish segment also set up the Gemibut Hazadim Society, for the burial of the dead and the relief of the respectable Jewish poor.[40]

The Scottish community asserted their identity through the formation of the Caledonia Society and the Jamaica Scottish Society. Both these performed mutual aid and benevolent functions and were designed to encourage the study of Scottish literature and music. Probably, however, they were more important as organisations for social intercourse. The highlight of the Caledonia Society's activities was the celebration of St Andrew's Day. In 1900, at the Myrtle Bank Hotel, 'the dining hall had been very prettily decorated by some braw Scottish lassies, who had placed a sprig of heather before each guest. The dinner was most appropriate to the occasion, beginning with Cockie Leckie soup and ending with Grampian pudding, all the chief delicacies of the land o'cakes coming between. The great dish, of course, was the Haggis which was solemnly carried around the table to the strains of the bag-pipes, and was followed by the inevitable 'wee drappie o't'.[41]

There is not much evidence that these obviously elite Scottish whites developed close associations with poor Scots in the island, except probably through the occasional act of benevolence. There were important divisions among whites on the basis of occupation and income. In the 1840s whites from Scotland and Germany were lured into the island as agriculturists. These imported whites were expected to occupy the highlands of Jamaica, in order to reduce access to these highlands by blacks who would thereby be forced to live within the 'civilising' nucleus of the plantation. The entry of these whites created white communities in Altamont (Scottish) and Seaford Town (German). The white settlers were cultivators of ginger and arrowroot, and as small farmers enjoyed equal or less success than their black counterparts. The assumptions of the colonial authorities seem to have rested on theories of competence based upon race. Governor Blake favoured the establishment of homogeneous white communities of agriculturists who would keep themselves distant and distinct from the black population. In fact, Blake believed that white agriculturists introduced into predominantly black communities would fail: 'I should not advise the advent of white agriculturists except in communities, on such a scale that the colonists would find themselves a part of homogeneous society, with a sufficient number of white neighbours to form their own social public opinion and standard of morals. Isolated white labouring agriculturists among a black population would certainly fail.'[42] In short, it was difficult to maintain the superiority of the white caste when it was not properly surrounded or protected from blacks. German settlers did not live up to the expectations of white elite society. The poverty of many of the settlers, and the realisation that whiteness at the level of German community settlement had not demonstrated white superiority, led Blake to conclude that the Seaford Town German community was a failure. The Germans lived very much like blacks in their adjoining communities. 'In intelligence,' complained Blake, 'they did not surpass the adjoining communities, nor do their energy compare favourably with the latter'.[43]

The fact that whiteness was associated with elite status was not lost on blacks in their own assessment of the poor Scottish and German farmers. Blacks referred to them disparagingly as 'white laba' (white workers). Nevertheless, poor whites exploited their whiteness to enable them to gain advantage in a society where the important thing was to be 'not black': 'But there are other whites not included in the Backra [class], especially when it is used in connection with intellectual and social greatness. They are described by the term "white laba", an abbreviation of and corruption of "white labourer". [They] include later immigrants of English, Irish, German origin, and a few Portuguese commonly called "poto" who all take rank side by side of the ordinary peasant, but take advantage of the native status of their more favoured kindred.'[44] Social class differences between whites could be bridged by common ethnicity, a fact noted by the historian Bryan Edwards in the late eighteenth century.[45]

There were whites who had always performed lesser administrative duties on sugar and banana estates such as bookkeepers and overseers. The bookkeepers were among the most exploited segment of the white labour force. In 1884 Rev. Henry Clarke reported that they earned between £30 and £60 per year, faced 'the hardest work and roughest treatment imaginable', and had a precarious existence.[46] One bookkeeper reported that two-thirds of his wage (20 shillings per week) was deducted for board and lodging on the estate. Some bookkeepers were not allowed to ride, paid their own fare from Britain, had no sanitary facilities on the estate, and no medical assistance. One bookkeeper who was ill for three months received no salary during the period. Bookkeepers were not encouraged to marry, since the estate had a vested interest in collecting a portion of their salary for room and board.[47]

Headmen of the estates provided bookkeepers with women on the estate. Beyond doubt, it was the bookkeeper's pigmentation that entitled him to that kind of attention. Pressure could be placed not only on the women employed on the estates but also on their families: 'I have known of girls to hold out a long time, others run away. The "weaker vessel" knows, Alas! that her whole family is dependent on the only Sugar Estate.'[48] The bookkeepers' sweethearts, once they had been secured, were paid through the blotter (the pay book) for work they had never done. Some bookkeepers kept, in polygamous style, both mother and daughter.

The major hope of the bookkeeper was to become an overseer, and it is clear that a number of them did so. Overseer positions were more or less reserved for whites. In 1884 an overseer could earn an annual salary of between £150 and £200, depending on the estate. The main problem of the overseer, and it was a real drawback, was that he had no job security. 'It is dangerous,' commented Rev. Clarke, 'for a man of family to hold the position.'[49]

An important segment of the white community which lived outside the formal plantation complex were the colonial bureaucrats imported from Britain. These whites occupied the upper rungs of the Jamaica Constabulary Force, which had been established by Sir John Peter Grant in 1867. Black men were not allowed to rise above the rank of constable, since the officer corps was by policy white. A first-class constable earned between £40 and £45 per year. This salary compared with £900 earned by the inspector general in 1879, and £300 earned by first-class inspectors. The deputy inspector general earned £300 per year plus £1 per day for travelling. A second-class constable earned one penny more per day (two shillings and fourpence) than the daily allowance for the sub-inspector's horse.[50]

There were white professionals, such as medical officers, some of them imported, and school inspectors, some of whom strengthened their economic position by investment in land. There were, moreover, churchmen, representing all the European Christian denominations in the island, who in theory, provided spiritual leadership for the Jamaican community.

The fact that Jamaica's Crown Colony administration showed marked preference for bureaucrats imported from Britain was a source of conflict between local and imported whites. Local whites described them as; 'transients', 'opportunists', 'without merit' and 'aristocratic destitutes'. The colonial bureaucrat was considered to be the entity through which Jamaica paid its tribute to the British Empire. Their high salaries were the subject of regular comment. Invariably, local whites concluded that expatriate salaries were too high. Frank Cundall, himself an expatriate bureaucrat, indicated that the colonial bureaucrat enjoyed a status and prominence which he never enjoyed at home: 'In England, a man may serve the State all his life and never come under public notice. In the West

Indies his every action is noted. His salary is freely commented on, his holidays duly chronicled, his promotions recorded, and his personality freely criticised.'[51] As Stanley and Barbara Stein have noted, colonial 'administration provided a highly visible structure of command',[52] and the colonial bureaucrat was the visible embodiment of imperial domination, in Jamaica's case underlined by whiteness. The expatriate bureaucrat's associations and interactions were primarily within the ranks of the white minority. It was generally acknowledged that however open-minded the bureaucrat was at the time of his arrival in the colony, his attitudes came to resemble closely those of the dominant local white segment, especially with regard to the black and coloured population. Despite their transiency, colonial bureaucrats, from governors to first-class clerks, invested in grazing pens, cinchona plantations and other economic enterprises. A survey conducted in 1884 revealed that land ownership among colonial bureaucrats ranged from 200 acres to over 2,300 acres.[53] For some bureaucrats the tropics became a kind of purgatory, monitored by the thermometer which Spinner described as 'the supreme ruler of the Englishman in the tropics against [whose] fiat none dares rebel'.

But the pretensions of the imported white bureaucrat was not lost on Spinner. In her novel, *Lucilla,* the heroine, a music teacher, who comes from a deprived area of Chelsea in London, is willing to marry daCosta, a wealthy brown plantation owner. She is, however, faced by the prejudice of colonial society, which is shocked at her association with him.[54] Spinner also shows that when a white bureaucrat (in this case a military officer) falls in love with a very sophisticated woman of colour, he takes her overseas beyond the reach of her local family.[55]

Local whites drew some distinctions between themselves and the colonial bureaucrats. They were usually more sensitive to local colour. The evolution of a separate consciousness was expressed through a recognition of a folk idiom which could be conveniently appropriated without violating the principle that Jamaica's culture was British. One result of this kind of thinking was the composition of a 'Jamaican anthem' sung to the tune of 'God Save Our Gracious Queen'. Another was the insistence that only locals understood the Creole, regarded as a 'quaint' Jamaican invention and at the same time an indicator of class origin. Local whites believed that expatriate magistrates' lack of knowledge of the vernacular could frustrate the ends of justice. Hence the following story.[56]

> Overheard in court
> A prisoner was before Justice Judge Little, charged with the theft of a pig.
> Judge: What did you do with the pig?
> Prisoner: John Cro' tek 'im, sah.
> Judge: Call up Mr John Crow!

A familiarity with Jamaican folk ways, such as the vernacular, could not, however, conceal the reality that Jamaican whites viewed themselves no less as Englishmen than their rivals in the bureaucracy freshly arrived in the island. The point was made forcibly by a black Jamaican who noted that whites identified with 'the soil and less so with the people of the land'.

> The Jamaican white man has his peculiarities as well as man everywhere under the influence of climate, local needs, blessings, thought, feeling .... At once he is the least Jamaican of everything pertaining to the country. He longs to return to England, if he is a native Englishman, and if he is not, he thinks at least he ought to visit that country; and he speaks of it as 'home', even when he has never visit d it. There are, however, some families among them, who, on account of their 'stake' in the country have become identified with this land for generations, but it is for the greater part an identification with the soil, and less so with the people of the land.[57]

In summary, the economic power of the white oligarchy conferred on them, with the blessing of the Colonial Office, significant political power and social and cultural influence. This social authority extended to most whites, regardless of their class or occupational position in the hierarchy. At the same time there were notable distinctions between whites in terms of place of origin, ethnic origin, wealth and ideology.

Notes

1. Jamaica Censuses, 1871, 1891, 1911.

2. William A. Green, *British Slave Emancipation. The Sugar Colonies and the Great Experiment, 1830-1865* (Oxford, 1982), pp. 310-11.

3. *Daily Gleaner,* 19 December 1903: Article by Mr Joyce, 'Why Young Men leave the Island'.

4. Ansell Hart, 'The Banana Industry in Jamaica', *Social and Economic Studies*, 3:2 (1954), p. 217 and Department of State C8.1/22, 3593/30 Miscellaneous Correspondence, J. E. Viera to US Consul, 28 March 1877.

5. Hart, *op. cit.*, p. 219.

6. *Jamaica Gazette*, Vol. 17, No. 39, 27 September1984, p. 288.

7. Hart, *op.cit.*, p. 219.

8. H. A. Will, *Constitutional Change in the British West Indies, 1880-1903*, (Oxford, 1970), p. 64.

9. *Ibid.*, pp. 62-63.

10. *Jamaica Council Minutes*, Vol. 23, 1986. Governors Message (No. 7), 'Jamaica Society of Agriculture and Commerce'.

11. National Library of Jamaica MS 317, Casserly Collection.

12. *Handbook of Jamaica*, (1908), pp. 493, 503.

13. *Daily Gleaner*, 11 June 1984.

14. Frank Cundall, *Jamaica in 1912*, (Kingston, 1912).

15. R. H. Tawney, *Equality*, (New York, 1961), p. 79.

16. Raymond Williams, *Culture and Society, 1780-1950*, (Harmondsworth, 1961), p. 129.

17. John William Root, *The British West Indies and the Sugar Industry* (Liverpool, 1989), p. 131.

18. Alice Spinner, *Lucilla: An Experiment*, (London, 1896), p. 5. Augusta Zelia Frazer, whose pen-name was Alice Spinner, accompanied her husband, a railway administrator, to Jamaica in the 1890s.

19. CO137/518, 1884. Norman to Derby (No. 1690) enclosing Gibbons' letter of defence.

20. National Library of Jamaica, MST 59. Livingstone Collection, Vol. 1, 1898-1903. H. P. Deans to Editor, *Daily Gleaner*.

21. Alice Spinner, *op. cit.*, p. 74.

22. CO137/545, 1891. E. Wingfield's summary of Mr Espeuts statement made at the Colonial Office.

23. Charles W. Mills, 'Race and Class; Conflicting or Reconcilable Paradigms?', *Social and Economic Studies*, 36:2, (1987), p. 100.

24. Stanley and Barbara Stein, *The Colonial Heritage of Latin America: Essays on Economic Dependence in Perspective*, (New York, 1970), p. 57.

25. W. J. Gardner, *History of Jamaica*, (London, 1873), p. 377.

26. Island Record Office, Jamaica. Wills probated in the Supreme Court, Vol. 135. Will of H. S. S. entered 6 March 1890 and of J. U. M. D., entered 22 February 1890.

27. Alice Spinner, *A Study of Colour*, (London, 1894).

28. *Daily Gleaner*, 22 March 1886 and W. A. Feurtado, *A Forty-five Year Reminiscence of the Characteristics and Character of Spanish Town* (Kingston, 1890).

29. Gordon K. Lewis, *Main Currents in Caribbean Thought*, (Kingston and Port of Spain, 1983), pp. 94-170.

30. Alice Spinner, *op. cit.*, p. 147.

31. Patrick Bryan, *The Jamaican People, 1880-1902: Race Class and Social Control*, (London and Basingstoke, 1991), pp. 33-62, passim.

32. *Daily Gleaner*, 13 January 1886, 'Womens Self-Help Society', Jamaica Archives, 'Upward and Onward Society of the Women of Jamaica. Second annual Meeting and Report', March,

1905. Kingston Educational Supply and Printers. See also *Daily Gleaner*, 17 December 1904, Report of Address of Mrs James Watson, President of Upward and Onward Society.

33. Kingston Charity Organisation Society, *Annual Reports*, 1900-50.

34. *Handbook of Jamaica*, (Kingston, 1928).

35. Patrick Bryan, *Philanthropy and Social Welfare in Jamaica*, (Kingston, 1990), p. 45.

36. Carol S. Holzberg, *Minorities and Power in a Black Society: The Jewish Community of Jamaica*, (Maryland, 1987), p. 28.

37. *Ibid.*, p. 28.

38. *Ibid.*, p. 29.

39. *Ibid.*, p. 65.

40. Bryan, *Philanthropy and Social Welfare*, p. 44.

41. *Daily Gleaner,* 31 December1900. 'Report of Annual Dinner of the Caledonia Society'.

42. Sir Henry Blake, *The Awakening of Jamaica*, National Library of Jamaica, *Jamaica Pamphlets*, No. 22 1890.

43. Jamaica Archives, 1B 5/18, Vol. 49, Blake to Chamberlain, No. 372, 14 November 1895.

44. J. H. Reid, 'The People of Jamaica Described', in R. Gordon, *et. al. Jamaicas Jubilee: or what we are and what we hope to be*, (London, 1888), p. 87.

45. Bryan Edwards, *The History, Civil and Commercial, of the British Colonies in the West Indies*, 3 vols, (London, 1801), Vol. 2, pp. 7-8.

46. Rev. Henry Clarke, letter to *The Times*, reproduced in *Colonial Standard*, 7 October 1884.

47. National Library of Jamaica, MST 59, Livingstone Collection.

48. Felix Holt, 'Confessions', *Jamaica Advocate*, 6 September 1902.

49. Rev. Clarke, *op. cit.*

50. CO 137/514, XC/A052699. Memorandum of Mr Matthew Joseph to Colonial Office.

51. Frank Cundall, *op. cit.*

52. Stein and Stein, *op. cit.* p. 69.

53. CO 137/517, 1884. Norman to Earl of Derby No. 348, 24 September 1884. Enclosure showing estates owned by civil servants.

54. Alice Spinner, *Lucilla*, p. 95 and pp. 274-75.

55. *Ibid.*, p. 112-13.

56. *Daily Gleaner*, 22 December 1899, Gleaner Christmas competition for the best local original joke.

57. H. J. Reid, *op. cit.*, p. 87.

7

In the Name of the People: Populist Ideology and Expatriate Power in Belize

KAREN JUDD

In September 1987, a week after the annual celebration of the '10th', or Belize's National Day, and the night before 'the 21st', Belize Independence Day, I sat late in a bar, flanked by the chairman of the opposition party and the editor of the party paper, the *Belize Times*. That morning, the paper had reprinted, for the fourth or fifth time, an excerpt from a well-known dissertation by a British historian, called 'The Belizean Elite'. Its thesis: Belize City Creoles celebrate a pro-British holiday, promoted in the nineteenth century by a self-interested elite, who historically sold out their black brothers and sisters in their grab for middle-class status, wealth, and property. Its major source: the opinions of a succession of British administrators, governors and Colonial Office clerks. Two well-known Creoles, one a long-term adviser to the party in power, the other a lawyer and politician with the opposition party, were getting into an increasingly heated argument, which at times threatened to come to blows over the identity of this Creole elite, an identity no one wanted to claim.

Seeing the young editor, an outspoken Latina, they turned their wrath on her. She said she would be happy to publish anything they wanted, but they were having none of it. One swung out wildly, this time at the opposition party leader. At that, they were ushered out to continue their argument outside. 'So what do you think of our Creole elite now?' she laughed.

Incidents like this are not uncommon in Belize, where Creoles, the racially mixed but predominantly black population, until recently occupied most of the civil service jobs.[1] City dwellers, they are often accused of disdaining agriculture for colonial lackey positions, and thus both of racial discrimination against Latinos and of 'selling out' their fellow blacks.

Creoles argue that political appointments as well as increased diversity within the public service have equalised Latino representation in Belizean public life, while leaving Latino commercial dominance untouched. But the charges of collaboration persist, revolving around images of Creole 'mimic men', more British than the British, imitating British occupations and celebrating a British dominance in the country. Those who level these charges are for the most part neither Latino nor white, but politicians and nationalists of various ethnic groups who regard the Creole middle class as an obstacle to progressive social change. As evidence, however, these critics cite the despatches of the colonial administrators, who were for much of the colony's history engaged in a struggle for control over the politics of the colony with ancestors of these Creoles. Themselves second sons, viscounts and marquesses, these Colonial Office aristocrats so discredited the ambitions of native capital that it is Creoles who must justify their history.

Meanwhile, whites, local and expatriate, stay above the fray. Unlike most Belizeans, for whom party affiliation is a major part of identity,[2] they stay out of politics, contributing funds to whichever party is in power and keeping their economic interests free of national or ethnic commitment. In this, they are continuing a long tradition. For today, as historically, British and US 'investors' siphon off the country's real wealth, their hold merely changing form with the changes in international capital accumulation Historian R. E. Runciman has argued that capitalism, far from being inevitable, must be 'selected'– nourished by either the state or a local ruling class.[3] He examines a number of historical situations in which capitalist practices failed to confer sufficient competitive advantages, among them Britain's colonies in Africa and the Caribbean, where, he notes, 'neither the colonial governments nor the metropolitan corporations were likely to benefit from promoting a strong, native capitalist class . . . .' (1995: 42)

British Honduras is surely the classic case. In some of the larger Caribbean islands, such as Jamaica and Trinidad and Tobago, export agriculture provided the basis for the development of a productive capitalist class, supplemented in the post-emancipation period by the growth of a local trading class. In British Honduras, by contrast, the extraction and export of timber dominated the economy for the greater part of the colony's history, retarding the development of agriculture and accompanying infrastructure such as roads and railroads. In this, the Colonial Office assisted, repeatedly vetoing the private construction of railroads, roads, ports, or industry out of fear of native self-interest, at the same time refusing to allocate the necessary Crown resources to open land for cultivation or encourage agriculture. In so doing they permitted the perpetuation of what amounted to debt servitude for black woodcutters on large tracts of metropolitan-owned land.

As a result, the colony passed from the nineteenth to the twentieth century with no roads and railroads nor electric lights, and almost without a local modernising capitalist class or a free wage-earning class. This not only allowed metropolitan banking houses to retain their grip on an almost exclusively extractive economy until the end of the Second World War, but it also virtually eliminated agricultural employment for the majority black population. Only in the post-war period have roads been constructed and only since the 1970s have sugar and citrus begun to replace timber as the colony's leading exports. To this day agriculture remains undeveloped, dependent on foreign investment capital and preferential access to foreign markets.[4]

While both black and white natives remained locked in a paralysing struggle with the Colonial Office to open the colony to agriculture and smallholding, a slow but steady migration of Latino residents from the neighbouring Mexican province of Yucatan which started in the 1860s, was changing the dynamics in the north. Yucatecan migrants, for the most part not wealthy, nevertheless were skilled agriculturalists, with, even more important, experience in hiring and supervising Mayan labourers. Local agriculture, stifled in the central part of country, slowly took hold in the north. But labour relations were more kin- and client-based than truly free. The same was true in the south, where Scots citrus growers had a ready supply of casual and migrant labourers from neighbouring Central America; growers supplied them with housing and supplies from a company store. Migrant workers still provide the major labour force, and growers remain dependent on foreign companies to process the fruit.

Today in Belize City, racism converges with clientelism to restrict the free market in labour. As Latino entrepreneurs, whose businesses are still primarily family-owned and run, increasingly challenge local white dominance in Belize City, their hiring preferences are for Latino workers, a practice shared by new North American firms for more overtly racist reasons (Bolland 1986). Thus Creoles find few new employment options, and consider that their only career lies in the public service, despite its low pay. Today, the government is the largest employer, and unemployment reaches as high as 40 per cent in some areas. Creoles for the most part find jobs in New York or Los Angeles. By saving the people from capitalism, it can be argued, the colonial rulers have bequeathed them no place to work.

This chapter looks at the 'de-selection' of capital in British Honduras. It focuses on efforts to open the colony to agriculture and transport, starting in the mid-nineteenth century, and highlights the efforts of those who sought to develop local capital. It reviews the British colonial authorities' denial of these efforts in the name of 'the people', resulting in a weak local capitalist class and an urban-based working class, unskilled in agriculture or industry. In it I will argue that the correspondence these efforts generated among the Colonial Office officials and local administrators has served to shape political discourse in Belize, particularly concerning the nature and role of the so-called Creole elite. Drawing on data from my research on elite Creole family histories (Judd 1992), I endeavour to distinguish the processes of class and racial identity formation, for both whites and Creoles, from the societal process of creolisation. In doing so I argue that the collapsing of the political and cultural process of creolisation with the very different process of economic consolidation has obfuscated the process by which whites, local and foreign, have continued to hold on to locally generated wealth.[5]

A woodcutting outpost

Belize is not unique among Caribbean countries, most of which, as R. T. Smith (1988: 13) notes, were controlled by a small white elite of planters, exporters and administrators, 'few of whom became a permanent part of the society'. The result was an association between economic class and a hierarchy of competing racial elites, none of whom could be considered upper-class. Unlike most of the Caribbean, however, British Honduras was never a plantation economy. Its location on the periphery of Spain's mainland empire, where Britain for long refused to claim an official colony, did not encourage permanent European settlement. Nor did the climate, which was not suited to cotton and was considered unsuitable for sugar. As a result, it did not develop a resident planter class. Instead, large tracts of virgin forests, accessible by river, made woodcutting an attractive alternative, first to adventurers, then to the London-based merchant banking houses. As the settlement grew, imported goods (everything from food to whiskey to cookware) increased, as did lumber exports, and eighteenth-century adventurers and pirates were replaced by nineteenth-century merchant capitalists, local partners or representatives of metropolitan banking houses.[6] Few put down permanent roots. Bolland (1979) has chronicled in detail the process by which the colonial authorities broke the economic and political dominance of the local settler class, which was all but extinct by 1850. Lacking opportunities to invest in either land or industry, most of the early woodcutters and entrepreneurs took their profits and went home. There were exceptions, among them Dr Manfield William Bowen, whose son Barry is one of the wealthiest men in Belize. Thereafter each decade saw a new wave of merchants and fortune-seekers from England or Scotland, and from each wave a few remained, giving rise to today's 'local whites'. But for the most part, whites were expatriates, including colonial administrators, London or Glasgow merchants, periodic military personnel and a constant supply of lawyers.[7]

The colony's former slaves, trained as woodcutters and unable to lease or purchase land after emancipation in 1840, continued to work in the forests, cutting first logwood and then mahogany for the European market. No longer slaves, they were more or less permanent debt contract workers, obliged to sign on as contract labourers season after season. While some gained experience as foremen or managers, none acquired agricultural know-how or entrepreneurial experience, since they lacked capital. Despite the rhetoric of emancipation, small plots of land sufficient to support a family were priced beyond the means of most labourers.

This became clear after 1860, when efforts were made to attract white confederate planters as well as former slave labourers as immigrants from the Civil War south. The US consul in British Honduras, Raymond Leas, pointed out that despite the fact that the US government had for some years been selling good agricultural land for $1.25 per acre (and Latin American countries were offering it to immigrants for free), land in the colony was priced at $5 per acre (cited in Cleghern 1967: 33-34).

Leas was not alone in pointing to the high price of land as an ongoing obstacle to development. That this price obtained for uncleared and inaccessible Crown lands as well as that offered by large landowners was interpreted by the local press as evidence of collusion between the largest landowner, the British Honduras Company (later the Belize Estate and Produce Company) and Colonial Office policy-makers. While one development-minded local administrator, Lieutenant-Governor Austin, eventually succeeded in getting the price of Crown lands reduced to $2.50 in 1866, his own sale of good private land to US immigrants at a nominal price was widely viewed in the colony as the cause of his recall shortly thereafter (Gibbs 1898: 151).

In fact, collusion was not needed, as the commonality of interest between Colonial Office and London-based landowners, notably the British Honduras Company, went very deep. Indeed, the dislike of Colonial Office administrators for native capitalists must be set against the history of this company. The original lands were first acquired by James Hyde, one of the colony's earliest settlers, who in the 1840s formed James Hyde & Co (later Hyde & Hodge), with a London merchant, John Hodge. Taking advantage of the Joint Stock Companies Act in 1856, Hyde and Hodge formed the British Honduras Company in 1859 and had transferred many of their lands to the new company by 1875. By then the company was entirely in metropolitan hands, and Hyde had long since returned to London. Renamed the Belize Estate and Produce Company, Ltd in 1875, the company gradually bought up most of the original settlers' holdings; by 1888 it owned about half of all privately owned land in the colony.

As Bolland has observed (1979: 184-86), the concentration of practically half of all freehold land in a single company allowed its metropolitan-based owners to virtually dominate the colony's development. Thus in 1871, its influence in the local Legislative Assembly resulted in the vote to become a Crown Colony, surrendering self-government and allowing London to take control of the colony's finances. In urging the interests of the British Honduras Company to the Colonial Office, its chairman pointed out that the claims of the company and those of the colony were 'nearly identical' (Robertson to Herbert, 9 June 1874, quoted in Cleghern 1967: 54).

Also in the company's interests was the inability of freed slaves to purchase land, obliging them to continue to seek the only work available, cutting mahogany. The contract labourers typically left their families in town while they worked in the forest camps (in six-month stints, broken only by Christmas). In town their children went to church schools, after which the most ambitious sought jobs in the city as clerks, teachers, or shop assistants. There they remained working their way up through the lower ranks of the public service as clerks and messengers, and becoming, by the late nineteenth century, a Creole middle class.

'It isn't British you know'

A review of the colony's newspapers for the last quarter of the nineteenth century and first quarter of the twentieth reveals a relentless cry for development from government critics and supporters alike. Certainly the most tireless was the editor of the *Colonial Guardian*, Frederick Gahné, a middle-class Creole who was born in Guyana and started the newspaper in 1882. Gahné saw the need for capital above all, most of which was exported. Week after week he pointed to the need to attract it by means of agricultural experimentation and diversification, opening the colony by road or railroad and improving existing steamship service (nearly the sole form of transport). A staunch nationalist, Gahné favoured local political autonomy as the best way to achieve these ends, but he was as critical of local as of official legislative representatives who seemed endlessly to fail to reach them.

Although the need for capital was noted by colonial critics and supporters alike (Gibbs 1883), Gahné was one of the few to point to the fact that capital flows tended to go in only one direction – out. For this reason, he supported a tax on exports, in effect on landowners. Granting that in 'properly organized countries' where landowners invest their profits in the country, taxes might restrict development, he wrote that here, 'where profits on exports are invested elsewhere, tax away' (*Colonial Guardian*, 29 July 1899).

Gahné perceived that a shortage of capital perpetuated the colony's dependence on government subsidies, thus the Colonial Office's continued ability to restrict development. A point of frustration was the subsidised mail service to the colony. How British Honduras got its mail involved negotiating several different interests, one of them being the export trade to the United States and Europe. British Honduras' commercial activity was too small to support commercial transport, especially in agricultural products; however, an annual government mail subsidy (amounting to $20,000 in 1867) made such a service profitable.

For reasons of empire, shipping had always been via Jamaica, the former seat of government of British Honduras. By the mid-1860s, as the colony's trade with the United States increased, the Legislative Assembly petitioned the authorities to subsidise a mail route via New York instead of Jamaica. This was turned down. With the increase in passenger service from New Orleans at the end of the Civil War, however, it became clear that shipping via New Orleans offered prospects for the cultivation and export of bananas, long stymied due to the lack of an efficient transport system to the US market (the highly perishable nature of bananas meant that New York was never an option in this regard). Thus a petition in 1867 to subsidise a mail route via New Orleans was accepted, and from 1867 to 1871 shipping to that port made trade in bananas possible, resulting in the beginning of banana cultivation on a small scale. The route was not so efficient for European exports, however, and as a result, metropolitan timber interests succeeded in getting the route returned to Jamaica in 1871 (Cleghern 1967: 45-46).

This shift was a setback for banana prospects in the colony, which required only small capital outlays and thus had always been attractive to small growers, even workers. Soon after, Lieutenant-Governor Barlee (1877-82), a strong-minded administrator committed to the development of agriculture in the colony, instituted a number of measures to that end. He changed the mail route to go via New Orleans, allowing Belize again to export to the US market.[8] Against the protests of the major landowners, he reduced the price of Crown land to $1 per acre, and instituted a standard $6 surveying fee. In so doing he hoped not only to attract immigrants, but, equally important, to stem the out-migration of the 'poorer classes', among them unemployed woodcutters, to neighbouring Honduras, where lands were much cheaper (*Colonial Guardian*, August 1882). In order to encourage sugar production, which was beginning in the north of the country by Yucatecan immigrants, he abolished the excise tax on sugar. He tried to impose a land tax, and sought to reform the system of land tenure, since the majority of sugar producers were tenant farmers on large estates, owned by absentee landlords who would not sell, leased for limited periods and 'carefully exclude from such leases anything that may bind the landlord to compensate the tenant for his improvements' (*Colonial Guardian*, 28 May 1882).

These efforts failed, due to the landlords' opposition and their lobbying efforts at the Colonial Office. Sir E. Brodie Hoare, MP, London representative of the British Honduras Company, regularly went to the Colonial Office to lobby against land tenure changes as well as land taxes. Following another tax protest in 1890, one official reminded the Colonial Secretary that 'this tax, though apparently ridiculous in amount, comes to so high a figure on the vast domains of the Belize Estate Co. that even the proposal to make it 1/2c per acre, or $3.20 a square mile ... was defeated in 1879 by the pressure of Mr. Hoare and his friends'. (Olivier to Wingfield 25 April 1890; CO123/194)

Barlee was not the only local administrator to come up against opposition from the metropolitan-based companies. Sir Alfred Moloney, governor from 1891 to 1897, shared the desire to stimulate agricultural development and recognised the potential of sugar cultivation in the north. He urged the construction of transport, which was non-existent apart from the occasional steamer on the coast. For agriculture elsewhere in the country he encouraged immigration as well as agricultural experimentation. But immigration depended on land access, which required a road or railroad system, while the land taxes necessary to construct such a system were continually rejected by the mahogany companies, who relied on the rivers for transport. A proposal that the government build a road from Belize City to Corozal, on the border with Mexico, was predictably declined, the result of a scornful assessment of the region's capacities by the Colonial Office's Sydney Olivier, who had visited the colony in 1890-91, and determined that 'no produce will come this way'.[9]

Moloney also supported various railroad schemes, including several private ones. While accepting the Colonial Office arguments that a privately built line would involve large grants of Crown lands to private investors, thereby making them unavailable to smallholders, he recognised that without a railroad, they would not be accessible to anyone but speculators anyway. Thus he argued that any scheme was better than none, since without a railway there was 'no hope for the future of the Colony of British Honduras'. (CO123/202, 18 April 1894)

Nothing better illustrates the conflicting visions of the colony's future as the history of efforts to develop a railroad, a history integrally intertwined with the fortunes of the colony's most notorious capitalist, C. T. Hunter, whose ill-fated development schemes have become the stuff of legend. Entrepreneur, deal-maker, rogue, C. T. Hunter came of age during the great railway mania that characterised Britain for 40 years after the opening of the Liverpool and Manchester Railway in 1830. Arriving in British

Honduras with a new wave of fortune-seekers in 1853, he was unique in the colony for his efforts to manufacture something – anything. Certain that a fortune could be made through energy and enterprise, he was one of the first to plant coconuts and experimented with machines to make coconut fibre and coconut oil, tried manufacturing cigars and patented a method for extracting gold and silver from ore. Rather than capitalist prominence, however, he gained increasing notoriety; he ran a hotel which was repeatedly fined for operating without a liquor licence, and for his 'foul and offensive privy'.

But nothing Hunter did equalled his canal dredging scheme, in which his efforts to cut costs by piling silt on the colony's streets precipitated an outbreak of yellow fever, and a breach of contract lawsuit which polarised the town and brought on a constitutional crisis. Indeed, in an era of canals and railways, Hunter was truly a man of his time. His schemes to build a railway, pursued through the entire shabby history of efforts to open the colony with a railway from Guatemala in the west to the Atlantic coast of Belize, ended only with his death, under the wheels of a London train, in 1906.

Although interest in a Belize-Guatemala railway began as early as the Anglo-Guatemalan treaty of 1859, with the promise of mutual efforts towards a 'cart-road', agitation for a railway to open up the colony to agriculture began in earnest in 1870, with the opening of a United Fruit railway in Costa Rica and the Honduras Interoceanic Railroad begun in 1869. In 1883 a US investor, Walter Regan, proposed to undertake a survey for a railroad from Belize City to Guatemala, which if feasible would require only a land concession. Upon completing the survey he recommended a southwestern route, through the colony's Sibun River valley, to the Honduras city of Cobán; he estimated a cost of $3 million, and requested land concessions of 12,800 acres per mile of railway.

A Public Meeting in June 1884 drew over 800 people in support of a railway. But there were rival routes. The Regan route went south, largely through Crown land, which would therefore not require financial compensation. An alternative went west, to Petén in Guatemala, largely through private lands; while shorter, it would involve compensation to private landowners. Among those who stood to gain in that way was Henry Fowler, administrator of the colony, who held considerable property along the Petén route; not surprisingly perhaps, he blocked the Regan plan. Fowler's successor, Walter Goldsworthy, supported the Regan plan, but his administration was first bogged down and ultimately discredited by Hunter's project to dredge the city's canals. Hunter himself, however, remained undaunted and in 1895, encouraged by the recent completion of a four-mile tramway in the south, advanced his own railway route, with backing from New York capitalists. This also went west, and thus could not open Crown land, but by this time the southern route had proved too mountainous, and Hunter insisted that his route would provide transport through the agriculturally rich Belize River Valley.

The Colonial Office objected to Hunter's proposal, as it had done to all private proposals, on the grounds that someone might make money: Sydney Olivier accused colonists of wanting a railroad 'in order that the lawyers, promoters, contractors, local landowners, merchants, shopkeepers or labourers there may handle some of the money employed in its construction' (quoted in Ashdown 1979: 96). While residents of the colony considered these to be excellent reasons, the Colonial Office felt that if a railway was to be built the government should build it. It then commissioned its own surveys, at the colony's expense, each designed to show that the proposed project would not in fact be able to pay for itself and therefore a railway could not be built (*Times of Central America*, 31 May 1895).

As a result, as Hunter stated in 1897, 'after 20 years there is no railway, tramway, telephone, telegraph nor postal service whatever into the interior. Belize is without a post-man to deliver letters, is only imperfectly lighted by a few oil lamps and has no water supply'. His revised proposal was endorsed by a public meeting in 1898 and finally by the editor of the *Colonial Guardian*, Frederick Gahné who, though an outspoken critic of Hunter's arrogance, especially regarding the canal dredging contract, nevertheless admired his efforts to break the paternalist grip of Crown Colony rule. In a perverse way, in fact, he succeeded; Hunter's canal dredging activities, his dismissal and subsequent breach of contract suit, and the governor's pre-emptory decision to pay in 1890 resulted in a demand for an unofficial majority and return of the electoral principle of government.[10] The Colonial Office dismissed this demand on the grounds that only Europeans were fit to govern the colony, and there were less than 400 of these.[11] In response, the local representatives, supported by a local People's Committee, walked out of the Legislative Assembly, precipitating a constitutional crisis that resulted in the restoration of local sovereignty in the form of an 'unofficial majority' (that is a majority of non-government officials in the local Legislative Assembly).[12]

In fact, it is possible that nothing Moloney proposed would have been agreed to by the piqued officials at the Colonial Office once he had conceded the unofficial majority in 1892. A proposal to add four elected members to the assembly in 1895 met with particular scorn, and a memo from the West India department called British Honduras the 'least suited of any West Indian Colony for the pretence of representative responsible government'.(CO123/210:2610) The memo accused the governor of having 'grovelled' before the People's Committee's demand for an unofficial majority and being subsequently on his belly in obeisance to a renewed campaign for the right to elected government.

With Hunter's death in 1906 went the last hope of a railway. Reviewing the whole sorry history in 1907 Gahné concluded that, like all improvements, it was 'negatived by the Clerks of the Colonial Office because "it isn't British, you know"'.

Local whites: foreign ties

Hunter's scandalous behaviour in dredging the canals allowed the Colonial Office to take the moral high ground while continuing to delay action on a railroad or open up Crown lands. Agriculture continued to stagnate as the British Honduras Company kept its stranglehold and the land tenure system remained unchanged. In 1915 the government finally introduced a location ticket system by which tenants could gradually purchase land. But this applied only to Crown lands. Private lands were held idle, and at the end of the Second World War the distribution of land had remained unchanged since the late nineteenth century. In 1927 some six per cent of landowners held 97 per cent of freehold land. Ownership had changed, however, as US investors purchased large estates for speculation. A 1959 survey indicated that only 5 per cent of the cultivable land was utilised. Yet in 1971 only three per cent of landowners held over 94 per cent of freehold land. In addition, all but one of those with estates of 10,000 acres or more were foreigners (Bolland 1986: 77). An effort to impose a land utilisation tax in 1966, by which undeveloped lands over 100 acres would be subject to a special tax, heralded as an act of 'economic emancipation', failed due to the success of the Belize Estate and Produce Company in getting its own lands exempted (*ibid.*: 79). In 1971 the company still owned almost one million acres, or almost 42 per cent of freehold land in Belize.

For those with capital, however, land could be purchased in abundance, especially in the south, in the Stann Creek Valley. In the late 1860s two Scotsmen, the brothers Alexander Findlay Bowman and Thomas Bowman, came to British Honduras. Alexander had been a sugar planter in Demarara, and after managing a sugar estate for the Belize Estate and Produce Company in Belize, he bought it and expanded into banana and cattle production. Soon after, as beet sugar cut into cane sugar profits, he converted it completely to banana cultivation. Thomas married into money and died young; one of his sons, Thomas Findlay, acquired the firm of John Harley & Co, a major merchant firm in Belize City, and the other, William Alexander, moved to Stann Creek Valley, becoming the town's largest merchant and the valley's largest landowner. The brothers and their partners (and later, relatives) the Prices and the Sharps, white planters from Jamaica, pioneered citrus growing in the valley.

By then a number of British and American planters were settling in the coastal and valley regions of the south. In 1905, pressured by the United Fruit Company, the British government actually subsidised a small rail line to transport bananas from the Stann Creek Valley (Bowman 1979: 23).[13] To do so, it dismantled the sole existing railway, a five-mile tramway up the Stann Creek Valley built by the British Honduras Syndicate, a group of local growers, in 1892.[14] Ignoring the demands of smallholders, the government also sold some 2,000 acres of land to United Fruit. United Fruit invested heavily in bananas, but William Alexander Bowman ordered the first grapefruit trees from Florida in 1913. Thus in 1918, when bananas were wiped out by disease and United Fruit pulled out, Bowman took over their holdings and planted citrus.[15] By 1943 he had 850 acres under cultivation, increasing to 2,000 acres in 1951. By then he was also supplying trees to other growers in the valley (*ibid.*: 22).

Planters, merchants, landowners, the Bowmans are as close as Belize has to a family elite. Over generations they have married well, adding British and American capital and avoiding Creole colour. Notably, they have stayed in Belize, breaking the tradition of re-expatriating family and fortune. Even so, they owe their success to their ability to attract first British then American shareholders. In 1947, Alexander's son Henry formed British Honduras Fruit Enterprises, with British shareholders, selling out in the mid-1950s to the Colonial Development Company (CDC). Then in 1962 he persuaded Salada in Florida to buy out CDC and build a modern citrus factory (*ibid.*: 28-29). Nestlé in turn bought out Salada in 1978, forming Belize Food Products, a wholly owned subsidiary. By then the renamed CDC (Commonwealth Development Corporation) was investing $6.4 million in the citrus industry (Bolland 1988: 84). Today Henry's son William is director and largest shareholder in Belize's other citrus processing plant, Citrus Company of Belize, as well as the largest private grower. In 1988 he formed a shipping company with a Florida businessman to ship citrus concentrate to Florida and Trinidad and Tobago.

Once dominant in cultural and political as well as economic life, however, the Bowmans stay out of the country's national cultural and political debates. Although they contribute their share to museum and scholarship funds, they do not see themselves as philanthropists; with other local whites they have left civic responsibility, from the Boy Scouts to the Red Cross, to urban Creoles and more recently, Latinos. Politically too, with the change to an elected government, they with other local whites have found it expedient to play a behind-the-scenes role, based on money and contacts, rather than enter the ethnically charged electoral fray. While William Alexander Bowman was active in the legislature in the 1920s and 1930s, his descendants found it more difficult after the long independence struggle and transition to self rule. Henry for a while combined loyalties to Queen and country, hosting the Queen at Stone Haven and representing British Honduras business interests in Britain. Loyalty to Britain appeared to prevail when as a member of the Belize delegation to talks regarding Guatemala's territorial claim, Henry felt obliged to inform the British that the Belize independence leader, George Price, had met the Guatemalans, thereby precipitating a breakdown in talks and engendering serious doubt about Price's loyalties in the minds of those, especially Creoles, who saw Guatemala as the greater menace.[16]

Another prominent local white, Barry Bowen, has increasingly relied on outside capital to finance his development projects. The eldest son of Eric William Bowen, great-grandson of the original doctor and one of Belize's earliest native capitalists, Barry Manfield Bowen inherited his father's entrepreneurial talent as well as his company. In 1987 he was both the wealthiest single individual and the largest private landowner in the country, and taken together his companies were the largest taxpayer and largest employer outside the government (King 1987: 65). In 1981, when he bought a controlling interest in Belize's largest merchant department store, his empire was worth some $23 million (Bolland 1988: 101), embracing some half-dozen businesses, including a Coca-Cola bottling works, the Belikin brewery and a crop-dusting operation. Then in 1983 Bowen bought the former Belize Estate and Produce Company, which by then still held over 700,000 acres, one-eighth of the total land in the country, for $7 million.[17]

Significantly, however, this last purchase, financed with a loan from a Panama banking firm, proved too much, and Bowen was obliged to seek foreign partners. Owing a large sum in back taxes, and unable to meet bank payments, he turned over a portion of the land to government in lieu of taxes and in 1985 negotiated a three-way deal with Coca-Cola Foods and two Texas businessmen, under which each partner received 200,000 acres and jointly owned another 100,000 acres. The deal infuriated local growers, who saw yet another handover to foreign interests. But the newly independent Belize government, then controlled by the long-time opposition party, the United Democratic Party, heralded it as a boost to the citrus industry, and again promised to exempt the new owners from local land use laws.[18]

The citrus growers succeeded in blocking the labour and price concessions promised by the government, however, with the result that Coca-Cola Foods, unable to get political risk insurance and the target of international environmental protests, threatened to pull out. In the end they donated 42,000 acres to the Program for Belize, a non-profit forest management group. Bowen, who maintains residences in Miami as well as Belize, sold 110,000 acres to the Program for $3.5 million, devoting the remainder to a forest-based ecotourism complex, Chan Chich.[19]

Citrus may still end up in foreign hands, however. Growers, who succeeded in blocking the Coca-Cola takeover, now face a challenge from another wealthy former foreigner, Michael Ashcroft, billionaire chairman of the UK/Bermuda ADT Group.[20] Ashcroft, following in the tradition of James Hyde, in 1987 set up Belize's first public holding company, Belize Holdings, of which he is director and majority (66 per cent) shareholder. One of the first undertakings of Belize Holdings was the financing of the purchase of Belize Food Products from Nestlé by a group of Belizean growers, in 1990.[21] Ashcroft was promptly heralded as the saviour of the Belizean economy by the Belize government, which by that time was controlled by the People's United Party, the party of independence and traditionally more nationalist.[22]

Belizean since 1987, when he was also granted citizenship in return for his investments, the 50-year-old international financier refers often to his childhood in Belize, but lives in south Florida and has an office in London, where he is a major Conservative Party fund-raiser. As well as shipping and offshore registers, Ashcroft controls the fate of more than one Belizean company including the Belize Bank, which has the exclusive franchise to sell offshore companies as tax havens to British and US residents, the country's telecommunications and power and electricity companies, its second largest hotel, and its leading local television producer.[23] He recently set up the Michael Ashcroft Foundation, which by financing high-school computer centres may be expected to deflect criticism by any government.[24]

Although a local public investment company could have major benefits for Belize, were it able to encourage the growing number of rich merchants who currently send their money abroad to reinvest in the country instead, the terms by which Belize Holdings operates in Belize indicate yet another form of metropolitan-based ownership. Coinciding with the rush to privatisation in the late 1980s, Belize Holdings came out a big winner: by the terms of the 1990 International Business Companies Act, all income earned by Belize Holdings and all personal income of its shareholders, Belizean or not, are exempted from all property or corporate taxes, sales tax, value added tax, custom or import duty indeed, all taxes of any kind, on revenue, profits or capital gain for 30 years. Although its subsidiaries are subject to 25 per cent of profits in income tax, compared to a local company's average of 45 per cent, its foreign owners and employees are also exempt from income tax.[25]

As the citrus industry, which nurtured the country's regional elite, is increasingly internationally owned, it brings full circle the history of government-sponsored expatriate capital accumulation described here. The independent country of Belize, far from changing the pattern of expatriate accumulation, has facilitated it. The remainder of this chapter looks at this against the ideology of creolisation.

Creolisation and its discontents

Creolisation is frequently defined as a New World synthesis of peoples and cultures. A term employed by scholars and nationalists throughout the Caribbean to describe the development of multiracial societies from a history of colonial oppression and slavery, it embraces a two-way process in which Europeans and the African, Indian, and Asian populations they exploited influenced each other over time, their cultures interacting in complex ways to make up new nations (Brathwaite 1971: 300). The creolisation as synthesis concept gained particular currency in the 1970s and 1980s as national intelligentsia embarked on a process of nation-building based on shared cultures (Bolland 1992: 53). In contrast to the model of a plural society which emphasised the unchanging nature of racial and ethnic hierarchy and conflict, the creolisation model stressed 'an evolving cultural unity' based on 'processes of integration and mutual adjustment between major cultural traditions of Europe and Africa' (*ibid.*: 58).

Turning from culture to people, the concept becomes more problematic, suggesting as it does a gradual blending of European and African and/or Asian populations into a single, creole population. Even those who have championed the cultural synthesis concept see its effects on people somewhat differently. Brathwaite (1971: 296), for example, sees creolisation as a process of cultural change 'based upon the stimulus/response of individuals within the society to their environment and – as white/black, culturally discrete groups – to each other'. Far from blending, peoples' cultural and ethnic identities come into sharper focus precisely in opposition to the changing status of the relevant other. For Creoles in Belize the relevant other depends on history and context, and has been at various times whites, Latinos or Garifuna.[26]

This dialectical process of identity formation is often forgotten, however, when analysing the emergence of a creole middle class in the late nineteenth century. Perhaps because of its importance in the political life of Caribbean countries, the emergence of this class, in Belize as elsewhere, is often not distinguished from the process of creolisation. Since in most places this class also occupied the lower ranks of the civil service, they often saw themselves, and endeavoured to get the British to see them, as rightful inheritors of the right to rule their countries. As this assumption was challenged, beginning in the 1960s in Belize by nationalist leaders of other ethnic groups and a different political vision, this creole middle class began to be identified as a creole elite.

Peter Ashdown, criticising the creole elite in Belize, names some dozen families who remained rich, landed, and self-interested, changing only their colour (1979: 7,18). Acknowledging that the mechanics of this process are unknown, he concludes we must assume that the way in which the 'white oligarchy' of the 1820s had become one suffused with colour by 1900' was by means of 'steady creolisation', a process he describes as increasing 'intermarriage between the descendants of the old Baymen and those of the free-coloured and ex-coloured and ex-slaves' (1978: 50,40). Reflecting widely accepted practice, he lumps Creoles of all shades together, on the basis that no family can have maintained itself as 'white' over time. While this may have some political utility, it is analytically confusing. Suggesting a line from a white colonial elite of landowners and merchants to today's creole middle class of civil servants and shopkeepers, it obscures the process of self-definition by whites as well as Creoles, and their very different location on the economic and political spectrum.

The word 'Creole' derives jointly from the Spanish *criar* – to nurture or raise – and the Portuguese *criollo*, meaning slaves born in the houses of their masters. Thus historically in the Caribbean as well as Latin America, it means anyone born locally, whether white or black. In Belize, the late nineteenth century saw both the white and the coloured middle class stressing shared local or 'Creole' identity in an effort to gain a degree of political autonomy from the British colonial rulers. By the mid-twentieth century, as middle-class black Creoles identified with the colony's history and traditions in an effort to take over the leadership, whites separated themselves, and began to call themselves 'local whites'. Later still, as non-Creole nationalists, more radical as well as ethnically diverse, denounced middle-class black Creoles as elitist and colonialist, membership in a local creole elite, with a tradition of long residence, had lost all political value and whites felt no pressure to claim their place. Today, Belize's self-identified 'local whites' simply do not participate in the political discourse of nation-building. This frees them from the process that identifies prominent families with one of the two major political parties. In part as a result, the family name is far more important to – and conveys far more about – Creoles than it does whites.

The break in 'white settler dominance' in the mid-nineteenth century was never repaired. In 1890, when a combination of white expatriates and Creole 'natives' joined to form the People's Committee and two years later succeeded in wresting a degree of political autonomy from the British Colonial Office in the form of an unofficial majority, they could never again attain the economic dominance of the early settlers. A loosely knit group of whites and Creoles, some of whom could trace their association with Belize back less than 50 years, they shared neither origin nor class interest; what united them was a desire to allow local interests to prevail in decisions governing the colony.

In the late 1800s, however, a small group of middle-class Creoles, including members of the People's Committee, began to self-consciously associate themselves with the colony and its future, forming literary and debating clubs and friendly societies, founding newspapers and writing for them, and speaking publicly about their place in history. Aware of the significance of the 100th anniversary of the Battle of St George's Cay, several of them formed a St George's Cay Centennial Committee, intended to get the British to recognise the anniversary as an official holiday. To this end they drew on every claim, both by descent and by sentiment, to identify themselves with the colony's history. The Battle of St George's Cay in 1798, in which residents and their slaves, backed by a small British force, succeeded in fighting off a far larger Spanish invasion fleet, was regarded by some as the basis for the British claim to sovereignty. The most prominent orators, Benjamin Fairweather, Wilfred Haylock and Henry Charles Usher, all claimed descent from those who had fought, and H. H. Vernon, as he seconded the resolution calling for a national holiday, referred only to 'our ancestors' (*Clarion*, April 8, 1898). Their most eloquent point was that masters and slaves had stood 'shoulder to shoulder', a theme echoed by the editors of both newspapers, in part, as Gahné pointed out, to refute the arrogant assertion of Lord Knutsford that because sufficient whites were lacking, Belizeans were not able to govern themselves.[27] A commemorative stamp proposed for the occasion featured a white soldier and a black soldier, both in uniform, clasping hands over a banner reading 'Shoulder to Shoulder' (enclosure in Newton to Chamberlain 29 June 1898).

The Battle of St George's Cay, in which the Spanish were repelled by a combined force of settlers and their slaves, represents the cultural expression of the Creole middle-class origin myth, described by Alexander (1984: 174) as the original union of a white master with a black slave, relating kinship and family to race, class and status. Not only does the story of the battle establish the original association of black slaves and white masters from which Creoles are meant to have descended, it does so in a way that overwhelmingly proves their patriotism and loyalty, and also, as I have argued elsewhere (Judd 1989), their claims as 'natives' or 'true Belizeans'.

Men of their time, they used their Baymen heritage to invent themselves as natives, and thereby play a role in the destiny of the colony they inhabited. These claims as natives link these 'prominent individuals' to the so-called creole elite identified by Ashdown in 1979, primarily those who asserted native identity in order to resist independence in the face of Guatemala's continuing claim to Belize. Yet this group makes up even less of a coherent class than the People's Committee of 1890. Of these four families, the Bowens, the Ushers, the Hydes and the Haylocks, can claim descent from the original Baymen who fought at the Battle of St George's Cay. Their family histories, however, exhibit very different trajectories. The Bowens, whose original white ancestor married into creole property, carefully 'whitened' in succeeding generations. Today, the Bowens along with later arrivals, including the Burns, the Hunters and the Bowmans, are self-defined 'local whites', seeking marriage as well as business partners in England and the United States. The Ushers and Haylocks, from a similar original union, followed the idealised path of creolisation, marrying locally, and becoming gradually more dark-skinned. Only the Ushers managed to hold on to wealth and property. The Hydes exhibit a third form. James Hyde, like William Usher, produced a Creole lineage, but Hyde returned to England in 1830, where he died in 1858, leaving his property to his white family in London. His creole son in Belize got little but a house in town.

The other nine families that comprise Ashdown's creole elite are Creoles of various classes and ancestry. Three of them, the Woods, Vernons and Fairweathers, like the Ushers and Haylocks, are light-skinned, middle-class and count their ancestors among the Centennial Committee of 1898. The Vernons and Haylocks, descended from petty bourgeois shopkeepers, are mostly professionals; they inherited too little to accumulate property and solidify elite status. The Woods, descendants of lawyers and newspaper men, proved that the professions cannot sustain elite status over time. The Fairweather ancestor was not white, early, or propertied; despite his claims in 1898, he was the son of a free-coloured man and a Miskito Indian who arrived in Belize long after the Battle of St George's Cay and became a master carpenter; any property he managed to accumulate was sold by his family to pay off his debts. Finally, the Goffs and the Ottleys, dark-skinned Creoles, have little money and less property; upstanding, intensely patriotic, they form the backbone of the lower middle-class creole tradition.

The grouping of these families together as those who have advanced their own interests at the expense of the country for generation after generation has considerably diluted the status of family and tradition in the public arena. The traditional Creole holiday of the anniversary of the Battle of St George's Cay was attacked by the nationalists in the 1960s as pro-British, a charge that is still levelled in a party political context. Indeed, the fracas in the bar with which this chapter began, was prompted by the reprinting of an article by Ashdown on the anniversary of that battle, which was designed to link middle-class Creoles with a colonial mentality.

Thus no one wants to be considered elite, and certainly not a memeber of the Creole elite. This represents a loss for Creoles, especially those whose ancestors struggled, with little wealth and less property, to become part of the political debate about the colony's direction and in so doing create themselves as actors in their own history (Judd 1992). It forecloses the public validation of racial and class pride they might take in this successful struggle.[28] For whites, it is convenient, allowing them to keep their economic dominance separate from the political debate. Few trace their origins before the present century, and only one before the mid-nineteenth century.

Equating family history with that of the country is not important to whites, who have no need to invent themselves as natives. Their power derives not from their economic dominance but precisely from their ability to divorce their legitimacy from their origins, their associations, their loyalties, even their residence.[29] Native-born or recent-ly arrived, whites are whites; membership in the 'old families' is as meaningless as dis-tinctions between true and other Belizeans. This is convenient not only for newcomers, but also for local whites, whose ancestors were most likely mixed.[30]

Divorced from local history and tradition, white status is more inclusive, at least geographically, allowing newcomers and old families equal membership. Today, US and British families who have arrived in Belize in the last two decades, make up the same social network as the Bowens, who descend from the Old Baymen.[31] Next to the Hunters, whose bad boy, C. T., fathered several creole children in addition to a 'local white' lineage, the Bowens come closest to the creolisation model – only in reverse. The 1808 interracial union between Manfield William Bowen, white doctor and magistrate, with Mary Hickey, an educated free-coloured woman who had inherited slaves from her white father, was repeated when his son formed a union with a free-coloured woman, Mary Elizabeth Hume, one of the largest property owners in the north (CO 123/23). Thereafter the Bowens attended to eliminating the Creole connection: interracial mar-riage became virtually non-existent over time.

Lisa Douglass (1991) points out the ways in which elite families define their histo-ry, sorting out legitimate and illegitimate lines as well as less than pure-white shades of colour. But she underestimates the influence of the colonial authorities in this process; their ability to inscribe both colour and legitimacy into the archival record is at least as powerful over time as the process of 'elite memory'. Indeed, in Belize at least, the will-ingness of family members to acknowledge 'outside' members provided linkages and connections that would never show up in the official records. This willingness, howev-er, at least for local whites, reflects their ability to stay out of damaging controversies. By not contesting the belief that all Belizeans have some coloured ancestry, they are less subject to attack and thus less noticeable; their uncontested status as white outside Belize, along with their international economic ties, small social networks and econom-ic elite status inside Belize are as a result also less noticeable.

A problematic category

The struggles over the significance of the Battle of St George's Cay today, as in the nine-teenth century, are carried on among elites, and primarily intellectuals and politicians. The people, including the broad mass of black and working-class Creoles, merely cele-brate. Similarly, the struggle for an unofficial majority, like the 30-year struggle for a railroad, was one between elites; specifically between the representatives of empire – at Government House and the Colonial Office – and articulate nationalists of all sorts,

whether unofficials, radical lawyers, capitalist adventurers, or local newspaper editors –
all those who wanted a more active role in the development of the colony. The 'people'
did not have a political voice until 1954, when the majority of the Legislative Council
was elected on the basis of adult suffrage.

Both sides claimed to represent 'the people' as well as 'the good of the colony';
their views of how this was done derived from their political ideology and their geo-
graphic and class location. Local nationalists believed both were best served by a more
aggressive capitalist development of agriculture and trade with both Central America
and the United States, rather than merely with Britain. Depending on their class interests, as merchants, planters, professionals, or shopkeepers, they differed over
land-tenure policy, franchise qualifications and taxation. The Colonial Office believed
the people were best represented by an enlightened class of gentlemen who would protect them from capitalist exploiters. While governors sometimes supported the inhabitants, and in the case of the railroad did so repeatedly, they were dependent on decisions
of the Colonial Office and ultimately the Treasury. Both offices were the preserve of
Britain's aristocratic younger sons, who looked down on merchants and other businessmen, regarded non-Europeans as unfit for self-government, and were ultimately respon-
sive to tight fiscal policy and the gentlemen representatives of London mahogany firms.

It should be noted that despite the concession of the unofficial majority, the Crown
retained the power of the purse as well as the final authority to make the laws. Crown
servants made up the officials in the Legislative Council and personally chose the officials. Moreover, the governor could overrule the unofficials if backed by the Colonial
Office, while all expenditure had to be approved by the Colonial Office and the Treasury
– hence the history of unbuilt roads and railroads. In the belief that better-off Europeans
were most qualified to govern, governors appointed resident managers of London merchant houses and European merchants and planters to the colonial legislature, then criticised them in the name of the people when they acted in their own interests.

Since the oft-quoted judgments of colonial administrators and Colonial Office
clerks have been crucial in Creole historiography, it is worth a brief examination of who
they were. Among the most genteel and privileged of the British public service were the
Foreign Office, where Robert G. W. Herbert, grandson of the first Earl of Carnavon, and
first cousin to his future chief at the Colonial Office, Lord Carnavon, was permanent
under-secretary from 1871 to 1892, and the Treasury, where Sir Michael Hicks-Beach,
eighth baronet, Sir G. H. Murray, kin to the Duke of Athol and Sir Edward Hamilton,
relation of the tenth Earl of Belhaven, held sway. Herbert wrote many of the scathing
judgments of the early 1890s, along with Sydney Olivier, later a baron and member of
the House of Lords.

Public school and Oxbridge products, these men – whether Tories (as most were) or Socialists, like Olivier – abhorred businessmen almost as much as 'the great unwashed', as Herbert called the majority of the colonists (Blakeley 1972: 39). They were chosen precisely in order that they could hold their own with the titled Colonial Secretaries of the 1890s, including Henry Holland, first Viscount of Knutsford, George Robinson, the Marquis of Ripon, as well as members of Parliament such as Sir Brodie Hoare and Baron de Worms, representatives of the Belize Estate and Produce Co. It is little wonder that when a public meeting in British Honduras resolved that the council be changed to a majority of unofficial members and elections be reintroduced, Herbert fumed this would be 'tantamount to surrendering the public interests to a small handful of disloyal and job-bing traders' (Herbert to Knutsford November 27 1890, CO 123/ 195).[32]

To uncover the continuing source of white economic dominance it is necessary to separate economic and political identities, historically and in the present. From the 1890s to the rise of the working-class and independence movements in the 1950s, government in Belize changed in composition from mainly expatriates to mainly Belizeans, from mainly whites to mainly blacks. So too did contending nationalist intellectuals and newspaper editors. Over this period, foreign (mainly British and American) commercial interests continued to hold the land and dominate the economy – a system which favoured the local commercial elite. But that elite changed primarily from a small group of white, local and British merchants, backed by British capital, to a small group of white local and American merchants, backed by US capital, although this group gradually expanded to accommodate Middle Eastern and Asian newcomers as well as the more successful Latino families. By contrast, the 'good Creole families' changed from being landed white resident gentry to various shades of black shopkeepers and lower-level civil servants, with little land or capital. The class and ethnic nature of this group, the so-called Creole elite, and their efforts to link their own history with that of the colony, can only be understood in this context.

The only major exception to the prevailing pattern of outside ownership is the state, which in Belize as elsewhere has become both major landowner and primary employer. The state sector, which includes education as well as the civil service, historically provided the major avenue of upward mobility for educated professionals. By the 1940s and 1950s Creoles began to obtain positions in the state bureaucracy, from which they might have been able to acquire land and other economic assets as the state took a strong role in national development in the post-colonial period. However, the resistance of most of the Creole civil servants to the terms and timing of Belize's declaration of independence in 1981 was such that rather than endure their opposition, the prime minister appointed advisers and aides from outside the traditional civil service. As a result

Latinos have been able to play an equal if not greater role in political and economic decision-making.

The recognition of the role of the state in the creation of an ethnically diverse petty bourgeoisie focuses attention on the ways in which this heterogeneous class, often considered a state-based elite, consciously and unconsciously operates to reproduce itself. A weak and fragmented working class encourages entry into the state sector (Thomas 1984), which increasingly recruits the sons and daughters of the working class; yet it offers few avenues of enrichment. The inertia characteristic of all bureaucracies stifles initiative and encourages the ambitious, once they have learned the rudiments of a profession, to go elsewhere to apply those skills. Those who have reached the top rungs of the civil service now encourage their children to aim higher; the traditional entry points of messenger or typist that enabled one generation to climb into this sector are not the jobs to which their better educated sons and daughters aspire. Thus the civil service that once provided jobs for children of Creole woodcutters and blacksmiths now provides them for the children of Garifuna fishermen and dockworkers (Wright 1986).

The constant flow of upwardly mobile young employees retards the development of common interests and thus of class consolidation and consciousness. Indeed the state, which offers opportunities for external education and eventual external employment in lieu of competitive wages and rewards for initiative, discourages the formation of class-conscious public employee unions. In Belize (as elsewhere), the Public Service Union's interests are often opposed to those of the industrial or agricultural trade unions (Grant 1966: 38; Kroshus Medina 1988). By draining workers out of the most exploited sectors of the working class and offering them a way up and ultimately out, the civil-service sector (the primary location of the petty bourgeoisie) becomes the ultimate 'escape valve'; its very openness simultaneously helps to keep an already weak working class weak and undeveloped and does not encourage the creation of a new class within its own ranks – since the acquisition of skills as a ticket out is in most cases worth more than the opportunities for advancement within the system or profit within the local economy.

It should be clear that the Creole elite of urban shopkeepers and civil servants occupies the class position of the petty bourgeoisie in Belize, lacking for the most part both property and wealth, at least in any sense that the term has comparative meaning.[33] Despite their basis in kinship ties, this group does not extend over several generations. Although many Creole families trace their ancestors to the early settlers, white or free-coloured, the 'elite' among them consist of only a handful of local merchant representatives, along with shopkeepers, carpenters, and clerks. The rest comprise a much more fluid group, whose ancestors had in the main worked themselves up, in successive generations, from unskilled woodcutters and skilled craftsmen – carpenters, blacksmiths, mechanics, and ship pilots – to low-level messengers and clerks in the civil service. Their middle-class status derived from education and the traditional, though declining prestige of the British civil service. Not only did most of these families not accumulate much in the way of wealth or property, they have, with few exceptions, historically lacked any opportunity to do so.

More even than class, therefore, the concept of elite is essentially relative, referring as it does to the top segment of any social category, from society as a whole to any occupational group. A Creole elite, rather than a group of kin-based Creoles who reproduce themselves as an elite group over several generations, means only those at the top of Creole, or Caribbean, society, at any given time. In Belize, as elsewhere, this chapter has argued, this elite is not Creole, but white.

Notes

1. The term 'creole' in Belize (as elsewhere) once identified native-born people, whites as well as slaves and free blacks. It now denotes people of varied ancestry, which always includes an African component. Creoles in Belize are distinguished from Garifuna (see also note 26), a black population whose ancestors descended from Carib Indians and escaped slaves on St Vincent. The native-born white population now call themselves 'local whites'.

2. Party affiliation runs in families in Belize; thus even those who claim they dislike both parties are invariably identified with one or the other.

3. Runciman defines capitalism as 'a mode of production in which formally free labour is recruited for regular employment by ongoing enterprises competing in the market for profit'. While formally free wage labour can and frequently does coexist with other forms, including debt servitude, kinship obligations or slavery, capitalism by this definition requires that free wage labour be dominant in the economy as a whole.

4. See survey in the *Financial Times*, 22 September 1992.

5. As Foucault (1984: 82) points out, genealogy as an analysis of descent cannot bestow meaning on history. Family histories are too fragmentary, too diverse, interrupted, multiple, various and accidental. They represent an accumulation of details that coalesce into meaning only within a shared context. In short, they tell their own stories; they cannot be used to prove a case.

6. Some of these operated as partnerships, with one partner conducting business in Belize and the other in London, where he could press his interests with the secretary of state. In time, however, the majority of them became centred on the metropolis, hiring professional estate managers to carry on the Belize side of the business.

7. In this respect British Honduras was very unlike Jamaica, where according to Douglass (1991), whites with families in Jamaica tended to stay on after emancipation, changing the white population from an 'expatriate to a resident community'. The 'British prejudice against commerce', which, she notes, opened the way for resident Jews and Scots in Jamaica, simply discouraged a resident commercial class in Belize.

8. In contrast to the monthly Jamaica service, the New Orleans service was every two weeks (Gibbs 1898: 157).

9. CO123/199 minute of Olivier 26 November 1892, on Moloney to Ripon. Olivier did not tolerate local upstarts and was dismissive of all locally elected members of the Legislative Council. Benjamin Fairweather, a creole of mixed Indian and coloured ancestry, 'counted for nothing' and R. H. Logan was described as 'a debauched creature' (CO123/210).

10. Hunters canal dredging operations, breach of contract suit and its arbitration, which provoked a walk-out of unofficial members, and the consequent constitutional crisis and demand for an unofficial majority, are described in Ashdown 1979.

11. The rejection, by the head of the Colonial Office, R. G. W. Herbert, outraged local creoles, and was reprinted frequently in Gahne's editorials: 'In a colony on the mainland of Central America, having relations with foreign countries for which the Crown is responsible, containing only about 400 inhabitants of European descent out of a total of 30,000, it is impossible for Her Majesty's Government to surrender its control over legislation and finance.' *Colonial Guardian*, 30 December 1890).

12. In the administrative structure governing British Crown Colonies, government officials were also a majority in the legislature, the rest, the so-called unofficials, being appointed by the governor to represent the masses (Smith 1982: 115). Because of these appointments, a number of authors have concluded that the colony's success in obtaining an unofficial majority, which lasted from 1892 to 1931, was not really significant.

13. The British relationship to United Fruit demonstrates that the colonial authorities' dislike of capital could be overcome, so long as the amount was large enough. In 1900 the shippers who held the mail contract were taken over by United Fruit, which had banana plantations in Central America. When the company declined to give preference to bananas grown in Belize, another company tried to get the contract, but the government insisted on paying a subsidy to United Fruit, despite the protests of its local members. Predictably, with the collapse of competition, United Fruit promptly raised rates to exporters. *Colonial Guardian*, 3 November 1900, 8 December 1900, 29 June 1901, 8 September 1901, 16 November 1901.

14. *Colonial Guardian*, 11 June 1892.

15. He later dismantled the United Fruit railway and sold the track and stock to the Belize Estate and Produce Co, which was constructing a private logging line (Wright 1977).

16. Guatemala's claim to Belize is based on the fact that Spain never recognised British sovereignty over the territory of British Honduras. A treaty between Britain and Guatemala in 1859 stipulated that Britain would build a road from Belize City to the border, which of course it never did. Although in 1992 Guatemala finally recognised Belizean independence, it still has not relinquished its claim.

17. *Financial Times*, 3 October 1985, which added that this was reported to be the largest single piece of potentially arable land in the whole of Central America.

18. Belize became independent in September 1981 under the leadership of the People's United Party (PUP), which lost to the United Democratic Party (UDP) in the elections of 1984. The UDP, which opposed independence under PUP leadership, was widely believed to be more pro-American than its rival.

19. For information on the Coca-Cola purchase, protests and pull-out, see: *Miami Herald*, 30 September 1985; *Financial Times*, 3 October 1985; *New York Times*, 11 July 1987; *Belize Briefing*, June 1987; *Houston Chronicle*, 2 November 1987; *Miami Herald*, 9 October 1988.

20. In July 1996 this electronic security and car auction company was purchased by fellow Florida billionaire Wayne Huizenga, owner of Republic Industries, for $4.4 billion. Ashcroft was to act as chairman for about a year, after which he was to remain a director of Republic Industries. *Sunday Times*, 7 July 1996

21. It was reported that Ashcroft would serve as chairman for approximately one year, after which he would remain a director.

22. The PUP won the national elections in 1989 and governed until 1993, when the UDP was returned to power.

23. See *Miami Herald*, 20 November 1994. With an announced NASDAQ equity of $136.6 million in June 1995, BHI holdings included a 75 per cent ownership in Panama Telecom Inc. in order to participate in the planned privatisation of the government-owned telecommunications industry, a $1.6 million interest in Grenada Electricity Services Ltd resulting from govern-

ment privatisation, construction and food processing interests in the Turks and Caicos and Cayman Islands, and food processing operations in Guyana. In December 1995 it also invested $7 million in Energia Global Inc., a US-based power project in Central America. See *Belize Times*, 25 June 1995, 17 December 1995.

24. The computers are part of the Information Technology Teaching Programme, a joint venture with the UDP government to which the Ashcroft Foundation has contributed $305,000 and the government $45,000. *Belize Times*, 3 December 1995.

25. See the London *Observer*, 23 June 1991.

26. Latinos, locally known as 'Spanish' came initially from Yucatan to the north, and increasingly Guatemala and El Salvador to the west. By 1991, they had become the majority population, making up 43.6 per cent, while Creoles had fallen to only 29.8 per cent. Garifuna, who came to Belize from neighbouing Honduras early in the nineteenth century, make up only 6.6 per cent. They retain a distinct culture, however, which is centred in the southern towns of Dangriga and Punta Gorda. At one time looked down on by Creoles as less cultivated, the two have become allies against the Latino 'aliens' in citrus growing areas (Kroshus Medina 1992: 8) have now joined Creoles in teaching and civil service jobs. Maya Indians, the other major population group, comprised some 11.1 per cent of the population in 1991 (Government of Belize 1992).

27. In 1898 he wrote: 'The one great cause that knit master and slave together in British Honduras, giving rise to a society more resembling the clans of Scotland than slavery – the master acting as Chief and the slaves as faithful and obedint clansmen was the undying hostility of Spain against those strangers who had dared invade and hold this portion of her extensive dominions'(2 April 1898).

28. The de-legitimising of the public arena for these families has pushed elite family pride inside in gendered ways. Thus men, who would be expected to represent the family in the public arena, had to be sought out at home, where they were glad to present family history to this outsider; while women, who might have been expected to control information in this domain,

more often introduced me to their men, deferring to them as having greater knowledge, or in some cases, as spokesmen. In at least two cases ultimate knowledge was acknowledged to rest with women, much older women, but they remained hidden, their knowledge jealously guarded and private. By contrast, at least two men represented themselves as knowledgeable when they were not.

29. In this they may be unlike whites elsewhere in the Caribbean. Douglass (1991) argues that whites in Jamaica equate family and nation, with the result that 'attachment to family is tied to their roots in Jamaica's past'.

30. Again unlike Jamaica, white identity includes no memories of a planter way of life. Mahogany camps, rather than country houses, were the prevailing residence pattern of early inhabitants, while nineteenth-century administrators and merchants lived in town.

31. It occasionally extends to families of Middle East origin, such as Palestinians, Syrians, and Lebanese, who arrived around mid-century, began as merchant traders, married women from local white or Latino families and entered import business, real estate, and tourism.

32. Information on Colonial officials is taken from Blakeley 1972: 32-42; Cannadine 1990: 239-44; Arnstein 1973; Roseveare 1969: 173-178.

33. While the US Embassy (1993) reported gross domestic product per head at $2,170 in 1992, but its distribution is unknown. The average income for paid employees was about $6,000 per year in 1988 (Bolland 1988: 94). Salaries for educated professionals average about $8,000-16,000 in the private sector and much less in teaching or the civil service. Secure housing is increasingly expensive and rents in what are considered safe areas of Belize City are equivalent to those in New York City. A 1995 declaration of politicians' assets reported only two or three millionaires whose net worth was over BZ$1 million, or US$500,000. *Amandala*, 26 November 1995, 24 December 1995.

Bibliography

Alexander, Jack, 'Love, Race, Slavery, and Sexuality in Jamaican Images of the Family', in R. T. Smith, (ed.), *Kinship Ideology and Practice in Latin America* (Chapel Hill: University of North Carolina Press, 1984) pp. 149-80.

Arnstein, Walter L., 'The Survival of the Victorian Aristocracy', in F. C. Jahèr, (ed.), *The Rich, the Well-Born, and the Powerful* (University of Chicago Press, 1973).

Ashdown, Peter, 'The Colonial Administrator as Historian: Burdon, Burns and the Battle of St. George's Cay', *Belizean Studies* 15:1 (1987), pp. 3-14.

—. 'Race, Class and the Unofficial Majority in British Honduras, 1890-1949', Ph.D. diss. (University of Sussex, 1979).

—. 'The Problem of Creole Historiography', *Journal of Belizean Affairs* 7, (1978) pp. 39-53.

Blakeley, Brian L., *The Colonial Office, 1868-1892* (Durham: Duke University Press, 1972).

Bolland, O. Nigel, 'Creolization and Creole Societies: A Cultural Nationalist View of Caribbean Social History', in Alistair Hennessy, (ed.), *Intellectuals in the Twentieth-Century Caribbean* (London: Macmillan, 1992)

—. *Belize: A New Nation in Central America* (Boulder: Westview, 1986)

—. *The Formation of a Colonial Society: Belize, from Conquest to Crown Colony* (Baltimore: Johns Hopkins University Press, 1977).

Bolland, O. Nigel and Assad Shoman, *Land in Belize, 1765-1871* (Kingston: Institute of Social and Economic Research, 1977).

Bowman, Henry T. A., *Emerald Valley and Twinkling Town*, (Belize: Stone Haven, 1979)

Brathwaite, Edward, *The Development of Creole Society in Jamaica, 1770-1820* (Oxford: Clarendon Press, 1971).

Cannadine, David, *The Decline and Fall of the British Aristocracy* (New Haven: Yale University Press, 1990).

Cleghern, Wayne, *British Honduras: Colonial Dead End, 1859-1900* (Baton Rouge: Louisiana State University Press, 1967).

Douglass, Lisa, 'The Power of Sentiment: Love, Hierarchy, and the Jamaica Family Elite'. Ph.D. diss. (University of Chicago Press, 1991).

Foucault, Michel, 'Nietzsche, Genealogy, History', (orig. 1971), reprinted in Paul Rabinow, (ed.) , *The Foucault Reader* (New York: Pantheon, 1984).

Gibbs, Archibald Robinson, *British Honduras: An Historical and Descriptive Account of the Colony From Its Settlement, 1670.* (London: Sampson Low, 1883)

Government of Belize, *1991 Population Census, Major Findings (*1992).

Grant, C. H., *The Making of Modern Belize* (Cambridge University Press, 1976).

Judd, Karen, 'Elite Reproduction and Ethnic Identity in Belize', Ph.D. diss (Graduate Center of the City University of New York, 1992).

—. 'Cultural Synthesis or Ethnic Struggle? Creolization in Belize', *Cimarron* 2:1-2 (1989).

King, Emory, *100 Years of Brodies in Belize.* (Belize City, n.p.,1987).

Medina, Laurie Kroshus, 'Class, Nation, and Ethnicity', paper presented to the 91st Meeting of the American Anthropological Association, San Francisco (1992).

—. 'Creating and Manipulating Power Within Dependency: The Citrus Industry in Belize', *Belizean Studies* 16:3(1988) pp. 2-13.

Roseveare, Henry, *The Treasury: The Evolution of a British Institution* (New York: Columbia University Press, 1969)

Runciman, W. G., 'The "Triumph" of Capitalism as a Topic in the Theory of Social Selection', *New Left Review* 210 (1995) pp. 33-47.

Smith, Raymond T., *Kinship and Class in the West Indies* (Cambridge University Press, 1988).

—. 'Race and Class in the Post-emancipation Caribbean', in Robert Ross, (ed.), *Racism and Colonialism* (The Hague: Martinus Nijhoff, 1982), pp. 93-119.

Thomas, Clive *The Rise of the Authoritarian State in Peripheral Societies* (New York: Monthly Review Press, 1984).

US Embassy, 'Economic Trends, Belize' (Belize City, 1993).

Wright, Christopher, 'Railroads of Belize', *Belizean Studies* 5: 4 (1977).

Wright, Pamela, 'Public Sector Work for the Garifuna: Class Formation, Ideology, and New Ethnic Symbols', *The Journal* (1986).

8

Ethnicity and Social Change in Curaçao

RENÉ A. RÖMER

Many of the societies currently described as multi-ethnic, came into existence as a consequence of the expansion of western European countries in the fifteenth, sixteenth and seventeenth centuries. From Portugal and Spain, and later from England, France and Holland, people spread over the world to the different continents. Wallerstein has argued that these migrations laid the foundation for what he called a 'world economic system' which shows relations
of dependency between these European countries and the societies that came into being as a
result of these migrations. Caribbean societies clearly exhibit the characteristics that
Wallerstein described. They are multi-ethnic and demonstrate dependency on western
Europe.[1] In this paper I will limit myself to the multi-ethnic aspects of these countries will
be discussed, with special reference to Curaçao, the largest island of the Netherland Antilles.

Curaçao was discovered in 1499 by an expedition under the command of Alonso de
Ojeda, one of the earliest *conquistadores*. The first *encomendado* (commander) of the island,
appointed in 1527, was Juan de Ampiés, who never set foot there. After unsuccessful efforts
by Lázaro Bejarano, de Ampiés' son-in-law, to develop the island in the sixteenth century,
the Spaniards lost interest.[2] The island was considered a useless island that could not be made
profitable, and so was easy prey for the Dutch, who had already penetrated the *mare claus-
trum* of the Spaniards in search of a foothold in the Caribbean from which the enemy (Spain)
could be attacked and salt could be obtained. In 1634 the Dutch took possession of the island
with only passive resistance from the Spaniards. Contemporary Curaçaon society has its origins in the colonisation that followed this conquest and subsequent developments. Little, if
any, evidence of Spanish colonisation is detectable in the present-day society.

We are indebted to Harry Hoetink for the first systematic analysis and description of the development of Curaçaon society.[3] The old society, as opposed to the new society that came into being in the twentieth century after the establishment on the island of the Shell refinery, had as early as the seventeenth century developed into a multi-ethnic society. It consisted of three main ethnic groups: the northern Europeans, who were predominantly Protestants, the Sephardic Jews who, originating from the Iberian peninsula, arrived in the island in the 1650s and 1660s from Amsterdam and Brazil, and the Negro slaves who were West African in origin. Through miscegenation between the two first-mentioned groups and the Negro slaves, a mixed-race group emerged which, in the seventeenth century had not yet developed a distinct identity. As a creole culture started to emerge through a process of the gradual merging of the different cultures, the identity of this mixed-race group started to take shape. The members of this group, more than those of the other groups, became bearers of this creole culture in which new customs and a new creole language, Papiamentu, emerged. One can say that by the late eighteenth century, a fourth ethnic group had developed which, although not homogeneous in the racial sense, was considered different from the existing ethnic groups and which considered itself different from the other groups. They were referred to as *de vrife lieden van de couleur* (the free people of colour), although in official documents we find that they were sometimes grouped with the slaves. That they were considered a distinct group is evident from Governor Feasch's establishment of a coloured militia for Otrabanda in 1749. This militia was even authorised to detain whites who did not adhere to the regulations which were introduced at that point.[4]

The process of racial and cultural mixing continued during the eighteenth century. By the beginning of the nineteenth century, Papiamentu had already developed its present morphology. The text of Monsignor Niewindt's catechism, first printed in 1825, shows little difference in syntax and grammar from today's Papiamentu. I mention Papiamentu here because this   creole language, over time, has played an important role in the gradual erosion of ethnic boundaries it has been. I have elsewhere referred to Papiamentu as the core of Curaçaon identity.[5]

Developments in the nineteenth and especially the twentieth centuries in the racial and cultural domains resulted in ethnic boundaries becoming increasingly blurred. This is certainly true of the Protestants, who were divided between the more aristocratic families, referred to in the sociological literature as the 'higher' Protestants, and the 'lower' Protestants, who were also considered different as whites from the lighter coloured people. The 'white honoris causa', as the novelist Boeli van Leeuwen called the lighter coloureds, who used to act as a kind of buffer group were gradually assimilated into the white group.[6] Quite a few of them who were originally Catholics accepted Protestantism for status reasons. The somatic image, the colour of the skin, the texture of the hair and other physical features helped, however, to maintain the fiction of a white Protestant group. The difference between white and light coloured which had, by the early nineteenth century, been characterised as more myth than reality, became increasingly artificial and gradually lost its social significance.[7] Although this development was already discernible by the beginning of the twentieth century, it was accelerated by the establishment of the Shell refinery on the island in 1915.

The establishment of the Royal Dutch Shell Company's refinery brought about fundamental changes in the social and economic structure of this mini-society.[8] The operation of the Shell refinery led to a substantial in-migration of whites from Holland, which disturbed the concept of 'whiteness' as understood by the local population, including the whites. These immigrants, who were European in their behaviour in contrast to the local whites, were called *makamba,* a pejorative term. There was also a substantial influx of Afro-Caribbean people who were contracted by the oil company because Curaçao could not supply the demand for labour. These workers were mainly Protestant but did not conform to the image of Protestantism as a white religion. Both groups of immigrants disturbed the *weltanschauung* of the core population (that is the population in its different segments as it had developed since the Dutch conquest of the island), for whom *grosso modo* whites were associated with Protestantism or Judaism and non-whites with Catholicism.

Initially, the differences in denominational affiliation and culture helped to keep the division intact. There was, on the one hand, the local creole culture and, on the other, British Caribbean or Surinamese creole cultures. Thus the Afro-Caribbean immigrants were different even if they professed a Protestant faith. Not only were they perceived as different by the core population but they also regarded themselves as different. They spoke another language, professed a different variant of Christianity, had other customs and, moreover, a different historical experience. Given these differences, the Afro-Caribbean immigrants can be defined as new ethnic groups, in the sense in which Alofs and Merkies have characterised the immigrants in the Aruban society, by referring to the immigrant associations as 'ethnic clubs'.[9] Green also refers to these immigrant associations as 'ethnic associations'.[10]

Confronted with these newcomers, the Curaçaon core population became more conscious of its common cultural heritage which had developed in the local creole culture, the product of the diverse cultural elements of the original ethnic groups. This was the first step in experiencing the creole culture as a national culture. The economic development which followed the establishment of the Shell refinery and the concomitant social mobility resulted in the further development of a white and coloured middle class that would become the bearer of this national culture. The situation was simplified because the original ethnic groups of the core population drew closer to each other in a new middle class, on the basis of a 'we' in-group feeling. The picture, however, became more complicated because of the presence of new ethnic groups. In this changing context, different designations such as 'we Curaçaon' (*nos yu di Korsou*) and child of the land (*yu di tera*) were widely used to distinguish the native-born from the newcomers.

The situation described above did not long persist. The children of the Caribbean immigrants quickly assimilated the local variant of a shared Afro-Caribbean culture, appropriating the local language, customs and folklore. They remained on the island after their parents left when Shell laid off employees as part of its streamlining and automation policy. In the 1970s the political parties ceased treating these descendants of the immigrants as distinct groups in Curaçaon society. Up to that point it had been the practice to have a separate Surinamese or European-Dutch or Caribbean (Windward-Islander) candidate on the voting list. That kind of development is less true of the European-Dutch who had established themselves on the island between 1920 and 1950. Their children generally returned to Holland, sometimes even before their parents, for post-secondary education.

What were the long-term consequences of these changes in the social structure there? It is important to note that race (somatic image) and religion were the two main elements in defining the original ethnic groups in Curaçao, both of which reinforced each other. Despite the gradual emergence of a national culture, religion (in addition to race) had long played an important role in distinguishing the different groups within the community. The Afro-Caribbean Methodists, Anglicans and Moravian Brothers, for example, were not welcomed in the Fort Church, the stronghold of the Dutch Reformed Church, not only because of the difference in religious denomination but also because of their racial antecedents. It is difficult to disentangle religions and racial considerations for religious arguments were often used to justify racial discrimination. This is clear, for example, from the colonial government's failure to compensate the Moravian Brothers for the salary of its first Negro minister on the same terms as his white colleagues, although he had similar qualifications. Before arriving at this decision, the governor had solicited the opinion of the United (Reformed) Protestant Church, whose pastor had made that recommendation as representing the general view.[11]

After the Second World War the erosion of ethnic boundaries based on race and religious difference) accelerated with the arrival from Europe of religious leaders who brought with them a completely different way of thinking. They had intimately experienced the folly of excluding people from social and religious institutions on racial or religious grounds. They were more liberal in their thinking and strove for more cooperation and unity between the churches. In 1962, for example, the Council of Churches was instituted, an organisation in which the different Protestant churches participated. In 1964 a second important step followed when the first non-white minister was appointed to the United (Reformed) Protestant Church. In 1974 a second non-white minister was appointed to the Fort Church. These developments had more than a symbolic meaning. In fact, the significance of the adjective 'Protestant' as the bond of a white ethnic group had become definitely eliminated. Whites and non-whites now professed their religion in the same church and participated jointly in its administrative bodies.

There was in this period yet another dimension of social change. With the arrival of a new European Dutch professional elite, the old Protestant elite lost its privileged position and gradually became part of the new middle class. As a result of the changes in the group's social status, its members have become increasingly assimilated to the creole culture. This does not alter the fact that, when it suits them, they stress their whiteness. Such an attitude is, however, generally not condoned and is considered an anachronism at a time when the Rotary and Lions Clubs, formerly bastions of white exclusiveness, count a high percentage of non-whites among their members. In this situation of social change, marriages between the descendants of the old elite and lighter coloureds are no longer the exception. The concept 'white Protestant' now denotes only a certain heritage, and no longer an ethnic group.

How did all these developments affect the Sephardic Jews as a distinct ethnic group? Did they have an eroding effect on the boundaries of this group too? Did the term 'Sephardic Jew' lose its meaning as the designation of an ethnic group with its own religion, history, culture and language? It is necessary to investigate whether the Jews became integrated into the wider society by participation in a more secular cultural tradition.

To Karner we owe a diachronic study of this group which deserves our attention.[12] Her main argument is that four generations of Sephardic Jews that she included in her survey gradually went through a process of secularisation. She analyses this process which took place during the twentieth century and led to the gradual loosening of the ethnic boundaries and its eventual disappearance. Karner divides her sample into four generations: 1855-80, 1880-1910, 1910-25, 1925-40. From the late seventeenth century until the end of the nineteenth century, Judaism was a source of pride within this group and consequently there was a strict adherence to long-established Sephardic customs. Endogamous marriage was regarded as highly desirable and children were named for their paternal grandparents. Sephardic families were determined to retain their cultural identity and religious convictions and, in general, maintain their heritage intact.

Two factors were of major importance for the survival of the Sephardic Jews as an ethnic group: the names, which should be considered as identifiable symbols of a common origin, and the Jewish religion, which was an even stronger unifying factor, setting the group apart from the rest of Curaçaon society. The generation born at the end of the nineteenth century (1880-1910) started, however, to exhibit a more secular attitude, breaking with the tradition of naming children after their parental grandparents by giving non-biblical names to their offspring. This first step on the path to secularisation took a more radical turn with the generations born between 1910 and 1925 and 1925 and 1940. The two most important developments were the cross-religion marriages, first of Jewish women with non-Jewish men and later of Jewish men with non-Jewish women.

Several factors explain this change of attitude. There were the changes in the economic and social structure of the island and the influence of education, both on the island as well as abroad. Parental influence that pressed for maintaining traditional values and norms was offset and, to a certain degree, even undermined by the system of public education which provided a forum in which regular contact among all social sectors took place. This childhood experience culminated in producing young adults with behavioural patterns that diverged appreciably from the norms of behaviour of earlier periods.[13] The establishment in 1941 of the first high school (a public school financed by the government) on the island meant that the youth from different segments of the society encountered each other on a new basis. Protestants, Jews and coloured Catholics all attended the only existing high school and had to compete on an objective basis. Catholic children, who were predominantly coloured, had traditionally enrolled in Catholic schools run by friars and nuns. Protestant and Jewish children had attended public schools. Although not many marriages can be traced to the school years, the social barriers between the groups definitely started to crumble as a result of this common experience. No less important was the fact that increasingly the young adults, after finishing high school, went to Holland and the United States for further education, away from the traditional environment. Liberal thinking on religious and social matters in the academic world in those countries did not fail to influence their attitude towards the long-held views of their own society. The idea of being basically different, mentioned by Shibutani and Kwan as an important element in ethnic self-identification, was gradually eroded.[14]

Other factors were the changes in the island's social and economic structure. Economic development resulted in social mobility, for positions that were previously held only by the whites in the society, in government by the Protestants and in commercial enterprises by the Jews, were gradually occupied by the new coloured middle class with college and university education. In the 1960s service clubs like the Rotary and the Lions began accepting as members coloured men with leading positions in the community. In theory, this more liberal attitude on the issue of colour does not necessarily imply a narrowing of social distance, but here it did result in changes in practice. Noticeable in the last 25 years are marriages, not only of Jewish men with non-Jewish (white) women but also with light-coloured native and foreign women.

What do these developments mean in terms of preserving an ethnic identity? As mentioned earlier, two important criteria for identifying the Sephardic Jews as an ethnic group in twentieth-century Curaçaon society are the use of original Sephardic names and the practice of Judaism. Although Sephardic names are still used, the evidence of the persistence of

Judaism depends on what is understood as its defining characteristics. The question arises because of the noticeable increase in the number of inter-religious marriages. If Judaism means more than attending services in the synagogue and celebrating the Bar Mitzvah and implies a way of life, then one might ask if non-Jewish wives do not find themselves in the extremely difficult position of having to educate their children in a religious tradition in which they were not brought up. This question is the more important since, according to Jewish tradition, it is the mother to whom the children's education is entrusted. She is responsible for passing on traditional Jewish beliefs and for teaching them to observe Jewish law, customs and ceremonies.[15] The conclusion that we can draw from this increase in cross-religious marriages among Jewish men with non-Jewish women is that Judaism in its true meaning is in decline, becoming no more than a religious tradition centred on the synagogue and with little influence on daily life in the family and in the community. This is partly due to the secularisation process that accompanied the modernising influence of the Shell refinery. The same process was also noticeable among Protestants and Catholics. The Jewish congregation is aware of this development and regards Hebrew lessons and Torah classes as countervailing influences.

In modern Curaçao the Sephardic Jews, like the Protestants, can no longer be considered as a distinct ethnic group. They are often referred to as the Curaçaon Jews or the Jews of the Netherland Antilles[16] because they are assimilated to the creole culture and identify themselves with what I referred to as the national culture, which is a core of common cultural elements they share with the middle class. The term national culture may be somewhat vague but it does comprise the language, music, dance, cuisine and local customs connected to important events in everyone's life.

No attention has been paid in this chapter to the Ashkenazi Jews and the Christian Lebanese immigrants who started to come to the Curaçao in the 1920s. Their presence on the island has been too recent to have influenced the cultural developments dealt with here in this paper. As far as religion is concerned, it can be argued that the process of secularisation that took place in the other ethnic groups is also applicable to them.

Up to this point, the social changes in Curaçaon society have been largely understood as being related to the process of modernisation which was prompted by the establishment of the Shell refinery. This was an evolutionary process of social change. Of a more revolutionary nature were the events that occurred on 30 May 1969, which have often been (and still are) referred to as the revolt of the 30th of May, when serious disturbances took place on Curaçao, especially in its capital, the historic city of Willemstad. A great number of striking workers marched into the city where they overpowered the police and stormed into the business centre, looting, destroying and setting fire as they went.

The immediate cause of this eruption was the deadlock in the negotiations for a collective labour agreement between the union (the Curaçaon Federation of Workers, CFW) and Wescar (Werkspoor Caribbean), a contractor working for Shell. The negotiations had been dragging on for months and had resulted in tensions on the labour front. CFW had received support from workers at several other companies. The real causes, however, were more deeply rooted and were intimately related to the racial social structure.

Despite the upward mobility which was made possible by the expansion of the economy, a significant part of the black lower class, the descendants of the slaves, did not profit from the new opportunities. Although this group has collectively benefited from economic growth in terms of an improvement in their general living conditions (the provision of electricity, running water, medical care and education), it has remained at the bottom of the social structure. The black man or woman remains the worker: a position in the social structure which is a vestige of the slave society.

In Curaçao, as in other Caribbean societies, it is difficult to distinguish between race and class; there is a correlation between socio-economic class and race. In a society marked by a substantial degree of social mobility, from which some coloureds have benefited, this must lead to social tensions. The effect of the disturbances of 30 May should be seen in terms of both racial and class consciousness. The black worker became conscious of his class position *vis-à-vis* the new middle class. The complementary reaction was the growth of a class consciousness within this new middle class which transcended ethnic and racial lines. In fact, one can say that the effects of the May 30 accelerated the process of social change which was already under way. A society originally divided along ethnic lines is increasingly giving way to a society differentiated along class lines.

Notes

1. I. Wallerstein, *The Modern World-System* (New York, 1974).

2. Carlos Felice Cardot, *Curaçao Hispanico* (Caracas, 1967), pp. 40-72.

3. Harry Hoetink, *Het Patroon van de oude Curaçaose Samenleving* (Assen, 1958).

4. J. Schiltkamp and T. de Smidt, *West Indisch Placaatboek* (The Hague, 1978), p. 265.

5. René A. Römer and Het Wij van de Curaçaoenaar, *Kristòf*, I (1974), pp. 49-60.

6. Boeli van Leeuwen, *Rots der Struikeling* (Curaçao, n.d.).

7. H. J. Abbriing, *Weemoedstonen uit de Geschiedenis van mijn Leven of mijn Reis naar Curaçao*, (Groningen, 1834). See also J. Hartog, *Curaçao, van Kolonie tot Autonomie*, II (Oranjestad, Aruba, 1961), p. 789.

8. René A. Römer, *Un Pueblo na Kaminda* (Zutphen, 1979).

9. Luc Alofs and Leontine Merkies, *Ken ta Arubano?* (Leiden, 1990), p. 106.

10. Vera Green, *Migrants in Aruba* (Assen, 1974), p. 65.

11. *Archives of the Government of the Netherlands Antilles.*

12. Frances Karner, *The Sephardics of Curaçao: a Study of Sociocultural Patterns in Flux* (Assen,1969).

13. Karner, *op. cit.*; Eva Abraham van der Mark, 'Marriage and family in a white Caribbean Elite', *Anthropologica*, XXII (1980), pp. 119-134.

14. T. Shibutani and K. T. Kwan, *Ethnic Stratification: a Comparative Approach*, (New York, 1965).

15. Leo Jung, *Essentials of Judaism* (New York, 1957), pp. 12-13.

16. Isaac S. Emmanuel, *Precious Stones of the Jews of Curaçao, Curaçao Jewry, 1656-1957* (New York, 1957); Isaac S. Emmanuel and Suzanne A. Emmanuel, *History of the Jews of the Netherlands Antilles*, (Cincinnati, 1970).

9

French Republicanism under Challenge: White Minority (*Béké*) Power in Martinique and Guadeloupe

FRED CONSTANT

Les békés[1] *sont des judokas. . .ils retombent toujours sur leurs pieds. (Békés* are like judo masters ... they always land on their feet.) With this critical metaphor, Jean-Luc Jamard (1983), after Jean Benoist (1972) and Edith Kovats-Beaudoux (1968), pointed out one of the most striking features of the social history of the French Caribbean: the remarkable persistence of the influence of the white minority, dubbed *békés*. The contemporary French Caribbean has been formed by five key historical processes: the abolition of slavery (1848); the gradual application of republican laws such as universal adult suffrage (since 1848 but particularly since 1870); the implementation of the law of *départementalisation*[2] in 1946 (full incorporation of the 'old colonies' into the French administrative and political system); the French national administrative reform of *décentralisation*[3] of 1982; and the Single European Act (*Acte Unique Européen)*[4] of 1993. At each of these moments, the *békés* succeeded in adapting, protecting and reinforcing the base which defines them as a white ethnic minority of power in a predominantly black insular society. On one hand, there is a fascinating continuity in the successful assertion of their economic dominance and in the stability of their political influence. On the other hand, *békés* demonstrate a surprising flexibility and adaptability through which they are taking advantage of the changing world. Given the growing dependency of French overseas departments on the financial benevolence of the French state and the widespread acceptance of the republican value of equality, it is impressive that such a pressure group, which is as well an ethnic minority, still forms the undisputed and unavoidable, economic elite of these particular territories.

However, this phenomenon remains little known and is still under-researched, not so much because it has not attracted the attention of social scientists but because of the difficulty of investigating such a highly politicised topic. Accounting for this original form of economic hegemony and political lobbying is certainly not a straightforward intellectual undertaking. For a long time the *békés* generated a passionately Manichean debate in which even hard facts – insofar it was possible to establish them[5] – were denied on grounds of principle. There have been two dominant approaches to the study of *békés* which can be called 'ideological' and 'angelic'. The first denies any legitimacy to *békés* considering them modern-day *négriers* (slave-holders) who use close ties to certain political circles in France to keep Martinique and Guadeloupe subordinate to the metropole (Cabort Masson 1987). The second considers *békés* to be full and equal citizens like any others, albeit ones with particular business acumen (Sablé 1972). To some extent it is still difficult to escape from these two ideological frameworks, which have more to do with politics than with scientific ethics.

Because of the inadequacy of standard approaches, this study is an attempt to break with these ideological predicaments in order to suggest an alternative analysis. A preliminary historical sketch is necessary to explain the differences between the *béké* question in Martinique and Guadeloupe. Then I will focus on *békés'* strategies to reassert their economic dominance and political influence. I will examine how and to what extent, lobbying by *békés* interferes in the policy-making process both at the national and local levels. In conclusion, I will make some final comments about citizenship, ethnicity, class and equality.

Historical background

There are few regions in the world where history has been so critical in shaping the present as in the Caribbean. Patterns of social interaction were based on uneasy, violent relationships between colour, class and income. Slaves were brought over from West Africa so rapidly that by the 1660s they were already outnumbering the whites. Martinican and Guadeloupean whites saw themselves as the sexual, as well as material, masters of their domains: the mulatto offspring of master-slave relations soon came to constitute an intermediate, yet crucially distinct, class between the white masters and the black slaves. Contemporary Martinican (and to some extent Guadeloupean) society still bears the traces of this tripartite white/mixed/black division whereby the land is owned by *békés*, the liberal professions are occupied by the lighter-skinned mulattos and the lower classes are largely composed of the darkest-skinned blacks. Yet there exist some significant differences in the socio-racial structure of the two islands, particularly in the relations of power between *blancs créoles*, mulattos and more recent white arrivals from metropolitan France. The French Revolution abolished slavery in 1794 (it remained for Napoleon, at the behest of his *béké* wife Joséphine, to re-establish it eight years later). While the *békés* of Martinique put the island under British sovereignty during the revolution in order to avoid the implementation of this short-lived reform, in Guadeloupe the French revolutionary commissioner Victor Hugues freed the slaves and crushed the resistance of the *blancs créoles*, whose survivors were forced to leave the island. Thus while in Haiti the abolition of slavery was to be a major event in the process of colonial emancipation, in Martinique continuity has prevailed over discontinuity in spite of the definitive abolition of slavery in 1848. In Martinique *blancs créoles* remain the economic, as well as social, elite of the island; however, in Guadeloupe their supremacy has weakened, due not only to Guadeloupe's revolutionary history, but to the greater influence there of metropolitan French capital since 1848. In addition, many of the *békés* in Guadeloupe are of Martinican origin (having settled there after the Revolution to fill the void left by the exile or execution of their Guadeloupean kin). The higher degree of outside control of the Guadeloupean economy has meant that its expansion has been slower than that of Martinique, where local control is far greater.

The introduction of French Republican reforms of 1870, such as the establishment of local elected assemblies in the Caribbean colonies, illustrates the capability of *blancs créoles* to turn the winds of change blown from mainland France to their advantage. The implementation of universal adult male suffrage from 1871 led the *blancs créoles* to change their political strategy. As they were an arithmetic minority, they were obliged to manipulate the emerging coloured political class in order to maintain their privileges and to adapt to political changes beyond their control. Since the last quarter of the nineteenth century, their political lobbying efforts have consisted in using their economic power as a political tool. The sources of this economic power, historically linked to slavery, were threefold. First, as the descendants of the colonists, they became the first landowners. Most of them were granted tracts of land free of charge, according to the provisions of the *concessions royales*, by means of which sugar islands were settled in the first place. Few of those who arrived in the islands as *engagés* (contracted workers) became full landowners after a period of three years. Second, they never stopped controlling the whole process of sugar-cane production and as such they were the biggest employers. The ex-slaves formed a cheap and abundant labour force without any legal protection. The sugar-cane production technology and the commercial networks were also under the white minority's control. Third, they established a banking system (*Crédit Martiniquais*, which is still in business) which gave them considerable financial autonomy. Because of this deeply entrenched economic power, it was not difficult for them to take advantage of the mulatto newcomers in politics and the low political awareness of the former slaves, now citizens. In Guadeloupe the situation was different for the reasons mentioned above, but the same type of arrangement between the mulatto politicians and the influential *blancs créoles* existed, albeit on a smaller scale.

The policy of assimilation, the gradual application of the civil and political rights to every one in the 'old colonies' came to a climax in 1946, when Martinique and Guadeloupe (as well as Réunion and French Guiana) were transformed into overseas departments. Since then the official policy has been *départementalisation* the administration of Martinique as an integral part of the French Republic, with, theoretically, all the corresponding rights, duties · and laws applicable to any French department. The *blancs créoles* campaigned vociferously against the incorporation of the 'old colonies' into the national administrative French framework. *Départementalisation* was opposed because it was perceived as a component of the (re)centralisation of the administration of Martinique and Guadeloupe and the start of the expansion of the state's presence in the islands. It was expected to reduce the extensive autonomy the white minority used to enjoy in the management of local affairs. *Départementalisation* was also rejected because the advanced legislation of a highly developed country (France) was regarded as unsuitable for small, remote, backward insular societies like Martinique and Guadeloupe. Thus *békés* were the first advocates of local autonomy and the concept of 'cultural differences'.

Finally, *départementalisation* was contested because it was seen as a shift from a paternalistic system with poor 'second-class' black citizens as clients to one where the disadvantaged were granted full and equal protection under the French state. The implementation of welfare legislation (such as social security and pensions) in the 'old colonies' was obviously contrary to their interests as entrepreneurs. The growing popular response to local parties and trade unions which promoted *départementalisation* was, of course, not congruent with their political interests. In other words, the white minority feared that *départementalisation* would achieve what the abolition of slavery had failed to carry out a century earlier: the transfer of power to the black majority. Local black politicians, however, very early foresaw the positive political consequences of an administrative reform they had been hoping for for almost a century. In their struggle against the white minority, the French state was their more efficient partner. Consequently, *départementalisation* became synonymous with decolonisation. It was expected to pave the way for an original form of political emancipation: decolonisation by integration.

For the reasons mentioned earlier, the *blancs créoles* did all they could to boycott or slow down *départementalisation*. Indeed, *the békés'* success in impeding the establishment of the social benefits of *départementalisation* has fed a general dissatisfaction with the process. Many resent the remaining inequities between the overseas departments and the metropole which persist, despite the ostensible full citizenship enjoyed by West Indians; for example, the minimum wage is lower in the islands than in metropolitan France. In addition, a high rate of unemployment (about 35 per cent) has engendered a wide-scale emigration to the mainland and an important influx of white (dubbed *métros*) civil servants from France into the insular public administration. Assimilation has also created concerns over cultural identity: are Martinicans and Guadeloupeans African, are they French or are they other? As Miles (1986:7) wrote: 'while all acknowledge that Martinique 'exists' by virtue of the enormous transfer of funds from France, it is a case of classical Latin American *dependencia* turning into Nietzschean *ressentiment*'. Taking advantage of confusion in local politics as well as contradictions in French national policies, the *blancs créoles* have challenged French republicanism: their resistance to *départementalisation*, and their adaptation to it, has favoured continuity over wide-scale transformation.

Welfare colonialism at work: The reassertion of *Béké* economic dominance and political influence

After 1946, despite the increasingly direct penetration of the French state and its value system, the white creole minority was to reinforce its dominant position in the 'old colonies'. The arrival from the mainland to the overseas departments of the doctrine of republicanism did not serve to effect fundamental change in the socio-racial structure of the insular societies. Nor did it promote a new philosophy of development which could have weakened the economic position of the *békés*. How can this continuity despite official change be accounted for? How can the reassertion of the white minority's economic dominance, despite the activism of politicians of colour who hold most official positions be explained? Such questions have generated a few serious studies but a number of controversies. Most studies stress the external factors which are deemed to protect and encourage the local hegemony of the *blancs créoles* and internal factors are evoked only to the extent that they are influenced by them.

The domination of the white creoles is attributed to several external forces, notably the role of the French state as 'broker': the alliance or collusion of the mainland bourgeoisie with the *Békés*, and the backing of national politicians. A monocasual explanation cannot account for the specific circumstances of space (Guadeloupe and Martinique) and time (before or after *départementalisation*) which have permitted the reassertion of *beké* dominance. Such commonly expressed views are of little help in explaining the case at point. The *Békés'* relations with the French state and with local politicians of colour reveal apparently contradictory trends. In some cases cooperation prevails over conflict, and in others, competition prevails. For instance, the dramatic rise in influence of Martinican and Guadeloupean nationalists at the end of the 1970s put the *beké* question on the local political agenda, while the Mitterrand administration placed the issue of economic development firmly back into the centre of the political debate. Furthermore, neither the *blancs créoles* nor the French form a homogeneous entity: both are highly fragmented organisationally and ideologically. The

French national state, the mainland bourgeoisie, or the national politicians have not always shared the views of the *blancs créoles* or served their private interests. To some extent, the latter have suffered from uneven capitalist development as well as from excessive government control.

It is possible to formulate a general hypothesis and point to common features and tendencies. The dominant position of the white minority is related to the skill of its leaders in taking advantage of state intervention at the periphery. Thus the critical capacity of the *blancs créoles* to convert French national public funds into private profits has been the key to their reassertion as an economically as well as politically influential minority. This approach has the advantage of bringing external and internal parameters to the analysis. It can be argued that as long as *départementalisation* was a challenge to *béké* hegemony, *békés* have challenged, and altered its implementation; but insofar as this process of full incorporation of the 'old colonies' into the French administrative and political system has coincided with their private interests, it has been strongly supported. The same dialectic may be observed with regard to local political parties. On the one hand, the *béké* lobby took advantage of left-wing dissatisfaction with *départementalisation* to lobby for more French national subsidies to local economic activities, mainly in the agricultural sector. On the other hand, the *békés* benefited from right-wing backing to obtain special national financial packages (block grants) to modernise the local economy.

Their control of land has been the main source of their adaptation to the changing politico-economic environment. Here two dominant strategies have been closely connected. The first has been to sell unproductive agricultural land when it was not possible to mechanise the exploitation of it or to build tourist resorts on it. This has been the main internal process by which *békés* have raised money in order to reassert their economic dominance. The second has been to exploit close ties to certain mainland political circles to increase state assistance in order to modernise the local agricultural sector. This external fund-raising has been the main source of the *békés'* penetration into tertiary-sector activities. The combination of these two strategies have raised a large amount of public funds which have been turned into private profits. Not only did this money help to modernise sugar-cane production and diversify agriculture (in the cultivation of commodities such as bananas, pineapples, citrus fruits and avocado), it has also been the main source of *békés'* investments in tourism, real estate and import and export. *Départementalisation* has entailed the rapid integration of an agricultural, tropical economy into a highly developed, industrially-based European one.

The economic and social results of this process have engendered some paradoxes from which the *blancs créoles* as economic entrepreneurs have benefited. On the one hand, it bought material advantages, such as a higher standard of living and a modern educational system for many people. On the other hand, these material advantages are artificial and illusory, based not on the productive forces of the country, but on a fostered dependence upon an ever-paternalistic 'neo-colonial' power. The local productive economy has virtually disintegrated, but the consumer society is comfortably implanted. The incentive to cultivate the land has disappeared, especially for the young, in the wake of the rapid, perceptible devolution of wealth to the fastest growing sector of the workforce, civil servants *(fonctionnaires)*. The *békés* are accused of having abandoned the employment-generating agricultural sector (while still possessing 50 per cent of the cultivable land in Martinique) to make their twentieth-century fortunes in modern industrial activities. They are often held to be responsible for the island's bleak trade deficit.

Some claim that Martinique's and Guadeloupe's growing dependence on the metropole for financial support is a 'false problem'. Considering the economic as well as political unity of the French Republic, it can be argued that analysing their economies as distinct entities does not make sense. As departments of France, their citizens benefit, even through transfer payments, from the productive capacities of the rest of the country. In this analytical framework, the *békés*, who are full and equal French citizens like any other Martinicans or Guadeloupeans, cannot be held responsible for the plunge in local productive capacity. As entrepreneurs, they are free to invest where the benefit is supposed to be most attractive, notwithstanding the consequences for the islands. However, others, especially those who advocate greater autonomy or independence, view the *békés* as a dangerous economically dominant minority whose private interests run counter to the imperatives of local development. In Martinique and Guadeloupe, those who take the latter view are a minority. Most people are primarily concerned with maintaining a fairly high standard of living, however illusory it may be.

Politics and policy making

In order to understand the contemporary influence of the *békés* on politics and policy-making, it is necessary to resort to history. Since the extension of universal adult suffrage overseas and the emergence of a political class of colour, the white minority has obviously no longer been able to hold public official positions. Thus *blancs créoles* felt obliged to intervene in the political process by dividing the new politicians. Given their control over the land as well as the economy, it was not difficult for them to convert their economic dominance into political influence. This process started openly in the nineteenth century and came to a climax in the 1950s. Clerc and Bougenot, *békés* of Martinique, succeeded for about 25 years in dividing the emerging mulatto republican political class by raising the racial issue: mulatto politicians were accused of betraying the blacks and becoming the *Békés'* allies (Constant 1988: 49-65).

The process of *départementalisation* resulted in two aspirations which are apparently contradictory. These may be defined as the 'right to roots' (geographically defined rights such as local autonomy and territorial identity) and the 'right to options' (rights rooted in universal principles such as liberalism and socialism). In some cases[6], the *blancs créoles* based their lobbying on the acknowledgement of their French citizenship and universal rights and values applicable to all French citizens; in others,[7] they based their lobbying on the excesses of the virtual completion of the integration process into France. Thus, the *békés* have alternatively or simultaneously advocated increased local autonomy from France and more protection of the French state, that is, a 'right to roots' and a 'right to options'. But the 'right to roots' they still demand (in rhetorically admirable terms) has more to do with their private local profit than with a self-reliance approach to development, which was in the 1970s, the core of the local political debate.

Contrary to commonly held beliefs, the *blancs créoles* gave support not only to the local right-wing political parties, but also to left-wing political parties. *Békés* are pragmatic above all: no ideological framework definitively structures their strategies, which are entirely devoted to the protection of their private profits. One can distinguish four historical sequences throughout in which they were successively in favour of more local autonomy from France and, on the contrary, in favour of more incorporation into the French national system; against the penetration of the European Community and in favour of it. Each situation is distinct and has led to different political alignments. In the 1940s they did their best to prevent the implementation of *départementalisation*. The main objective was to keep Martinique and Guadeloupe under colonial rule, which meant second-class citizenship and a low-wage local economy. At that time the *blancs créoles* were contesting the legitimacy of France's integration of a tropical, rural economy and society into a highly developed, European one. In the 1960s when *départementalisation* began to be criticised by its former local left-wing advocates, the *békés* used their close ties to certain right-wing political circles in the mainland to keep Martinique and Guadeloupe subordinate to France. Demands for local autonomy gave way to an unmitigated allegiance to France, a rhetorical adherence to its political institutions, its universal liberal values and the policies of *départementalisation*. In the 1970s, the European Community became a growing preoccupation for the white creole minority, which feared the penetration of foreign international firms into the small overseas economies and the end of their long economic monopoly. Right-wing politicians were pressed to protect the overseas departments from this invasion.

As long as the European Community appeared to be a threat to the white minority's economic dominance, it was criticised and contested. But since the 1980s, when the *blancs créoles* began to benefit from European Community funds, they became pro-Europe as far as their private profits were concerned. At each of these periods, the *blancs créoles* offered their financial assistance to national (white) and local (black or mulatto) politicians as long as they supported their views. Both at national and grassroots levels they often succeeded in imposing their personal and informal views as the official policy of Republican France. To a significant extent, European and French economic and financial actions in the 'old colonies' have been converted into private profits.

Looking ahead

In forecasting future developments, two significant trends are already discernible. First, there is a trend towards the reinforcement of *blancs créoles* as a separate social and economic group. Second, there is an opposite trend toward their integration into the wider society. These contradictory phenomena will be discussed before examining their political implications.

Are the *blancs créoles* becoming more integrated into the wider Martinican and Guadeloupean society? Are they now more commonly recognised by the numerically dominant civil society of colour as equal members? Two recent developments must be taken into consideration. To start with, there is a growing professional migration of younger *békés* to the French mainland or North America. Many of them have decided to escape the traditional professional activities of the white minority in favour of other activities such as architecture, journalism or medicine. After graduate study, most choose to settle outside their native island. Although kinship networks and family ties remain strong, they are much more open-minded than their parents with regard to the tradition of segregated social intercourse. There is also, particularly in Martinique, a rapprochement between young, dynamic *békés* and the wealthy, educated milieu of colour. Associated with mulatto economic entrepreneurs, they are forming an emerging and influential multi-ethnic bourgeoisie, especially in local professional institutions such as the Chamber of Commerce and Industry, where such close cooperation is becoming increasingly common. These multi-ethnic joint ventures, although still exceptional, are putting an end to the traditional closeness of the white minority, but this rapprochement is still limited to business, and has not been accompanied by matrimonial alliances[8] or private socialising. It may, however, indicate a new trend. Alternatively do the *blancs créoles* continue to view themselves as separate from civil society and maintain distinct boundaries of cultural and social identity? Although they can of course no longer maintain the full extent of the colonial privileges they once enjoyed, the changes described seem to be superficial when compared with the remarkable continuity of the core of white minority economic dominance which consists of matrimonial strategies and financial hegemony.

Racial purity is still a central feature in the matrimonial strategies of the *békés*. There is tight social control over marriages and those who do not respect the rule of endogamy are excluded from the group. Until now, the white minority has been structured along this racial principle, which is linked to its internal hierarchy. Matrimonial strategies are also closely tied to economic strategies. We have seen how the *blancs créoles* succeeded in taking advantage of the changing economic and political environment. From the abolition of slavery in the nineteenth century to the incorporation of the French Antilles in the European Community in the twentieth, they converted public funds into private profits, advocating more local autonomy, more integration into the French administrative system, as it suited their economic interests.

Of these two contradictory trends, which will prevail? Will they result in the realignment of the socio-ethnic stratification of the elite and in significant changes in social and political behaviour? The two chief approaches to the study of the *békés*, 'ideological' and 'angelic', are linked to the 'two France paradigm' (Miles 1986), which posits two faces of France, one good, the other bad. The good France is republican France, the France of the Revolution, the France which abolished slavery, the France which decolonised, the France which gave Martinicans and Guadeloupeans the suffrage and citizenship. It is the France of *liberté, égalité, fraternité* – the France of the Left. This France denies legitimacy to *békés*, who are held to be responsible for Martinique's and Guadeloupe's economic decline. Because they have preserved a tradition of segregated social intercourse and financial hegemony in the islands, they have become the universal targets – if not scapegoats – of all the left-wing political formations, and are frequently accused of keeping the territories subordinate to the metropole. The bad France is, on the contrary, the colonial, reactionary, slave-holding, Napoleonic, imperialistic France of the right. If the good France has granted rights and freedoms, it is the bad France which has taken them away; it is still threatening to do so through an insensitive, culturally imperialistic version of assimilation. That is the France that protects the *békés'* interests against the predominantly black population and considers maintaining economic hegemony to be the best hope for Martinique and Guadeloupe.

Paradoxically, it was the election of the socialist, François Mitterrand, as president of the French Republic in 1981 which was to attenuate the analytical usefulness of the 'two France paradigm'. With the accession of the left-wing guardians of the Good France to the control of a state largely fashioned by the right, and the transformation of the left from an opposition to an administration, previously clear ideological distinctions became blurred. In the wake of the presidential elections, the Antillean left (except for the radical fringes) changed its rhetorical attitude towards France, white metropolitan French resident in the island, and even the long-lambasted *békés*. Preference for a reconciliation with the white minority started to prevail over the traditional rhetoric of hostility, which has substantially decreased. Nowadays, *békés* are no longer denied any legitimacy. Their recognition as dynamic entrepreneurs seems to be widespread. If they happen, from time to time, to generate controversies, these controversies are now focused on the modalities by which they may best contribute to the economic development of the islands.

Notes

1. It is difficult to give an up-to-date estimate of the demographic weight of the *blancs créoles*. According to Kovats-Beaudoux (1968) Kovats-Beaudoux (1972) and Cabort Masson (1993), there are about 3,500 in Martinique and less than 500 in Guadeloupe. In both islands, but particularly in Martinique, there is an internal hierarchy (*grands békés*, middle-class *békés*, *petits blancs*) based on the combination of two main factors: wealth and patronymic (and to some extent education). There are about 150 *blancs créoles* surnames, of which 16 represent almost 50 per cent of the total population. Thirty-nine per cent of the *blancs créoles* settled before 1713, 22 per cent settled between 1713 and 1789, 35 per cent arrived in the nineteenth century. The *grands békés* represent between 10 and 15 families and are said to be the oldest and wealthiest. The middle-class *békés* are much more numerous. They are said to be less wealthy and more recently settled in the islands. The *petits blancs* are mostly employees in *grands békés* businesses.

2. France is divided into 101 departments, which are the main executive and administrative unit of the country. Four of these departments – Martinique, Guadeloupe, French Guiana, Réunion are overseas departments (*départements d'outre-mer or DOM*). These overseas departments participate in France's presidential elections and their inhabitants are entitled to the same political rights and freedoms as all citizens of mainland France. Thus all Martinicans and Guadeloupeans are legally French citizens.

3. The greatest change in this respect, to date, has been the narrowing of the control of the prefect, and the corresponding transfer of power, authority and responsibility to locally elected institutions. This reform is based on a return to, and respect for, regional and cultural characteristics throughout France that centralised government and administration have stifled since Napoleon, and on the will to expand democracy, enlarge local responsibility and simplify government.

4. The *Acte Unique Européen* is the act mandating the European Community's (EC) efforts to eliminate economic barriers among member states and construct a unified Europe. As departments of France, Martinique and Guadeloupe are affected by decisions of the EC, and participate in elections to the European Parliament.

5. Official statistics on the *békés* as a socio-economic class are not kept, but a casual inspection of the major import firms on the island confirms the continued economic predominance of at least a fraction of the class of indigenous white (familiarly referred to as the 'ten or fourteen families').

6. For instance, in 1992 the airports in Martinique and Guadeloupe were blockaded by banana-producer associations on strike. The issue was whether the European Community would accept the banana-export crop from those islands as a European protected product or not. Germany had imported cheaper bananas from Costa Rica, ignoring the rule of community preference, by which a European Community member must give preference to any other member state's product. As a result, the *blancs créoles* organised an impressive demonstration to urge the French state to implement the 'escape clause', which can only be invoked by a Community member in the case of a vital national issue. As full and equal French citizens *békés* were demanding the protection of local banana production by the French government. After a week-long airport lockout, the government acceded to strikers' demands.

7. For instance, in the past, unless they agreed to conclude joint ventures with the white creole economic elite, most French mainland (*métro*) investors in Martinique and Guadeloupe were obliged to give up their projects. It is often said that fifty-one per cent of the capital of such ventures must remain under local white minority hands. This local protectionism – illegal under French and European law – has been (and is still, to some extent) allowed by the authorities concerned on the grounds of local particularism. In the exceptional cases when this protectionism has happened to fail, the issue has been politicised in nationalist terms by the *békés* lobby. However, while centralisation was severely criticised, the state was urged to cover any losses.

8. The desire to preserve ethnic or racial homogeneity is still well-grounded even if it is no more an obstacle to professional joint ventures.

Bibliography

Allen, Mark, 'The Agri-Business Bourgeoisie of Barbados and Martinique', Society for Caribbean Studies Conference, Swanwick, Derbyshire (1980).

Benoist, Jean and Edith Kovats-Beaudoux, 'Les Blancs Créoles de la Martinique', in, Jean Benoist (ed.) *L'Archipel Inachevé. Culture et Société aux Antilles Françaises* (Presses de l'Université de Montreal, 1972), pp. 106-132.

Constant, Fred, *La Retraite aux Flambeaux. Politique et société en Martinique* (Paris: Editions Caribéennes,1988).

GROMSCA (Groupe de recherche sur l'organisation et le milieu des sociétés de la caraïbe), *Reproduction des hiérarchies sociales et action de l'Etat: le cas des Antilles françaises* (Maison des Sciences de l'homme, CORDES,1977).

Jamard, Jean-Luc, 'Les Blancs créoles de la Martinique: minorité ethnique privilégiée et classe dominante?', *Information sur les sciences sociales* 19 (1980) pp. 167-97.

'Les *Békés* sont des judokas ...', *Les Temps Modernes* 39 (1983), pp. 1872-94.

Kovats-Beaudoux, Edith, *Une minorité dominante: les Blancs créoles de la Martinique* (Université Paris-Sorbonne, Thèse de troisième cycle, 1968)

Masson, Guy Cabort, *Les puissances d'argent á la Martinique* (France: Laboratoire de l'AMEP 1987, 1993).

Miles, William F. S., *Elections and Ethnicity in French Martinique* (New York: Praeger, 1986).

Sablé, Victor, *Les Antilles sans complexes – Une Expérience de décolonisation* (Paris: Maisonneuve et Larose, 1972).

Notes on Contributors

Hilary McD. Beckles is Professor of History at the University of the West Indies, Cave Hill campus, Barbados. His publications include *White Servitude and Black Slavery in Barbados, 1627-1715* (Knoxville, 1989); *Natural Rebels: A Social History of Enslaved Black Women in Barbados* (New Brunswick, 1989); and *A History of Barbados: From Amerindian Settlement to Nation-State* (Cambridge, UK, 1990).

Bridget Brereton is Professor of History at the University of the West Indies, St Augustine campus, Trinidad. She is author of *Race Relations in Colonial Trinidad, 1870-1900* (Cambridge, UK, 1979); *A Modern History of Trinidad, 1783-1962* (Kingston, 1981); and co-editor of *East Indians in the Caribbean* (New York, 1982); and *Engendering History: Caribbean Women in Historical Perspective* (Kingston, 1995).

Patrick Bryan is Professor of History at the University of the West Indies, Mona campus, Jamaica. He is the author of *The Jamaican People 1880-1902* (London, 1990) and *Philanthropy and Social Welfare in Jamaica* (Kingston, 1993).

Fred Constant is Professor at the Institut d'Études Politiques, Université Robert Schuman de Strasbourg. His publications on the French Caribbean include *La Retraite aux Flambeaux. Politique et Société en Martinique* (Paris, 1988).

Michael Craton is Professor of History at the University of Waterloo. His publications include: *A History of the Bahamas* (London, 1962); with James Walvin, *A Jamaican Plantation: The History of Worthy Park* (Toronto, 1970); *Sinews of Empire: A Short History of British Slavery* (New York, 1974); *Searching for the Invisible Man: Slaves and Plantation Life in Jamaica* (Cambridge, Mass., 1978); *Testing the Chains: Resistance to Slavery in the British West Indies* (Ithaca, NY, 1982). The first volume of a social history of the Bahamas, with Gail Saunders, appeared as *Islanders in the Stream: A History of the Bahamian People* (Athens, Georgia, 1992). *Empire, Enslavement and Freedom in the Caribbean* (Kingston, 1997).

Howard Johnson is Professor of Black American Studies and History at the University of Delaware. His publications include *The Bahamas in Slavery and Freedom* (Kingston, 1991) and *The Bahamas from Slavery to Servitude, 1783-1933* (Gainseville, Fl., 1967).

Karen Judd is an anthropologist who received her PhD from City University of New York. Her dissertation was on elite families and ethnic identity in Belize. She has taught anthropology and women's studies at colleges throughout the City University system and currently works as a writer and editorial consultant, specialising in women and development and human rights issues.

Brian L. Moore is Senior Lecturer in History at the University of the West Indies, Mona campus, Jamaica. He is the author of *Race, Power, and Social Segmentation in Colonial Society: Guyana after Slavery, 1838-1891* (New York, 1987); *Cultural Power, Resistance, and Pluralism: Colonial Guyana, 1838-1900* (Kingston, 1995).

René A. Römer has served as Professor in Sociology of the Caribbean at the University of the Netherland Antilles and is currently a part-time Professor at the University of Groningen, The Netherlands. From 1983 to 1990 he was Governor General of the Netherland Antilles. His books include: *Cultural Mozaic of the Netherland Antilles* (1977); *Un Pueblo na Kaminda* (1979); and *Korsou* (1981).

Karl Watson is Lecturer in History at the University of the West Indies, Cave Hill campus, Barbados. He is the author of *The Civilised Island, Barbados: A Social History 1750-1816* (Barbados, 1979).